Understanding Poverty

Second Edition

Pete Alcock

Consultant Editor: Jo Campling

MACMILLAN

First edition 1993
Reprinted 1993, 1994, 1996
Second edition 1997

Published by
MACMILLAN PRESS LTD
Houndmills, Basingstoke, Hampshire RG21 6XS
and London
Companies and representatives
throughout the world

ISBN 0–333–69279–9 hardcover
ISBN 0–333–69280–2 paperback

A catalogue record for this book is available
from the British Library.

This book is printed on paper suitable for recycling and
made form fully managed and sustained forest sources.

10   9   8   7   6   5   4   3   2
06   05   04   03   02   01   00   99   98

Copy-edited and typeset by Povey–Edmondson
Okehampton and Rochdale, England

Printed in Hong Kong

For Dan and Tom
Chris and Anna

Contents

Contents

List of Figures and Tables

Figures

Table

List of Abbreviations

AA	Attendance Allowance
CAB	Citizens' Advice Bureau
CB	Child Benefit
CDP	Community Development Project
CPAG	Child Poverty Action Group
DHSS	Department of Health and Social Security
DIG	Disablement Income Group
DLA	Disability Living Allowance
DSS	Department of Social Security
DWA	Disability Working Allowance
EAPN	European Antipoverty Network
EC	European Commission
EPA	Educational priority area
ERDF	European Regional Development Fund
ERM	Exchange rate mechanism
ESF	European Social Fund
EU	European Union
FC	Family Credit
FES	Family Expenditure Survey
FIS	Family Income Supplement
GLC	Greater London Council
HB	Housing Benefit
HBAI	Households below average incomes
ICA	Invalid Care Allowance
IEA	Institute of Economic Affairs
IFS	Institute for Fiscal Studies
IS	Income Support
LIF	Low income families
LIS	Luxembourg Income Study
LSE	London School of Economics
MA	Mobility Allowance
MSC	Manpower Services Commission
NA	National Assistance
NAB	National Assistance Board
NACAB	National Association of Citizens' Advice Bureaux
NCIP	Non-Contributory Invalidity Pension

NI	National Insurance
OECD	Organisation for Economic Co-operation and Development
OEO	Office of Economic Opportunity
OPCS	Office of Population Censuses and Surveys
PSI	Policy Studies Institute
SB	Supplementary Benefit
SDA	Severe Disablement Allowance
SERPS	State Earnings Related Pensions Scheme

Preface to the First Edition

What thoughtful rich people call the problem of poverty, thoughtful poor people call with equal justice a problem of riches (R. H. Tawney, 1913).

I set out to write a book about poverty in Britain with Tawney's famous words echoing in my mind. I felt that in one short sentence he had summed up the main issues involved in both the political and the definitional debates on poverty in modern society. After completing the task I had not changed my view on this; and if this book achieves the goals I set for it, it will be by explaining to those who are new to these debates, or to those who wish to revisit them, why Tawney was right eighty years ago and why today we are still struggling to come to terms with the implications of his analysis.

The title of the book expresses these goals. The book is intended as a textbook, providing students of social policy, sociology and related disciplines with an analysis of the various debates that have been conducted in Britain and beyond on the problem of poverty, and of the policies that have been developed in response to these. The book therefore discusses research on poverty carried out in Britain and elsewhere; but it is not a report of research and it is not itself based on any new or original research. As we shall see, especially in Part II, both existing research and the academic and political debates that flow from it involve major contradictions and conflicts of view – most fundamentally over the very meaning of the word poverty itself.

Academics and politicians have not come to an agreement what poverty is or what should be done about it. Indeed they frequently talk at cross purposes about the size and seriousness of the problem. What all are agreed on, however, is that poverty, where it does exist, is a problem, and a problem that requires policy responses to deal with it. This book is a guide to the various ways in which the problem of poverty has been defined and measured, and to the policies that have been developed in attempts to respond to it. It assumes some knowledge of the social science context of the debate on social phenomena, but presumes no prior acquaintance with writing on or research into poverty and related issues. I hope that the understanding that it provides is accessible and self-explanatory. What it does not provide, of course, is any simple answer to the problem itself – beyond that which is implicit in Tawney's early insights.

I should like to thank a few people who helped in the writing of the book. Saul Becker, at Loughborough, read through a first draft and provided helpful comments and suggestions, some of which I followed. Chris Pond of the Low Pay Unit acted as reader and offered many useful comments. Jo Campling encouraged me to begin a project that I had been thinking about for some time, and helped me to secure the publisher's interest in ensuring that it saw the light of day. Academics writing about poverty are often criticised for talking about the problem rather than doing something about it: writing this has not lessened my commitment to the latter, and I hope it might encourage that commitment in others too.

PETE ALCOCK

Preface to the Second Edition and Acknowledgements

The second edition of this book is the product of significant revision and updating to reflect recent evidence on the developing problem of poverty in Britain and recent policy responses to this. The book has been revised throughout and many new references included. There has also been some restructuring, in particular the discussion of 'the underclass' has been moved alongside other material on the distribution of poverty, and there is a new chapter dealing directly with the causes of poverty. Other major changes include discussion of the now widely recognised and debated problems of social exclusion and social polarisation, a review of the importance of poverty dynamics in the measurement and definition of poverty, and brief coverage of the recent extensions to local antipoverty action in Britain.

New research evidence includes in particular the findings of the various projects involved in the Joseph Rowntree Foundation's Inquiry into Income and Wealth in the early 1990s. What this and other research depressingly confirms is that, in the short period between writing the first edition of this book and revising this for the second edition, the problem of poverty in Britain has continued to worsen rather than improve. It is to be hoped that any future editions might have a more uplifting story to tell.

PETE ALCOCK

The author and publishers wish to thank the following who have kindly given permission to use copyright material: John Hills and the Joseph Rowntree Foundation for Figures 1.1 and 2.1 from J. R. Foundation Inquiry into Income and Wealth, Vol. 2; London School of Economics and Political Science for Figure 4.1 from LSE/Welfare Programme Discussion Paper WSP/16 by A. B. Atkinson; Oxford University Press for Figures 8.2 and 8.3 from *The Economics of Inequality* by A. B. Atkinson, Figures 2.2 and 3.2, 1983.

Every effort has been made to trace all the copyright-holders, but if any have been inadvertently overlooked the publishers will be pleased to make the necessary arrangement at the first opportunity.

Part I

The Context of Poverty

1

What is Poverty?

Is Poverty a Problem?

> Poverty means going short materially, socially and emotionally. It means spending less on food, on heating, and on clothing than someone on an average income. . . . Above all, poverty takes away the tools to build the blocks for the future – your 'life chances'. It steals away the opportunity to have a life unmarked by sickness, a decent education, a secure home and a long retirement (Oppenheim and Harker, 1996, pp. 4–5).

> The evidence of improving living standards over this century is dramatic, and it is incontrovertible. When the pressure groups say that one-third of the population is living in poverty, they cannot be saying that one-third of people are living below the draconian subsistence levels used by Booth and Rowntree (Moore, 1989, p. 5).

Many people, including academics, campaigners and politicians, talk about the problem of poverty, and underlying their discussion is the assumption that identifying the problem provides a basis for action upon which all will agree. However, as we can see, people do not all agree on what the problem of poverty is; and thus, not surprisingly, the action they wish to encourage or to justify is not at all the same thing. Most people of course claim that their understanding of poverty is the correct one, based on logical argument or scientific research. However, as our exploration of the problem of understanding poverty will reveal, there is no one correct, scientific, agreed definition because poverty is inevitably a political concept – and thus inherently a contested one.

Many commentators perhaps do have a clear idea of what they think should be done about poverty, and thus their description and definition of it provide a justification for this. In political debate the ends and the means – and the terms – are always inextricably intertwined. Thus what commentators mean by poverty depends to some extent on what they intend or expect to do about it. Consequently academic and political debate about poverty is not merely descriptive, it is prescriptive. Poverty is not just a state of affairs, it is an *unacceptable* state of affairs – it implicitly contains the question, what are we going to do about it?

Therefore the first thing to understand about poverty is that it is not a simple phenomenon that we can learn to define by adopting the correct approach. It is a series of contested definitions and complex arguments that overlap and at times contradict each other. It is differently seen as a big phenomenon or a small phenomenon, as a growing issue or a declining issue, and as an individual problem or a social problem. Thus in understanding poverty the task is to understand how these different visions and perceptions overlap, how they interrelate and what the implications of different approaches and definitions are. In a sense we learn that the answer to the question – do you understand poverty? – is: that depends what you mean by poverty.

If, however, we recognise that poverty is essentially a contested concept, then why is it that academics and politicians continue to seek an accepted definition or argue that their approach is the correct one? Why can we not simply agree to differ, or suggest perhaps that poverty, like beauty, is contained only in the eye of the beholder? This may, at least for some of the more academically minded, appear an attractive and indeed a logical means of avoiding entering into the cut and thrust of political debate. However it is in practice not a viable response. We cannot sit on the fence on the poverty problem or suggest that the problem is merely one of academic or political debate, because implicit in the disagreements about the definition of poverty are disagreements too about what should be done in response to it – intrinsic to the notion of poverty itself is the imperative to respond to it. Different definitions require different responses, but all require some response. All are thus debates about what to do about the problem. Or to put it another way, although poverty is a contested problem, it is still a problem; and the one thing that there is no disagreement over is that *something* must be done about it.

This is not to suggest, however, that all those writing about poverty are proposing new action now. Some discussion of poverty in Britain in the late twentieth century, for instance, focuses on the argument that no further action is needed because the problem of poverty has already been dealt with by past action. Indeed this was the view popularised by prominent members of the Thatcher government in the late 1980s, as revealed by the quotation from Secretary of State John Moore (1989) at the beginning of this chapter. Nevertheless this is not an approach that denies that poverty is a problem, nor that action is required in response to this. Even John Moore recognised that poverty, where it existed, was a problem. His argument was that this problem had already been overcome by past and continuing policy developments, notably the provision of social security benefits to meet basic needs, and that further action to extend this was therefore not necessary. Thus by implication, if social security were removed altogether, then poverty would return – although this is not what Moore was advocating.

Poverty is a problem, therefore, however it is approached; and when we understand the differences between approaches to the problem, then we can begin to make judgements about what we ourselves think the *real* problem is. Poverty is also a basis for action, or policy. Policy change flows from changing views of the problem of poverty, and academic and political debates about poverty have provided a central basis for the development of social policy in Britain – and of course in other countries too.

There may seem to be something of a logical contradiction in this link between problem and policy, however. If the way in which poverty is defined depends on the policies proponents are advancing to deal with it, then this suggests that in a sense the policy determines the problem. This may seem like a circular argument – a kind of academic 'chicken and egg' conundrum. However it is really only an acceptance of the interrelated nature of all social phenomena in the real world. We are living in a world where academics and politicians are seeking to define the problem of poverty, and where there are a range of policies which have been introduced in response to one or other version of the problem. What is more the introduction of these policy initiatives has had an effect on poverty as previously conceived – with some, such as John Moore, even claiming that they have removed it.

This means that an understanding of poverty requires us also to undertake an understanding of the social policies that have been developed in response to it and have thus removed, restructured or even recreated it. Indeed there are many who argue that poverty is largely, if not entirely, a product of social policies, or social and economic policies, pursued by states in order to control and discipline their citizens. By creating and then containing the poor states can control others through fear of poverty, a point to which we shall return shortly. Certainly it is the case that, in Britain in the 1990s, the problems of determining who is poor, how poverty is experienced and how it may or may not be escaped have been heavily influenced by past policies with a long and complex history.

Identifying Poverty

Poverty is a complex problem and it is a product, in part at least, of the impact of political process and policy development. It is also a political or a moral concept – it implies and requires action. Poverty is thus not the same as *inequality*, although the two concepts are closely connected. The most important distinction between the two is that whereas poverty, as we have seen, is a prescriptive concept, inequality is a descriptive concept. Inequality is simply a state of affairs – and probably an inescapable if not even a desirable one. Opinions are hotly disputed, of course, about how much inequality is acceptable – or rather about the extent of inequality that should be tolerated. There are those who argue strongly that certain levels of inequality should be acceptable and indeed desirable (Green, 1990), and others who argue that significant inequality is unacceptable and even destructive (Field, 1989). But the dispute here is about the extent of inequality, not the existence of it.

In the 1990s the debate on the distinction between poverty and inequality has been complicated by the identification of wider conceptualisations of poverty to include a recognition of *social exclusion*. As we shall discuss further in Chapter 6, social exclusion is a term that refers to circumstances of deprivation and disadvantage that extend beyond lack of material resources, and people may be socially excluded even if they are not materially poor. However social exclusion, like poverty, is a prescriptive concept – it suggests an unacceptable state of affairs requiring policy action. This is also true of the 1990s concept of *social polarisation*, which is a broader conceptualisation of inequality implying not just differences in levels of resources but also the development of undesirable gaps between social groups.

For many commentators, and for most of those who will be discussed in this book, it is this political and moral terrain in which the debate on poverty, exclusion and polarisation is situated that makes it so attractive for study and argument. It is because poverty is not just one aspect of inequality, but the unacceptable extreme of inequality, that it is so important to study it; and it is because the identification of poverty requires policy action to respond to it that both academics and politicians have been concerned to identify it. It is the moral and the political thrust of poverty research that is its great attraction, and as such it has attracted some of the most eminent and important academics and politicians concerned with social policy in Britain and beyond.

Such a political focus was certainly important for one of the pioneers of modern poverty research, Booth, who undertook a massive study of poverty in London in the 1880s with the clear intention of bringing the scale of the problem and its intensity to the attention of politicians and policy makers, who would then be forced to react to it (Booth, 1889). This was also the concern, albeit initially on a smaller scale, of the most famous of British poverty researchers, Seebohm Rowntree, in his study of York in 1889, which was repeated in the 1930s and the 1950s (Rowntree, 1901, 1941; Rowntree and Lavers, 1951). Rowntree paid much attention to arriving at a precise definition of poverty (an issue we will discuss in more detail in Chapter 5), in order to demonstrate, conclusively he hoped, that those who were poor were unable to provide for themselves and therefore needed support or improvement.

The use of carefully defined and measured research evidence on poverty in order to provoke policy response is an example of the political context of the concept discussed above. It became an approach widely developed by Fabian academics and politicians throughout the twentieth century in order to put pressure on governments and political parties to develop social policies to help the poor. More recently this has included the work of academics, notably from the London School of Economics (LSE), such as Titmuss, Abel Smith and Townsend. In the early 1990s, one hundred years after Rowntree's initial research, the Joseph Rowntree Foundation, commissioned a series of major research projects on poverty and inequality in Britain – although, as we shall see shortly, the findings from this research suggested that despite a century of research the level of poverty remained high and growing (Barclay, 1995; Hills, 1995).

Townsend in particular has been one of the most influential of poverty researchers in the latter part of the twentieth century. He developed the argument that poverty continued to exist and grow even in a more affluent Britain because poverty was not as narrowly defined as Rowntree had initially conceived it, but also encompassed the broader notion of relative deprivation within a society of changing norms and customs (Townsend, 1979); and it is this approach that was taken up in much of the Rowntree Foundation research in the 1990s. This, of course, is an example of how different definitions of poverty can be advanced in order to make the case for new and different policy responses; and it has been developed further in the 1990s with the debates on social exclusion, as we shall see later.

In addition to academic debate, however, the campaigning work of organisations such as the Child Poverty Action Group (CPAG) in presenting facts and figures on poverty to a public audience has also become a part of a constant pressure on governments to change or adapt policies to provide more resources for the poor. The CPAG regularly provides updated figures on the 'facts' of poverty in Britain (see Oppenheim and Harker, 1996), as well as more considered analysis of the differing aspects of poverty (Golding, 1986; Smith and Noble, 1995), or the changing context of policy (Becker, 1991; Simpson and Walker, 1993).

All of this research and political activity on poverty has been carried out by academics and campaigners who have been seeking to establish *objective* definitions and evidence of poverty in order to influence policy debate. However academics are not poor themselves, and the definitions and measurements they have developed frequently ignore the *subjective* views on poverty that are held by poor people themselves. There has been relatively little attempt to involve poor people and their subjective experience of poverty in the debate on definition and measurement. This point has been taken up by Beresford and Croft (1995) and we shall return to discuss it further in Chapter 13. However its influence may be contradictory.

To perceive oneself as poor, of course, is to put oneself within an undesirable or negative situation – to be the victim of an unacceptable state of affairs. Those who are poor by some objective criteria may therefore understandably not want to identify themselves and their experiences with such a negative, exclusionary and even stigmatising situation. It may not be much comfort to admit to being poor, and thus some people may deny it, even though they would welcome the benefits that would flow from policies designed to improve or ameliorate their position. What is more, people at the bottom of the income distribution in Britain may not see themselves as poor, particularly if they make comparisons with those elsewhere in the world who face starvation and destitution, or even with those else-

where in Britain who are worse off than themselves – relative judgements of poverty are shared by the poor too.

Subjective definition, therefore, does not necessarily mean that
poverty will be seen to be a more significant or more pervasive
problem, and few would suggest that the subjective experience of the
poor should entirely replace the objective research of the academics in
identifying poverty. At the same time, however, research on poverty
that ignores the experiences of poor people is likely to paint only a
partial picture of the problem; and as we shall see later, it is increasingly the case that means of incorporating experience alongside
measurement are being developed in academic debate.

The History of Poverty

Poverty exists within a dynamic and changing social order; and to
some extent, as we have suggested, it is created by, or at least *recreated*
by, the social and economic policies that have developed over time to
respond to or control it. Thus the history of poverty is also a history of
the policies directed at or developed for the poor. As Vincent (1991)
discusses in his history of poverty in Britain in the twentieth century,
this interrelation between poverty and policy has consistently shaped
the position of poor people within all aspects of the broader social
structure.

It is possible to extend the history of poverty as far back as the
history of society itself, but most of those writing historically about
poverty in Britain trace the current development of poverty and
poverty policy from the period of the gradual replacement of feudalism by capitalism as the modern economy began to develop in the
seventeenth and eighteenth centuries. Indeed in his book on the
history of poverty in Britain, Novak (1988) argues that it is only at
that point that poverty was created. This is because at that time the
majority of people were separated from the land and became workers,
and thus lost control over the means of producing material support
and became dependent on wages from paid labour. After that those
who could not work for wages could not support themselves and thus
were poor.

Poverty, it is argued from this perspective, is therefore a product of
capitalism, and it is sustained and recreated by capitalism in order to
provide a discipline – through fear of poverty – for workers to

maintain their commitment to the labour market. For Novak, therefore, poverty is caused by the logic of the capitalist wage labour market and is maintained by capitalism, as he further argued in 1995 (Novak, 1995); it will thus only be eliminated when capitalism is replaced by some other economic system.

There are, however, some serious problems with such a strict Marxist approach to the understanding of poverty, in particular its failure to perceive or discuss poverty within other economic systems and its rejection of any attempts to ameliorate or reduce poverty within capitalism. It is also oversimplistic in its assumption that modern economies such as Britain experience only a capitalist economic order. Arguably the British economy has only ever been partly capitalist. Elements of feudalism survived alongside capitalism during the early period of capital development; and more recently collective or state-owned forms of production have developed within capitalism – prompting some commentators to refer to modern Britain as a 'mixed economy' (Crosland, 1956). Consequently poverty in Britain is the product of a range of economic and other social forces, and not only of the structural exclusion of the capitalist wage labour market.

However the link between poverty and the development and control of the wage labour market is an important, indeed a crucial one. Clearly exclusion from paid labour is likely to lead to poverty when there are no, or few, other sources of material support. At the same time the employers of wage labour will wish to maintain a ready and willing surplus of workers to undertake paid employment at the lowest possible cost. State policies to respond to the problem of poverty have always been directly influenced by such demands, and have created a legacy of policy priorities that have shaped images of the problem of poverty and the needs of the poor.

Thus early laws dealing with the landless poor, dating from 1349, branded them as vagrants and subjected them to controls to prevent unwanted competition for their labour. Through a series of later statutes, in 1530, 1536 and 1547, these controls became more extensive and also began to invoke a distinction between those who were poor and unable to work and support themselves, such as the elderly or sick, and those who were poor but were able in theory at least to support themselves. It was a distinction later represented in the categories of the 'deserving' and the 'undeserving' poor. The latter were assumed to be idle, indolent and possibly criminal and were therefore subject to punitive policies of control designed to encourage or force them into employment and self-sufficiency.

During the time of Elizabeth I this approach was encapsulated in the Poor Law Act of 1601, the aims of which, according to Golding and Middleton (1982, p. 11) were work discipline, deterence and classification. The Poor Law was the most important policy development dealing with poverty until the end of the nineteenth century; and it was a development that focused in particular on control and deterence. This could be seen most clearly in the growth of the institution of the workhouse or Bridewell. Workhouses were institutions to which poor and destitute individuals could be sent to be provided for if they could not provide for themselves. This was a form of poverty relief, but the regime within workhouses was extremely harsh and punitive so as to discourage both present and potential residents from perceiving them to be a desirable alternative to employment and self-sufficiency.

However workhouses could not provide for all the poor, especially in rural areas at times of low wages and high prices. Thus after 1795 the Speenhamland system of the local parish topping up agricultural workers' wages to meet higher prices was introduced, and spread rapidly. This was an indiscriminate and costly form of support for the poor, however, and it did not include direct disciplinary measures of control or encouragement of self-support. It was considered by the Royal Commission on the Poor Law, set up in 1832, and with the Poor Law Amendment Act of 1834 'outdoor relief', as Speenhamland payments were called, was ended, parish control of the Poor Law was replaced by central and uniform administration, and the workhouse test of encouragement to self-sufficiency was intended to be invoked for all the poor.

Central to the philosophy of the 1834 Poor Law was the notion of 'less eligibility'. This was the belief that the support provided by the state for the poor should confer a lesser status than that of the lowest labourer, in order to encourage all the poor to seek any employment rather than remain dependent upon the state. As the 1834 report put it: 'The first and most essential of all conditions . . . is that his situation on the whole shall not be made really or apparently so eligible as the situation of the independent labourer of the lowest class' (quoted in Novak, 1988, p. 46).

The workhouse test was of course the epitome of the idea of less eligibility, and its punitive regime underlined the punitive attitude towards poverty – or rather pauperism – upon which the Poor Law was based and which dominated nineteenth-century Victorian attitudes towards the problem of poverty. The predominant assumption was that poverty was the product of the interaction of the twin problems of indolence and vice, and thus state policies should seek to counteract their influence by encouraging self-sufficiency and penalising dependency. That this also enforced labour discipline amongst the workers by putting them in fear of losing their jobs and falling into poverty was also no coincidence. State support for the labour market through social policy, as well as through the laws of contract and combination, was part of the agenda of reform of nineteenth-century British government. Despite the protestations of adherence to the ideals of *laissez-faire*, therefore, early responses to the problem of poverty created a policy framework that resulted in definite attempts to shape and control the lives of the poor.

As we shall see in Chapter 14, although the gradual replacement of the Poor Law by other forms of insurance-based social security and national assistance in the twentieth century has removed some of the harshest aspects of the workhouse test, the notions of less eligibility and labour market discipline have continued to dominate state policy responses to poverty and to maintain the priorities developed in these earlier forms of state control. Modern social security benefits have by and large been maintained at low levels of payment in order to prevent any competition with low wages, and benefits for the unemployed have generally required recipients to demonstrate that whilst receiving state support they are also seeking employment. Thus state policies have continued to be predicated upon support for the labour market and the attempt to divide the poor from the employed.

In practice employment has never of course been a guaranteed means of avoiding poverty. As Bowley's studies in the early twentieth century were already revealing, many of those who were poor were in full-time work (Bowley and Burnett-Hurst, 1915), and similar evidence of the problem of the working poor is still widespread today (see Gosling *et al.*, 1994). Furthermore many of those who are poor and out of work are far from feckless idlers revelling in dependency. They are looking for – and hoping for – work, but are unable to find it. Thus the distinction between the employed on the one hand and the feckless and dependent poor on the other is a false one. However it is a distinction that has maintained the apparent distinction between the poor and the employed, dividing and classifying those in the lowest classes, and controlling and disciplining the poor at the same time as supporting them.

State responses to poverty that control and discipline the poor have therefore created and shaped particular images of both the problem of poverty and the policy response to it. How we view poverty and how we change or develop these policies are in part determined by these legacies of history. The divisions between the working and the non-working poor, and between the deserving and the undeserving poor, exercise a strong influence over images of poverty in Britain today. This will be discussed in more detail in Chapter 2.

Thus current debate and discussion is situated within a powerful legacy that shapes our perception of poverty and presents the poor as a separate group from those who work and are able to provide for themselves. Poor people's problems are thus seen as largely the product of their own idleness or inability. This is accentuated by the fear that overgenerous state support for the poor may only compound this problem by encouraging indolence and dependency. There are overtones of racism in this legacy – poor people are presumed to include a disproportionate number of foreigners who have come to Britain to benefit from that generous state support. Donnison's (1982) book *The Politics of Poverty* has a cartoon on the cover that neatly encapsulates the images of poverty that we have inherited from history. It features an obviously poor tramp begging for money, in return for which he promises to confirm the prejudices of passers-by. In reply to someone giving him a coin he says 'Yes. I'm on Social Security. . . . No. I've never done a hand's turn in my life. . . . Yes. I'm of Irish extraction'.

The Extent of Poverty

Poverty is a political problem, and therefore the nature of the problem is the result of the particular political context within which it has developed. This inevitably means that discussion of the extent of poverty largely takes place within one particular political context, usually within one country, and that comparison of poverty across national political boundaries cannot readily be undertaken. We cannot simply count the number or proportion of poor people in Britain in the 1990s and compare them with the number in France or the United States, or still less Brazil or Ethiopia. What is understood by poverty, and who would be counted as poor in these other countries, is likely to be very different from in Britain because of their different political and economic circumstances and histories.

Because of the incomparability of definition and measurement therefore, international approaches to the problem, or problems, of poverty have not been widespread, although this is also a product of the low level of development of international action on a range of social and economic concerns. Well-publicised cases of destitution or starvation, such as those experienced in Eastern Africa in the 1980s and 1990s, have been the focus of international concern and action. There are also international agencies, such as Oxfam and Christian Aid, that seek to coordinate international efforts to relieve poverty in different parts of the world. Academics such as Townsend (1993, 1995) are also challenging us to recognise the gap between the poor and the rich at the global level. Nevertheless international assessment of the extent of poverty across the world as a whole is relatively underdeveloped.

Within the developed world, however, measurement and definition are more common and international comparisons of poverty have been made and are being expanded. George and Howards (1991) have recently contrasted poverty in Britain and the United States, and the Luxembourg Income Study (LIS), which will be discussed in more detail in Chapter 8, provides an important new source of information about poverty in a wide range of developed countries in the 1980s and 1990s. Mitchell (1991) has utilised the LIS database to contrast income transfer policies in ten welfare states.

Furthermore, as will be discussed in Chapter 4, the development of cross-national economic and social policy amongst the member countries of the European Union (EU) has also led to the development of significant investment in the provision of data on poverty and anti-poverty policies in all EU countries, and to the development of community-wide policy initiatives to combat poverty, such as the establishment of three EU programmes to combat poverty and the European Observatory on National Policies to Combat Social Exclusion, which closed in 1994 (Robbins *et al.*, 1994), and the funding of the European Anti-Poverty Network (EAPN).

Despite such developments, however, it is still the case that most discussions on the extent of poverty in Britain, and in other EU or overseas countries, focus on the problem within the country, rather than on the broader international context. What is more, attempts to measure the extent of poverty are much simpler when restricted to the problem of poverty within one political and economic system. Although, as will be discussed in Part II, defining and measuring poverty in Britain are in practice highly complex and highly contested exercises.

Leaving aside these debates for the time being, however, there is the further problem that even within one country, and despite the continuing impact of past history, the extent of poverty and the conception of it also change over time. In part this is perhaps a welcome feature – the problem of poverty ought to change as new debates and definitions develop and new policies are introduced. However these changes make it extremely difficult to compare past data on poverty with present figures in order to make a comparison or judgement about the effects of changes over time.

This was revealed most graphically in Rowntree's three studies of poverty in York in the 1890s, 1930s and 1950s. Although similar methods were used to survey a similar population, on each occasion there were changes in the definition of poverty. As will be discussed in more detail in Chapter 5, these changes were consciously made and readily justifiable, but they did mean that on each occasion different forms of measurement were being taken. Furthermore when Abel Smith and Townsend (1965) sought to dispute Rowntree's findings on the extent of poverty in the 1950s, their argument was based quite explicitly on the use of different criteria to define and measure the same problem.

Despite these problems, however, some attempts have been made to measure and compare poverty over time. Fiegehen *et al.* (1977, ch. 3) used a range of definitions and methods to compare changes in poverty from the end of the Second World War to the mid 1970s, and concluded that the extent and depth of poverty had reduced over this period. In a wide-ranging article in 1988 Piachaud attempted to adapt data from a range of poverty studies to develop a constant relative poverty level that could be used to compare poverty in Britain from 1899 to 1983. Despite the methodological initiatives that Piachaud developed, however, his conclusions about changes in poverty levels over time were fairly tentative. Although there was evidence of a significant decline in poverty following the Second World War, trends since then appeared to have fluctuated and increases were revealed in poverty levels in the early 1980s (Piachaud, 1988). However since then the trend towards increasing poverty in Britain has developed significantly.

As stated above, the research on poverty and inequality in Britain commissioned by the Joseph Rowntree Foundation one hundred years after Seebohm Rowntree's original poverty research in York provided a symbolic benchmark against which to compare trends in the growth or decline in the extent of poverty. The research projects that comprised the wide-ranging Inquiry into Income and Wealth (see Hills, 1995) could not extend their period of comparison back to the

1890s, but many of them did compare changes over three decades from the 1960s – and over this period the findings revealed much evidence of similar, if depressing, trends.

A study of income distribution between 1979 and 1990/91 showed that whilst the better-off had improved their position over this period, the poorest had drifted further behind (Jenkins, 1994). Another study used family expenditure data to reveal that although there had been fluctuations in the level of inequality in the 1970s and 1980s, these were dwarfed by the growth in inequality in the 1980s (Goodman and Webb, 1994). This trend of growing inequality after 1979 can be clearly seen in Figure 1.1, which is taken from Hills' (1995) summary report of the research and charts the relative shares of disposable income of the poorest fifth and richest fifth of households from 1978 to 1993.

The changes in the distribution of income revealed by the Rowntree research were a product of growing wage differentials as well as higher levels of unemployment (Gosling *et al.*, 1994). Nevertheless rising unemployment led to a significant increase in poverty and inequality, especially for those households where no adult member was in paid work (Gregg and Wadsworth, 1994). As a result of this the proportion of the population in poverty increased dramatically over the 1980s and

FIGURE 1.1   *Shares of disposable income, 1977–93*

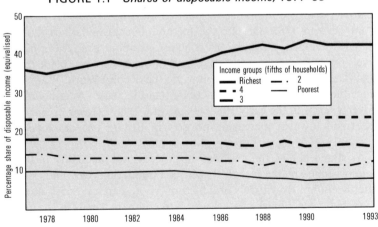

Source: Hills, 1995, p. 24.

early 1990s. The Rowntree research revealed that the proportion of the population receiving an income below half of the national average income increased from 7 per cent to 24 per cent between 1977 and 1991 (Hills, 1995, p. 33).

These figures were confirmed by the government's own annual statistics on changes in household income in the 1980s and 1990s (DSS, 1995a). The government figures showed an increase in the proportion of the population receiving less than half the average income, from 9 per cent (5 million) in 1979 to 25 per cent (14.1 million) in 1992/93. This was an increase in relative poverty, of course, and over the same period the average standard of living did rise. However the government statistics also compared the changes in real income experienced by each decile (10 per cent) of the population against the real value of that income in 1979. After taking account of fluctuations in housing costs, these figures revealed that although the population as a whole experienced a 38 per cent rise in income over this period, the bottom 10 per cent experienced a *fall* in real income of 17 per cent – see Table 1.1.

These are high levels of poverty indeed, and in contrast to earlier evidence of a gradual decline in poverty and inequality in the earlier part of the century following Rowntree's original research they

TABLE 1.1   *Rises in real income between 1979 and 1992/93 (including the self-employed) (per cent)*

	Income before housing costs	Income after housing costs
First (bottom)	1%	–17%
Second	8%	1%
Third	13%	6%
Fourth	17%	15%
Fifth	23%	24%
Sixth	28%	29%
Seventh	32%	34%
Eighth	40%	40%
Ninth	48%	48%
Tenth (top)	62%	62%
Total population	37%	38%

Source: *Poverty*, no. 91 (Summer 1995), p. 17.

demonstrate a significant increase, both relatively and absolutely, over a short period of time. They also compare interestingly with developments in other advanced industrial countries. In the United States, where similar social and economic policies to those in Britain were pursued in the 1980s, there have also been growing inequalities resulting from a decline in the incomes of the poor and a major increase in the wealth of the top 10 per cent (see Phillips, 1990, ch. 1). However the growth in inequality in Britain since the beginning of the 1980s has been more rapid than in any other industrialised country except New Zealand (Hills, 1995, p. 65).

Therefore – leaving aside the problem of definition and measurement, to which we will return in Part II, and the difficulties inherent in making international comparisons – both research evidence and official statistics reveal continuing high levels of poverty in Britain at the end of the twentieth century despite a hundred years of growing affluence and welfare reform. As the CPAG and others have argued therefore, they continue to create a case for further action to be taken to eliminate or alleviate the problem. As we shall see throughout the rest of this book, however, both the extent of the problem and the nature of the action to be taken are more complex than these basic figures suggest. Both definition and action depend on evidence about the distribution of poverty and on perceptions of the causes that lay behind this. We shall explore these in the following two chapters.

2

The Poor and the Underclass

Ideologies of Poverty

Poverty is a political concept. As explained in Chapter 1, it does not just describe a state of affairs, it also implies that some action must be taken to remedy it. What is more the political actions that have been taken to remedy it, in Britain as elsewhere, have had a cumulative effect in reshaping and recreating the concept of poverty itself. Implicit in the development of both definitions and policies, and the inter-relationship between them, however, are assumptions about the circumstances and experiences of the victims of poverty. The politics of poverty is also the politics of the poor – both who is poor and why they became poor or remain so; and behind these political debates are ideological views of the poor – images and attitudes that govern how we approach the processes of definition, measurement and policy development.

We all perceive poverty, like other social phenomena, through an ideological framework, and for each of us that framework and those perceptions of poverty are unique. However, although unique they are not isolated. Our perceptions and attitudes are governed in large part by broader social influences, in particular the ideologies of powerful social figures and social forces, which receive publicity through the media, through politics, through education and through other social interactions. The public images of poverty are central in determining private perceptions, a relationship that was explored by Golding and Middleton (1982) in research on public and private attitudes to social security dependency and abuse in the 1970s.

Most obviously, ideologies of poverty are a product of history – they develop out of past ideologies. Golding and Middleton open their report with a review of the history of social security and poverty policy in Britain over the last few centuries, demonstrating, as we saw in Chapter 1, that current perceptions have been shaped by past percep-tions and the policies and practices that have flowed from these. Not surprisingly, therefore, Golding and Middleton found that perceived divisions between the non-working and the working poor, and the deserving and the undeserving poor, continued to exercise a very powerful influence on public and private ideologies of poverty. The particular focus of Golding and Middleton's research was on the growing fear about social security abuse, as popularised by newspapers and politicians in the 1970s. They explain how media reporting of only one or two established incidents of social security abuse was able to carry the implicit, or at times explicit, message that these were only the tip of the iceberg of widespread social security abuse. Abuse was the product, the media implied, of idle and feckless claimants seeking to enjoy a comfortable living without working, which they were readily able to do because of the ineffective administration of an overextensive and overbureaucratic benefits system – and because even for those not actually defrauding the system, benefits were so generous that they encouraged a life of indolent dependency, which could even extend to Spanish holidays on the 'Costa del Dole' (see Golding and Middleton, 1982, pp. 106–7).

Two particular 'news' stories encapsulated the ideological concern and preconceptions that dominated media coverage of poverty and benefits issues during this period. One was the case of a Liverpool claimant, Derek Deevy, who was charged with fraudulently receiving benefits totalling £57, although he claimed to have received over £36 000 in false claims. Among the features of the reports of this case were attempts to portray the apparent ease with which he had duped a naive and ineffective social security system out of tens of thousands of pounds of taxpayers' money. In other words social security support was portrayed as a 'soft touch'.

The other case concerned a genuine claimant in Cornwall who had both a legal and a common law wife as well as twenty children. There was no suggestion of fraud in his case, but he was nevertheless claiming a large weekly social security payment and living, it was claimed, a life of 'gentle glee' at the taxpayers' expense (ibid., p. 92). The images portrayed by these two stories were those of an overgenerous and easily outwitted social security system providing support, not to alleviate hardship and deprivation, but to maintain a comfortable life of idleness that was far more desirable than that enjoyed by many of those at work who, through the rising taxes on their hard-earned wages, were being expected to finance this.

It was not only the media that fanned the flames of anticlaimant hysteria during this period however. MPs too used their high political profile to draw attention to the so-called problem of abuse and to encourage pressure for punitive action to be taken, and government ministers also reinforced the ideological climate of suspicion. In the early 1970s Conservative Secretary of State Keith Joseph had established a committee to investigate the 'abuse of social security benefits' (Fisher Committee, 1973), and later Labour minister Stan Orme established a departmental coordinating committee on abuse (Golding and Middleton, 1982, p. 79). In the 1980s and 1990s these concerns continued and there were a number of attempts to 'crack down' on social security fraud and abuse by deploying additional staff on detection work (see Smith, 1985).

Of course the media and the political campaigns against social security abuse were in part a particular product of the social and economic circumstances of the 1970s and 1980s, as Golding and Middleton point out (1982, ch. 8). These were periods of rapidly growing unemployment and low wages due to economic recession and of a tax burden that was increasing, especially for those lower down the income scale. This was fertile ground for the exploitation of fears about what came to be called 'scrounging'. Golding and Middleton's study revealed the close links in these fears between media and political concerns, and public and private ideologies of poverty – and the consequences these have for perceptions of the causes of poverty and the policy solutions to it.

Their research also included a survey of attitudes towards welfare conducted in Leicester and Sunderland in 1977. This revealed a high degree of hostility to social security claimants among a large proportion of respondents. In particular hostility was directed at scroungers and those claimants, in some cases in very large numbers, who were accused of abusing state support. When asked about who deserved to receive social security support most respondents mentioned the old and the sick, only 5.9 per cent quoting the unemployed (ibid., p. 169). Furthermore the survey revealed that the highest estimates of abuse and the greatest resentment towards claimants came from those in low-paid, low-skilled employment (ibid., pp. 169–72).

Thus attitudes towards poverty reveal the distinctions between the working and the non-working poor and the deserving and the undeserving claimants that are the legacy of the history of poverty and poverty policy in Britain. What is more these are continually shaped and reshaped by ideologies of poverty contained in the media and other public forums, as one of Golding and Middleton's respondents revealed:

There are some genuine ones but the majority just bleed the country dry. The ones who have not worked for a long time should be made to do some kind of work and not claim benefit. 80% are scroungers. It's just what you hear, what's on TV, what's been in the papers over the last few weeks (fitter's wife, quoted in ibid., p. 173).

The ideological divisions also exploit the contradictory experience of real economic relations. For instance it is the low paid in low-quality jobs, paying taxes and working hard for little reward, who most resent those apparently benefiting at their expense, although this may be a notion of 'benefit' ill-informed by knowledge of the realities of dependency on social security. Golding and Middleton found that respondents underestimated family needs and overestimated benefits levels (ibid., p. 188). Such hostility may also rather misjudge the sources of the real hardships that low-paid workers are experiencing; for instance even reduced benefit levels would be unlikely to do much to reduce the burden on ordinary taxpayers or to improve the pay and conditions of unskilled workers.

Golding and Middleton's evidence was reinforced by other research into popular ideologies of poverty in Britain in the 1970s. In 1976 the EU included a survey of perceptions of poverty in a regular six-monthly opinion survey in member states (EC, 1977). One of the questions asked was about perceived causes of poverty. This revealed that in Britain a large proportion (43 per cent) believed that laziness and lack of willpower was the main cause – a much higher proportion than in all other countries, where structural causes were more frequently quoted. Another question asked was whether too much or too little was being done for the poor by the state. In Britain 20 per cent said too much, twice the proportion in any other country, with only Denmark and Luxembourg registering double figures at 10 per cent.

The EU survey revealed, therefore, that ideologies of poverty are very much the product of the particular forces at work in particular societies. They are the product of particular histories and current circumstances rather than universal truths (or untruths). Thus as history and circumstances change, so too do ideologies. As we have seen, poverty and inequality have increased in Britain (and in the EU) since the 1970s, and yet benefit levels and public support for the poor have been cut. A repeat of the survey in 1989 found laziness and unwillingness less often cited as causes of poverty in Britain than in 1976, down from 43 per cent to 18 per cent. There was also a much higher proportion (70 per cent) believing that public action to combat poverty was inadequate (EC, 1990). A further survey in 1993 did not break down the answers to the causes-of-poverty question by country, but across all twelve EU members – those citing laziness as a cause had decreased from 17 per cent in 1989 to 11 per cent (EC, 1994).

Ideologies of poverty provide an important backdrop to both academic and political debate. Academics and politicians may seek to influence popular ideologies, but they also share in them, and share in their reproduction. Golding and Middleton (1982, p. 199) point out that structural explanations of poverty are largely absent from popular debate because perceptions of poverty are linked to experiences of poverty and thus to the individuals who are, or are seen to be, experiencing it. The focus on poverty as an individual experience is also a predominant feature of many studies of poverty and much debate about the circumstances of the poor. Most academic studies do not directly reproduce the simplistic assumption that poverty is largely the result of individual idleness, condoned or encouraged by state largesse. However the focus on the question of who is poor and attempts to discern potential links between particular social groups and the experience of poverty can lead to forms of analysis that risk treating the victims of poverty as the authors of their own misfortune, and even as a separate group from the rest of the society in which their poverty is found.

Who is Poor?

It is important to know who is experiencing poverty and to examine whether those in particular social groups or social circumstances are more or less likely to suffer from it. It is also important to be able to see whether this distribution of poverty is similar or different in different societies and whether it varies over time within one society. This is not just a matter of sociological interest either, for the identification of poverty is linked to political action, and the identification of particular individuals or groups as disproportionately experiencing poverty may suggest that policies should be focused or targeted upon them in particular. However, as we have suggested, such an approach can lead in some cases to a pathological view of individual circumstances as the causes of poverty, rather than the symptoms of it.

The history of poverty in Britain, as we saw in Chapter 1, is linked to the development of the capitalist economy and the resulting impact of the regime of wage labour. Once removed from the land as a source of support people were at risk of poverty in a wage-based economy if they did not have capital resources or a wage (and an adequate wage) from employment. Risk of poverty is therefore related to class status. It is those in the working class, and especially those without recognised skills or qualifications on the margins of the labour market, who are most likely to be unemployed and poor. Indeed in a wage economy, for the vast majority of people to be unemployed also means to be poor – although this is not of course an iron law, as unemployed lottery winners and members of the aristocracy reveal.

Unemployment is also disproportionately experienced by particular categories of potential, or hopeful, workers. Those who are sick or suffer from a disability may find it difficult to secure waged labour because it may be assumed that they cannot perform effectively. Members of minority ethnic groups, in particular black people, may also be excluded from the labour market by the prejudice held by employers. Older people are excluded from the labour market by the widely held assumption that after a certain age they will want to, or will be required to, retire from work. All these groups experience particular problems of poverty, which we will discuss in more detail in Part III.

However, whilst in a wage labour economy unemployment increases the risk of being poor, at the same time employment provides no guarantee of escaping it. Many workers have found that all needs cannot be met from the low wages which they earn, especially if they have dependants to support. Even those in waged work may therefore be at risk of poverty, and low wages frequently fall below the state social security benefit levels. This is particularly likely to be the case for temporary or part-time workers based in particular sectors of the labour market, such as catering and cleaning in the service sector. This type of employment is also more likely to be undertaken by women, ethnic minority members or those with disabilities, thus reproducing among the working poor the social divisions that characterise the distribution of unemployment.

Research on poverty has consistently revealed that pensioners, the sick, the disabled and the unemployed – those outside the labour market – constitute the majority of the poor in Britain. However the proportions in these different categories have shifted over time, and this is particularly the case in the last quarter of the twentieth century. As Figure 2.1 (taken from the Rowntree Inquiry into Income and Wealth), reveals, since the early 1980s the number of employed and

FIGURE 2.1   *Individuals earning less than half the average income, by economic status, 1961–91*

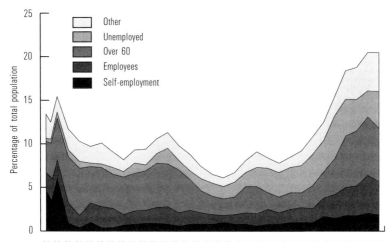

Source: Hills, 1995, p. 34.

self-employed people among the poor (defined as those earning less than half the average income) has grown significantly. Likewise the number of lone parents has grown over this time and they are at a high risk of poverty.

The changing composition of the poor is a reminder that poverty is both created and recreated by the social structures and social policies within which it is situated – it is a product of history. However the recent significant growth in the number of certain categories of poor people, such as the unemployed and lone parents, has been seen in some quarters as evidence that major social changes in the distribution and causes of poverty have been taking place in recent times in Britain and other advanced industrial countries, with important implications too for the nature of antipoverty policies to respond to this.

Temporary and relatively predictable exclusion from the labour market, for example because of sickness and retirement, has been associated with acknowledged risk of poverty linked to life-course events and changes in the life cycle. These events were identified by Rowntree in his early research on poverty, and we shall discuss them further in Chapter 7. They also give rise to a form of antipoverty policy linked to the need to protect people against such predictable life-cycle events, based on the redistribution through state support of resources across the life cycle – with contributions being paid at times of employment and benefits being received at times of exclusion. This is sometimes referred to as 'horizontal redistribution', and as we discuss in Chapter 14 it is linked to social security protection through social insurance.

However lone parents and the unemployed – especially the long-term unemployed, who have been the most rapidly growing group in the 1980s and 1990s – are not temporarily excluded from the labour market, they are more or less permanently removed from it. For them insurance protection based on benefits in return for contributions is not an effective form of protection as they are unable to make the required contributions; they are thus more likely to depend on social security benefits financed out of ordinary taxation and targeted directly at the poor – this will be discussed in Chapter 14. Provision of such support is referred to as 'vertical redistribution', a transfer of resources from those in employment to those who can prove they have no means of support.

The change in the composition of the poor referred to above has resulted in an increase in the number of people not protected from poverty by social insurance, due to long-term exclusion from the labour market or reliance on inadequate wages within it. Certainly the number of poor people having to rely on social assistance benefits has been growing dramatically in recent times. The number depending on income support, the basic assistance benefit in Britain, increased from four million in the 1970s to ten million in the 1990s, and this phenomenon has been repeated in most other European countries (Room *et al.*, 1989). Some commentators, especially those working for the EU, have thus begun to refer to these growing groups as the 'new poor' (Room *et al.*, 1990), and to suggest that the processes shaping both the risk and the experiences of these groups are different from the life-cycle events of past generations.

The changing experiences of new poverty, argue commentators such as Room, have moved beyond the narrow confines of material poverty and low income to encompass a broader process of 'social exclusion', which brings disadvantage and discrimination across a wide range of social activities (Room, 1995) (this will be discussed in more detail in Chapter 6). However the identification of a new form of poverty has been taken up by some as suggesting that the changes in the distribution of poverty are the product of changes in the activities and attitudes of poor people, and that new poverty is not just a product of shifts in types of employment and social security support, but evidence of fundamental alterations in social structure and class formation.

The Underclass

In the 1990s the debate on the changing composition of the poor has therefore sometimes taken a wider and more sinister path than simply counting and comparing the number of different social groups among the poor. The growth of new poverty has been seen as the product of new social forces, which it is argued affect particularly those groups that have come to constitute some of the largest elements among the poor – although, as we shall see shortly, these forces are not actually new at all. Identification of these social forces is based to a large extent upon pathological perceptions of the causes and dynamics of poverty within society, as we shall discuss in Chapter 3. They have been associated most dramatically, however, with suggestions that the new poor now occupy a different place within the class structure of late twentieth-century Britain – they are no longer the unemployed working class, but a separate underclass.

A number of studies of social divisions and the impact of poverty on certain social groups have sometimes referred to these groups of poor people as constituting an underclass at the bottom of, or even below, the rest of society. As early as 1973 Rex talked of black communities in Britain becoming a segregated underclass, which he later described as being 'cut off from the main class structures of society' (Rex, 1979, p. 86). In his major study of poverty, Townsend (1979, p. 819) suggested that the elderly experienced an 'underclass status', a status that he later (p. 920) extended to include the disabled, the chronically sick, the long-term unemployed and lone parent families. In a book dealing more generally with the labour market disadvantage of different social groups, Oliver (1991b, p. 133) argued that disabled people constitute an underclass in modern industrial society.

All these writers were using the concept of an underclass to describe the circumstances of particular groups in poverty. Their focus was largely on the exclusion experienced by such groups, their inability to participate in many social activities and their feeling of being trapped in a position of deprivation. Implicit in this, however, was the suggestion that perhaps the circumstances of such groups took them outside traditional class and social stratification approaches, based largely on labour market divisions, and left them as a distinct social class below the working class. This idea of the underclass as a new social class was taken up more directly by Runciman (1990), who linked it to the declining role of employment in the manufacturing industry in the late twentieth century and the economic changes that would inevitably flow from this. It was also discussed by some of the contributors to a debate on the concept initiated by the Policy Studies Institute (Smith, 1992).

It has perhaps been taken up most prominently, however, by the Labour MP and former director of the CPAG, Frank Field, in a book published in 1989 entitled *Losing Out? The Emergence of Britain's Underclass*. In this book Field argued that in the 1980s the universal values of citizenship that had underlain the postwar welfare state had been abandoned in favour of policies that had led to social polarisation and the emergence among the poor of a new British underclass. He identified the underclass as constituting three groups of people in particular: the long-term unemployed, single parents and the poorer elderly. Field also identified four causes of the emergence of such an underclass: the rise in unemployment, the widening of class divisions, the exclusion of the poor from rising living standards and the change in public attitudes away from altruism and towards self-interest.

Field's account of the emergence of this new British underclass was an outspokenly sympathetic one, and his clear aim in publishing the book was to seek to sway political opinion in favour of shifts in policy that might reverse the trends he had identified. Field was well-known for his views on poverty and social security policy. He was aware, however, that the notion of an underclass had been taken up and used rather differently by other writers, notably Dahrendorf, who in 1987 had talked of high unemployment as being related to the growth of an underclass in Britain, but who also associated this with undesirable characteristics and fatalistic attitudes amongst those affected.

Field was aware that there was 'a danger of these characteristics being interpreted as the "causes" of the problem itself, and from this it is only a short step to falling into the syndrome of "blaming the victim"' (Field, 1989, p. 6) although he himself later indulged in such causal association and moral judgement in his discussion of the problems of poor female lone parents. In practice, however, the 'danger' of associating description of the characteristics of an underclass with explanation of its causes, and moral judgement of the attitudes and behaviour of those within it, is one that is inescapably intertwined within all attempts to categorise those who experience poverty and deprivation as a separate social category, as a review of the history of the underclass concept reveals.

The Legacy of Pathology

The attempt to identify the individual or social characteristics of the poor as the source of their poverty implies a pathological model of the causation of poverty, as we shall discuss in Chapter 3; and the association of such pathological approaches with depictions of the poor as a separate or isolated group in society has been a recurring feature of debates about the problem of poverty in modern industrial society. Despite the renewed interest, this is not a new phenomenon; and in Britain, as Morris (1994, chs 2 and 3) discusses, the trend can be traced back at least as far as the early studies of poverty of the late nineteenth century.

In his seminal studies of poverty in London, Booth (1889) distinguished a group among the ranks of the poor whom he regarded as a 'residuum' of criminal or feckless characters who were a blight on the rest of the poor and lower classes. Stedman Jones (1971), writing about class structure and class struggle in the last two decades of the nineteenth century, described the fear of both middle-class and 'respectable' working-class commentators that the residuum would constitute a threat to social stability by undermining the work ethic and threatening social order. Part of the characterisation of the residuum, and part of the fear they supposedly generated, were the assumptions that they did not share the values and aspirations of the rest of society and that this cultural alienation, and the poverty that resulted from it, was transmitted within the underclass from generation to generation.

Macnicol (1987) takes up the development of this notion of intergenerational pathology or inherited deprivation by looking at the investigations by eugenicists during the interwar years into the evidence of genetic transfer of disability or deprivation. In many studies the distinction between physical disability and social deprivation was confused or overlooked, and it was only with the realisation of the horrors that eugenic approaches had led to in Nazi Germany that the prominence of this research began to decline.

In the United States in the 1960s the pathological tradition was taken up once again in response to the rediscovery of poverty within the

affluent postwar American society (Morris, 1994, ch. 3). One significant catalyst for this reemphasis on the categorisation of the poor was
the detailed research carried out by Lewis (1965, 1968) into the lives of
poor Puerto Rican families. Lewis described how such families, and the
communities in which they lived, had learned partly to cope with their
high level of poverty and deprivation by suppressing expectations of
greater wealth, or even secure employment, and developing a culture
that focused on the day-to-day strategies adopted by poor families and
individuals to survive without affluence in an affluent society. Lewis
referred to this as a 'culture of poverty' and his main concern was
merely to identify and describe it as a social phenomenon.

However the idea that poor people in affluent American society
might have a separate culture of poverty, which therefore prevented
them from ascribing to or achieving the wealth that was available to
others, quickly became adapted as a pathological explanation of the
persistence of such poverty. Because poverty in the United States is
experienced much more by black people, especially those living in
black inner city neighbourhoods, this pathology also acquired a racial,
or racist, dimension (Jennings, 1994). For instance Moynihan (1965,
p. 5) talked of the 'deterioration of the Negro family' as the cause of
poverty among black Americans, and Wilson (1987) identified poor
blacks as belonging to an underclass isolated from other sections of
the American community.

The reemphasis on pathological explanations of the poverty that
was rediscovered in affluent America in the 1960s was followed by a
significant change in emphasis in the policy responses to the problem,
as we shall discuss in Chapter 15. This resulted particularly in a change
in focus towards the families and communities of the poor rather than
towards the broader social and economic structure of which they were
a part. Such a change was also experienced in Britain in the 1960s and
1970s following the renewal here too of pathological approaches to
poverty, based in part on the debates in the United States.

Evidence of social pathology could be found in the Plowden Report
(1967) on primary schooling, which resulted in the later development
of 'education priority areas'. However perhaps the most famous
British example of the pathology of poverty during this period were
the views Conservative minister Keith Joseph expressed in a speech to
the Pre-School Playgroups Association in 1972. Joseph referred to
poor people as having 'problems of maladjustment' and suggested that
such inadequacies might be transmitted intergenerationally via what
he described as a 'cycle of deprivation'.

Despite the failures of the policy developments of the 1960s in the United States, the pathological approach to poverty returned again in the 1980s, with direct reference to sections of the poor (black) population as an underclass. This was first identified in the work of Auletta (1982), who talked about nine million people constituting an underclass with undesirable and socially disruptive values. It was taken up particularly however by Murray (1984), a right-wing political scientist, who argued that welfare benefits had helped to create a culture of dependency that attracted some people into underclass status, identifying in particular the supposedly growing number of young female lone parents who had chosen a life of parenthood on welfare benefits rather then accept the responsibilities of marriage. Murray argued that through such – inadequate – single parenting a culture of deprivation and dependency was transmitted to subsequent generations, thus recreating an isolated and hopeless class of welfare recipients.

In 1989 Murray was invited over to Britain by *The Sunday Times* newspaper to investigate the possible development of an underclass in Britain similar to that he had identified in the United States. The high level of poverty and welfare dependency had suggested to some that this might be the case. The problem of a potential underclass had been referred to by Dahrendorf in 1987, and a number of incidents of social unrest in inner city areas with high levels of deprivation had resulted in press reports suggesting links between hopelessness and lawlessness among unemployed benefit dependants.

Murray's findings were published by the right-wing policy group, the Institute of Economic Affairs (IEA), together with commentaries by critics (Murray, 1990). His conclusion was that things were not as serious in Britain in the 1980s as they were in the United States, but that a new underclass was emerging as a result of increasing levels of illegitimacy and single parenthood, high levels of criminality and the dropping-out of the labour force of young unemployed male school-leavers who had never developed the habit of employment. His account was both bleak and forthright, identifying the underclass as a 'type of poverty' and suggesting that the current policy responses were likely to accentuate rather than relieve the problem. It also contained clear moral overtones disapproving of the characteristics he identified as causing underclass status, such as illegitimacy and fecklessness.

These moral issues were taken up by Murray even more directly when he returned to Britain five years later (Murray, 1994). This time he singled out single mothers as the major cause of changing attitudes and values among the new generations of the poor, and blamed overgenerous social security benefits for encouraging women to become single mothers. As in 1990, Murray's views were challenged by other commentators, who condemned his pathological approach as an example of blaming the victims of poverty for their plight; but it was Murray's opinions that received the widest coverage in the popular press.

The work of Murray is the clearest and most recent example of a long historical tradition of the pathologisation of poverty in academic research and political debate. It focuses on the culture of poverty as an explanation of the problem of deprivation, and subsequently as a justification for a particular policy response to it. As Ryan (1971, p. 8) put it in a book entitled *Blaming the Victim*:

> First, identify a social problem. Second, study those affected by the problem and discover in what ways they are different from the rest of us. . . . Third, define the difference as the cause of the social problem itself. Finally, of course, assign a government bureaucrat to invent a humanitarian action programme to correct the difference.

In blaming the victim, therefore, poverty becomes the problem of the poor people themselves, and identifying them as occupying a distinct status as an underclass as a result of this provides a spurious socio-economic justification.

Cultural Divisions and the Poor

Murray (1990, 1994) and Field (1989) provide quite different usages of the underclass concept in the context of poverty in Britain at the end of the twentieth century. Their political traditions and political motivations in resurrecting the term and applying it to groups of poor people are very different, and largely conflicting. Murray is a right-wing theorist and wishes to identify poor groups as a separate social category in order to demonstrate that their separation is the cause of their poverty. Field is on the political left and wishes to identify them as separate in order to persuade policy makers to develop measures to reintegrate them.

Moreover these different usages are not new or unique to the recent debates on the underclass. Researchers who have studied the 'culture of poverty', such as Lewis (1965, 1968), have frequently done so in order to describe rather than condemn the isolation and separation of the poor. Attempts to identify the social divisions and social characteristics of poverty do not always identify these as causes of deprivation, and even pathological approaches to poverty do not all carry with them adverse moral judgements of the characteristics associated with those found to be poor.

However the 'long and undistinguished pedigree' (Macnicol, 1987, p. 315) of the concept means that its associations with pathological explanations of the problem of poverty are never far below the surface of academic and political debate on the underclass. Thus, as Dean (1991, p. 35) has argued, 'It represents, not a useful concept, but a potent symbol'; and in an understanding of poverty this potential symbolism must be recognised and understood. This means that the social divisions and cultural differences that characterise poor groups must be understood within the broader social and economic context in which those groups, and their deprivation, are situated, and that assumptions about the transmission of poverty should be critically examined in the light of empirical evidence. Mann (1992) provides a history of this context and of the role of social divisions within broader welfare policy in Britain, and Morris (1994) discusses recent debates and research evidence.

In fact the research that has been carried out into the transmission of poverty between groups or across generations has largely contradicted the 'cycles of deprivation' thesis that underlies many pathological approaches towards the poor. Following Keith Joseph's identification of the problem of intergenerational transmission, in the 1970s a major research programme was commissioned by the government and the Social Science Research Council to investigate the evidence on inherited deprivation. The researchers found the problem to be significantly more complex, both theoretically and methodologically, than had been suggested in Joseph's notion of a cycle (Rutter and Madge, 1976), and the overall conclusion drawn by the researchers was that there was no evidence to support the thesis of intergenerational transmission of poverty (Brown and Madge, 1982).

More recently research examining the social circumstances and individual attitudes of poor people on the margins of the labour market has also cast doubt on the existence of an underclass as a separate and isolated social group (Morris, 1995). For a start evidence suggests that there are significant differences within this group between the relatively large number who over time are moving in and out of employment and have close links with the labour market and the smaller number of very-long-term unemployed (Morris and Irwin, 1992). Therefore not all of those outside the labour market are subject to economic exclusion, so – as Gallie (1988) has argued – there is no automatic link between economic circumstances and social differentiation.

The assumptions about separate value systems and cultural divisions among poor people are also suspect when contrasted with the findings of empirical studies of the lives of poor people. Townsend's (1979) major study of poverty in Britain revealed that poor people had very similar hopes and values to those who were better off in British society – their problem was that they were frequently prevented from realising these and had learnt, in most cases reluctantly, to cope with this plight. In a study of poor families in north-east England in the late 1980s, Bradshaw and Holmes (1989, p. 138) concluded:

> But at a time when British poverty is again being discussed in terms of an underclass, it is of crucial importance to recognise that these families, and probably millions more like them living on social security benefits, are in no sense a detached and isolated group cut off from the rest of society. They are just the same people as the rest of our population, with the same culture and aspirations but with simply too little money to be able to share in the activities and possessions of everyday life with the rest of the population.

In fact studies of attitudes towards poverty that focus not only on the poor and deprived but on the whole of society, reveal that the relationship between the exclusion of the poor and the problem of poverty is rather different from that discussed in pathological approaches to deprivation. Golding and Middleton's (1982) study found considerable evidence that those who were not poor, and in particular members of the working class who felt themselves to be struggling hard to avoid poverty, were those who identified poverty as a problem that poor people had brought on themselves. For instance a forty-year-old male teacher provided a classical example of using the cycle of deprivation thesis to blame the victims of poverty: 'Poor people often have foolish parents, those who don't encourage industry and thrift, they have confused priorities' (Golding and Middleton, 1982, p. 197).

What research such as this reveals is that the separation and cultural isolation of the underclass is not the problem of the poor who supposedly inhabit it, but of the rest of society, who see in it some justification for their (slightly) higher social status. There is no hard evidence to suggest that there are economic or cultural differences between the poor and the rest of society. However, for those who suggest that there are, there is the moral comfort of believing that the problems of poverty and exclusion that poor people experience are 'theirs' rather than 'ours'.

3

The Causes of Poverty

The Dynamics of Deprivation

Implicit in much of the debate on the emergence of an underclass or new forms of poverty in modern society are assumptions about the causes of poverty. Once we recognise that poverty exists, then we know as social scientists that it must have a cause (or causes); and if we can identify the cause of poverty, then that should give us a basis to develop a policy response to it. For underclass theorists such as Murray (1990, 1994) poverty is seen as the product of individual weakness or fecklessness. This is a pathological model of social causation, and it implies a policy response that focuses on individuals and seeks to change their attitudes or behaviour – as we shall see in Chapter 15, such policies have been developed in Britain and other advanced industrial countries.

However this pathological model of individual causation is not shared by all, and indeed Murray's position is challenged by some of the critics featured in his books. Some of these critics argue that poverty is not the product of individual weakness or failure, but rather it is the result of the complex operation of social forces. Social forces include the actions of classes, groups, agencies and institutions that interact within a particular social and economic order. These forces, and the social and economic order within which they operate, change over time – they are dynamic, not static. However they continually create and recreate the social circumstances that people experience, and within which some people are poor. Such an approach focuses not on individuals as the authors of their own fortunes (or misfortunes), but on the structural forces that have shaped those fortunes – in other words on a structural model of social causation.

Such a structural approach was taken up by Ferge and Millar (1987) in a book that included studies of poverty in a range of different countries in both Western and the then socialist Eastern Europe. The authors in this book argue that an approach that focuses on particular groups of poor people, as the underclass thesis does, ignores this changing structural context and process, which, in the title of the book, they refer to as the *Dynamics of Deprivation*.

The important point about the phrase the 'dynamics of deprivation', however, is the attention it draws to the changing context in which poverty, or deprivation, is experienced. Poverty, like all social phenomena, is the product of social change; and if we want to identify the cause of poverty, then we need to examine the dynamics of social change. In their different ways both the pathological and the structural approaches to explaining poverty do this, although they focus on starkly contrasting aspects of it. In his 1978 study of the explanations of poverty Holman sought to identify and contrast a number of different perspectives, which we can classify as either pathological or structural approaches; a similar distinction was later made by Spicker (1993, ch. 6). We will examine some of these approaches below. The suggestion by Holman and others is that some perspectives may be preferable to others in explaining the causes of poverty. However it may be the case that many have a role to play in explaining poverty, for indeed it is likely that the poverty we find in Britain today is the consequence not of the actions of one individual or agency, but of the interactions of many different causes.

Pathological Causes

The first category of explanation that Holman (1978) refers to in his book is 'individuals and poverty'. This includes the pathological explanations of indolence and fecklessness adopted by some underclass theorists, as we discussed above. It also includes *genetic* explanations, which seek to relate social status with supposedly inherited characteristics such as intelligence, and *psychological* approaches, which explain individuals' (non)achievements by reference to acquired or developed personality traits. These are potential explanations of poverty and they do include a dynamic, albeit a largely immutable one, deriving from nature rather than nurture. In many cases such individual explanations imply a rejection of social or structural explanations, and they can be criticised as approaches that seek to blame the victims for their own poverty.

Proponents would argue, however, that genetic or psychological approaches do not imply individual blame, they merely establish causal links. However there are serious questions as to whether the evidence to support those links has been satisfactorily established, especially since, as Holman (1978) discusses, most of those who might appear to have inherited the characteristics associated with poverty do not themselves become poor.

A second category of explanations, which have also been interpreted by critics as a case of blaming the victims, are those that focus on the family or the community as the cause of poverty. One of the most well-known proponents of such approaches is the former Conservative Social Services Minister Keith Joseph (1972). As we saw in Chapter 2, Joseph referred to this as a 'cycle' of deprivation' in which the inadequate parenting, lowered aspirations and disadvantaged environment of families and communities became internalised as part of the values of their children as they grew up. Thus when these children reached adulthood their expectations and abilities were lowered, and they more readily expected and accepted the poverty and deprivation of their parents and acquaintances.

As discussed earlier, such an approach has been very influential in recent debates on the emergence of an underclass as a product of social isolation and the adoption of a culture of poverty. This has also been reflected in the development of antipoverty policy, as we shall discuss in Chapter 15. Although this approach avoids ascribing poverty to individuals, it still contains a pathological model of poverty creation and recreation. It is the poor themselves who, it is suggested, produce and reproduce their poverty, but collectively through the culture of the family and the community.

This does not explain the broader circumstances in which families and communities are situated, nor how they came to be poor in the first place. Nor does it explain how some individuals and families manage to escape the culture of poverty. The research commissioned by Joseph in the 1970s to investigate the operation of 'cycles of deprivation' raised these questions when it concluded that most children of poor homes did not repeat the poverty of their families and communities, and that most of those who were poor did not themselves come from such deprived backgrounds (Brown and Madge, 1982). This suggests that explanation should focus on the creation of such backgrounds, and not just on the behaviour of individuals within them. This takes us beyond the pathological and onto the structural level.

Structural Causes

Poverty is a product of dynamic social forces, as we have discussed; and in modern welfare capitalist countries state policies have been developed over time to combat or reduce poverty. If, therefore, despite these policies poverty persists then perhaps explanation should look not to the failings of the poor but to the failings of antipoverty policies and to the agencies and institutions responsible for making them work. If the victims of poverty are not to blame, then the blame must lie elsewhere. A focus on agency failure directs attention towards those who are supposedly charged with eliminating poverty.

In particular, of course, this means the social security system, and there are many who have pointed to the failure of social security to remove poverty (MacGregor, 1981; Donnison, 1982; Spicker, 1993). For instance many claimants do not receive the benefits to which they are entitled. Benefit publicity is poor and benefit agencies are often hostile and apparently suspicious of the rights of potential claimants. Complex rules on entitlement exclude some in need and even those who do receive benefit may not receive sufficient to meet their needs as they or others define them. Benefit policy and benefit delivery may therefore contribute as much to the experience of poverty as to its elimination; and as C. Walker (1993) discusses in her analysis of assistance benefits, social security may even be seen as a way of 'managing poverty'.

This is not to suggest, however, that social security policy has no impact on the level of poverty. Clearly without social security provision the extent and depth of poverty in Britain would be much worse; and social security also has objectives other than the elimination or relief of poverty, as we shall discuss in more detail in Chapter 14. Furthermore social security is not the only area of policy implementation that may be accused of contributing to the reproduction of poverty. Housing policies, in both the public and private sectors, have obviously failed those poor people who are homeless. Health policies, or the lack of them, may have resulted in sickness and disability, leading to poverty. Social services may have failed to assist with, or may even have added to, the problems that have brought individuals and families into poverty. Indeed all agencies, be they state, voluntary or those in the private sector, who contribute to the range of social services within the welfare state may be accused of failing in their tasks as long as poverty persists among their clients or potential clients.

This may be the fault of individual officers within these agencies experiencing low morale or falling down on their jobs; or it may be the fault of the structure and operational practices of agencies, which make them unable to achieve success whatever their workers may do. However it may also be the fault of the policies with which the agencies have been charged; or, as some have argued (see Novak, 1984), perhaps a misconception of what such policies are seeking to achieve. Social security systems, for instance, are concerned with controlling and disciplining the poor as well as, or perhaps even rather than, removing their poverty. This is a matter of policy, however, and not merely institutional practice.

Focusing on such policy failure, or the failure to develop appropriate policy, is an approach to explaining the dynamics of poverty that moves beyond the level of individuals, communities or agencies – or rather moves to the level of those individuals and agencies who, through political action, claim to be prepared and able to influence social policies and social structures. As MacGregor (1981) argues, policies to combat poverty are the product of political decisions, and as we have discussed, poverty is a political concept. The identification of poverty is linked to political action to eliminate it; thus if poverty remains then politicians have failed either to identify it accurately or to develop appropriate policies in response to it. In such an approach therefore, poverty is the result of political failure, or the failure of political will.

Of course not all politicians would admit that they had failed to eliminate poverty. Indeed, as we have seen, members of the Conservative governments of the 1980s were outspoken in their claim that poverty, as they defined it, had been eliminated through the policies developed and implemented by themselves and previous governments. What this reveals, as we know however, is that political debates on poverty policy cannot be separated from debates on the problem of poverty itself. But this does not negate the value of approaches that seek to explain the causes of poverty within the dynamics of political decision making. Indeed quite the reverse is true.

The question of who takes political decisions and how their decisions are put into practice is obviously crucial in determining the circumstances of people living within that political system, including the poor. There is a powerful logic to the argument that we need look no further than politics and politicians to find the causes of poverty – they run the country, they are responsible for the problems within it.

For a long time sociologists have pointed out, however, that no matter how powerful politicians may seem, or may even believe themselves to be, they do not control all aspects of the societies they claim to run. Indeed politicians have little or no control over many events, both of a day-to-day nature and of major social and economic importance – and sometimes they are quick to point this out when referring to the actions of other governments or international agencies. Politicians may be prepared to accept the blame for the continued existence of poverty, but it is far from clear that they are entirely responsible for it.

One of the main reasons why politicians cannot control all aspects of society, or certainly all aspects of welfare capitalist societies such as Britain, is the fact that many of the social events in them are the product of economic forces and economic decision making that politicians do not control. In practice most politicians would probably admit this and would claim that their aim is to *manage* the economy. However they would probably readily admit that this is an aim which they can at best only partly achieve; and even that partial achievement may depend to a large extent on what they, or we, mean by 'manage'.

In a largely market-based economy within an international context in which economic planning often takes place at a supranational level, national politicians cannot act freely and cannot change or influence all economic forces. The vagaries of national and international forces thus affect people in ways that politicians cannot control. Such forces can create poverty, which politicians may have intended or hoped to avoid, and conversely they can reduce poverty without direct political action being taken.

This is obviously the case with the poverty associated with the high levels of unemployment resulting from the international economic recessions in the 1930s, 1970s and 1980s. It was also the case for the relatively low levels of poverty associated with periods of economic boom, such as in the 1950s. Poverty is not just the result of unemployment caused by economic recession, however. Economic decline also results in (1) lower wages, leading to poverty for some in employment; (2) earlier retirement and lower pensions, thus increasing poverty among the old; and (3), perhaps most importantly, pressure to cut public spending on benefits, leading to less state support for the non-employed and employed poor.

Changes in national and international economic forces therefore can and do cause poverty. This may suggest a kind of fatalism that assumes because there is nothing even politicians can do about it, then we must simply 'grin and bear it' and hope for better times ahead. Recognition of the importance of economic forces does not necessarily imply fatalism however. Economic forces are largely the products of decisions taken by people, and the consequences of these decisions are to a very large extent predictable – and they can, or could, be changed. Indeed they can be changed as a result of pressure from politicians. The point to understand is not that politicians cannot control economic forces, but rather that they *must* seek to control economic forces if they wish to influence the events that economic forces largely determine. Policy responses that merely focus on the consequences of economic forces therefore will and do fail; but policies that seek to prevent these consequences by seeking to influence economic forces ultimately can and will succeed – a point that will be returned to in the final chapter.

As was suggested in Chapter 1, there are those who argue that the interaction of political will and economic forces cannot solve the problem of poverty because it is this which is its cause. This is the essence of the argument developed by Novak in 1988 and to which he has returned more recently (Novak, 1995). Poverty is produced by the operation of a capitalist wage labour market because to operate efficiently that wage labour market needs poverty, or rather poor people existing on the fringes of it. Fear of poverty acts as a disciplinary force on workers and provides evidence that just as hard work and obedience will bring its rewards, so will idleness or inactivity lead to punishment. Much the same sort of approach concludes Holman's (1978) review of explanations of poverty. He refers to it as a structural explanation in which poverty is merely the converse of wealth within a stratified society; if we accept the one then we must also be prepared to accept the other.

The danger of adopting wholesale such structural approaches, however, is that they can tend to be little more than statements of the obvious. Poverty is the product of an unequal or capitalist society; therefore only if we change the society will poverty cease to exist. As an explanation of the cause of poverty this tells us everything and nothing. As a programme for policy action it is hopelessly unrealistic. Of course it is the socioeconomic structure, and the political process that reproduces this, that causes poverty. But it is a complex and ever-changing structure and it is far from immutable. The structure can be changed, and particular aspects of it can be reformed or restructured. The structure of society includes the political actors, the institutions and agencies, and the families and communities of other explanatory models. All are in part responsible for the circumstances in which particular people (including the poor) currently find themselves – and all can change, or be changed, in ways that will alter those circumstances and the prospects of individuals within them.

The search for the cause of poverty cannot therefore be confined within one or other of these causal frameworks; it must encompass the interaction of them all. At the same time, therefore, the solution to the problem must involve action and change at a number of different levels of society. Of course such action has been taken in the past, and will be taken in the future. Policies to combat poverty do already exist, as we shall see in Part VI, and they draw on different aspects of the causal frameworks discussed above. However they are also informed by the broader political or ideological perspectives that influence the exercise of political power. These ideological perspectives overlay the causal frameworks discussed above, and influence the way in which the policies they suggest are translated into action through the political process. They are therefore an important element in understanding the dynamics of deprivation and exclusion.

Ideological Perspectives

Understanding ideological perspectives on welfare and their influence on the development of social policy and political debates would involve an investigation and analysis of theory and philosophy that are beyond the scope of this book. The influence of ideological perspectives on the development of social policy have been outlined by the author elsewhere (Alcock, 1996a, ch. 7), and the major ideological perspectives on welfare are discussed in more detail by George and Wilding (1994). Nevertheless it is worth briefly discussing here some of these major ideological perspectives and the different implications they have for the development of antipoverty policy, for all have been influential at different times in structuring recent policy and debate on poverty in Britain. The four most important perspectives are neoliberalism, conservatism, social democracy and revolutionary socialism.

Neoliberalism

In recent years neoliberalism has been associated with the writings of the new right on welfare (Barry, 1987; Green, 1987; and see Levitas, 1986). It also rose to prominence in Britain in the 1980s because of the support neoliberal policies received from some members of the

Thatcher governments, including the prime minister herself (see Gamble, 1989). However neoliberal thinking has remained a significant, if less prominent, strand in political theory throughout the twentieth century. It was presented in the 1940s as a criticism of the rapid moves towards state welfare provision in the country (Hayek, 1944), and was raised again later in the writing of the American critic Milton Friedman (1962).

In general the view of the neoliberals is that state activity in the economy should be kept to a minimum in order to avoid interfering with the operation of the market, and in particular that the state should not meddle in social affairs but rather should leave individuals and families to provide for themselves as and how they wish. Further than this their belief is that rather than helping to solve the problem of poverty, state intervention has only made it worse, in particular by encouraging dependency and undermining self-sufficiency.

This argument was outlined in a short and pithy article by the Thatcherite minister Rhodes Boyson in 1971, called *Down with the Poor*, and it was later pursued in more depth by the American political scientist Murray (1984). Both argued that the state should not interfere with the dynamics of poverty, and that as a consequence therefore all state support for the poor should be withdrawn. However this extreme position has never been seriously pursued by governments in Britain, including the Thatcher governments of the 1980s, as new right theorists themselves have recognised (Green, 1996). Nor has it been pursued in other developed capitalist countries. Of course lack of state antipoverty measures is not uncommon in some developing countries, although this is not generally the product of neoliberal political theory, and it has not resulted in the absence of poverty. As a recipe for structural change to combat poverty, therefore, the neoliberal message is a relatively simple one – reduce state support and encourage self-sufficiency. What this might achieve however is debatable.

Conservatism

Conservatism is a loose term that is used to cover a fairly wide range of political approaches, from those of Conservative governments in Britain, including for the most part even the Thatcher governments of the 1980s, to those of European Christian Democrat governments, such as in Germany, Belgium and the Netherlands in the 1980s. Supporters of conservatism believe in the need for state intervention, in particular in matters of social policy, in order to ameliorate or even counteract the problems arising in a predominantly market-based economy. In the case of poverty this means recognising that it is, at least potentially, a problem requiring state action. However conservatives generally do not wish to see too much state interference in the operation of the market economy, especially the labour market, and in particular they do not want social policy to become an expensive drain on public expenditure.

In general therefore conservatives have tended to operate what is sometimes called a 'casualty approach' to poverty (Townsend, 1984). The poor are the casualties of the market and their symptoms of suffering must be relieved by the state. This is referred to as relieving, rather than preventing, poverty; and it leads to measures to target state support on those individuals or communities that are positively identified as poor. Commentators have called these 'selective' approaches to poverty relief, and contrasted them with the 'universal' approaches preferred by social democrats (see MacGregor, 1981, ch. 5). As we shall see in Chapter 14, these differences also lead to rather different conceptions of the role of state policy in combating poverty.

Conservatism has been a powerful force in British politics throughout the twentieth century, despite the introduction of strong welfare state provision in the period immediately following the Second World War. In the last two decades in particular, selectivism has come once again to dominate the politics of poverty in Britain. This has not been without its problems however – nor its contradictions. For in Britain selectivism has had to compete with universalism within the field of welfare politics, as conservatism has competed with social democracy.

Social Democracy

Social democrats include, by and large, the Labour Party in Britain and much of the Liberal Democratic Party. The governments of Scandinavian countries such as Sweden, Denmark and Norway have also been social democratic ones throughout most of the postwar period. Perhaps the main difference, both in broad political terms and in the field of welfare politics, between social democrats and conservatives is that whereas conservatives operate with a minimal model of social policy when dealing with the casualties of the market economy, social democrats seek to intervene, or interfere, in the market economy in order to prevent the problems occurring in the first place. Thus for them social policy objectives should be related to economic policy measures, a point to which we will return in Chapter 16.

In the case of poverty this means intervention in the labour market to reduce unemployment and to improve pay and conditions through minimum wages and support for child care, and the provision of comprehensive benefits through social security for those outside the labour market and for additional costs related to such things as child care or disability. Social democrats generally believe in providing benefits on a universal basis to all those who satisfy certain conditions, without imposing a test to determine whether they are poor. However they generally expect those able to take employment in the labour market to do so; and in order to encourage them to do so they may provide both positive incentives, such as state-supported training schemes, and negative incentives, such as availability for work tests as a condition of receiving benefits.

Revolutionary Socialism

Revolutionary socialists, as the name suggests, believe in the revolutionary transformation of capitalist society into socialist society, arguing that this will remove the poverty that in capitalist society results from the operation of a punitive labour market. The failure of the socialist countries of Eastern Europe and the Soviet Union, which became internationally apparent in the 1990s, has significantly undermined the appeal of socialism as a solution to the problem of poverty in capitalist societies; but it has not entirely undermined the revolutionary case. Many argue that these were not in any event proper socialist countries, in particular because they did not pursue collective policies to achieve egalitarian aims but merely reproduced inequalities through state appropriation of wealth and influence.

Crucial to the socialist case is the removal of the capitalist labour market, which they identify as the cause of poverty through unemployment and low pay, and the replacement of this with a system of state-provided support for all, together with the confiscation and redistribution of the wealth of the rich. Although this may seem a distant, even a Utopian goal there are some who argue that the consistently high levels of unemployment in capitalist countries in the latter part of the twentieth century, and the increasingly obvious environmental costs of uncontrolled growth in profit-oriented production, mean that the alternative of a non-productive, non-market social order is becoming ever more attractive (Gorz, 1982, 1991).

What is more the idea of a distribution of basic resources to all, irrespective of labour market position, is now supported by a wide range of opinion, extending beyond the socialist revolutionaries themselves (see Van Parijs, 1992). Thus whilst revolutionary socialism would still require a radical transformation of the social and economic structure of existing welfare capitalist countries, its vision of a society in which the distribution of resources does not depend primarily on the labour market is perhaps no longer such a distant prospect.

The problem with such broad summaries of these different approaches is that they are really only caricatures of a wide range of complex and contradictory political theories and arguments, which in practice frequently overlap and merge. Thus the views of many fit only uncomfortably into one category or another. However they do provide a brief guide to the major differences within the approaches to social reform propounded by political theorists and political actors; and they provide a guide to the framework within which political action to challenge the causes of poverty is likely to be discussed and implemented. In Part IV we will examine in more detail the major policies that have been developed to respond to poverty in Britain in the latter part of the twentieth century and assess how successful the differing approaches have thus far been in tackling those causes.

4

Poverty in Europe and Beyond

International Comparisons

Most discussion of the problem of poverty, and certainly most research into it, takes place within national boundaries. However poverty is of course an international, or rather a global problem. There are gross inequalities in the resources available to peoples in different parts of the world and within all countries, and this results in deprivation in relatively affluent countries and in severe deprivation in some less affluent ones when compared with wider international standards. We live in a profoundly unequal world in which the extreme poverty that leads to starvation and early death is unfortunately still quite common.

Such international inequity and extreme poverty are not new phenomena, but the increasing development of international contact through international agencies and international trade are making it an ever more immediate problem for a wider community of nations. Also the increasing scope and depth of the communications media are bringing more knowledge of the problem into the homes and consciousness of ever more people. Poverty is thus now an international problem, and politicians and academics are increasingly beginning to realise and argue this (see George, 1988; Townsend, 1993, 1995).

Recognition of the international dimension of the problem of poverty, however, brings with it problems of definition and analysis extending beyond the issues that have dominated national debate and research in countries such as Britain. As discussed in this book, the problem of understanding poverty in a country such as Britain involves appraising a complex range of debates and assessing confusing and sometimes seemingly contradictory evidence. To develop this understanding on to an international scale requires extension and expansion of both theoretical definition and empirical measurement. This is an important development, but it is one that cannot be given adequate attention here. This is primarily a book about poverty in Britain, not about poverty in the world; and whilst it is essential to recognise the wider international context of the problem it is not possible to do justice to the broader issues involved within the confines of a text such as this.

However, because of the increasing importance of international contacts and international cooperation, it is no longer possible to understand poverty in Britain without some understanding of the international context within which British inequality and deprivation is situated, and of the growth of international initiatives in antipoverty policy and strategy. In Britain in the 1990s this international context includes in particular the European Union (EU), of which Britain is a member state. Study and debate on poverty in Europe is now well established and EU initiatives to challenge poverty in member states are a significant feature of antipoverty policy. As will be discussed below therefore, the European context of British poverty and anti-poverty policy is likely to be of increasing importance to any under-standing of the problem and the responses to it.

International comparisons in the study of poverty are therefore increasingly relevant; however they are inevitably fraught with diffi-culties. In a survey of poverty rates in a range of OECD countries, Atkinson (1990b) pointed out that comparisons must take account of the problem of comparability of data across national boundaries, for surveys carried out either independently or by national governments may not necessarily use the same bases for definition or measurement in different countries. This is of course a serious methodological and analytical problem, and Atkinson discussed four of the main problems involved in it in a little more detail. These are:

- The use of different indicators of poverty.
- The application of different poverty lines to income or expenditure distributions.
- The adoption of different units, families or households for measure-ment.
- The choice of different equivalence scales to compare the resources available within units.

These present problems for the analysis and comparison of data from research studies a single country, but such problems are magnified several times when analysis or comparison seeks to transcend national boundaries.

Nevertheless progress has been made in recent years in the international analysis of data on poverty. The Luxembourg Income Study (LIS), for instance, now provides an international data base on poverty from seventeen advanced industrial countries in the EU and beyond (see de Tombeur and Ladewig, 1994). Significant effort has been made within this to overcome, or at least to recognise, some of the problems of the comparability of data across countries, and within the limits of this the LIS permits academics and politicians in participating countries to contrast the levels and distribution of poverty in different nations and assess over time the impact of differing antipoverty policies in differing social contexts, as Mitchell (1991) has demonstrated. This has implications for our understanding of the problem of poverty in Britain, and it has implications for the development of antipoverty policy too. In the 1990s therefore the international, and in particular the European, dimension of British poverty policy is of more significance than it has ever been in the past.

Poverty in Europe

Despite the existence of wide cultural and political differences, which have often divided Europe over the last hundred years and more, the economic and social development of most Western European countries has followed a pattern that provides for closer comparison and cooperation than exists between many other groups of countries throughout the world. Further, since the collapse of Eastern Bloc communism in the late 1980s this pattern is likely to be imported in some form to many Eastern European countries over the next decade or so. Thus the growth of capitalism and industrialisation, the development of political democracy and the establishment of welfare states have produced within European countries patterns of poverty and poverty policy that permit a relatively easy comparison to be made between trends and achievements.

The relative homogeneity of Western European socioeconomic structures has been consolidated considerably since the end of the Second World War by the economic and social unity provided by the creation and development of the EU. Initially covering six countries (France, Italy, West Germany, Belgium, the Netherlands and Luxembourg) the European Economic Community, as it was then called, has expanded to cover fifteen countries comprising most of Western Europe; and it has transformed itself in to a political as well as an economic union – the EU. In the process of this the EU has expanded from being a predominantly economic and trading partnership to become a focus for joint economic and social planning across a wide spectrum of financial and welfare issues, and it is heading towards greater social and political unity at the turn of the century (Hantrais, 1995).

In the EU in particular therefore, it is possible to identify common problems of poverty and inequality and common strategies for responding to this, and these can be compared between different nation states with some degree of complementarity. All countries have experienced the impact of industrialisation and the creation of labour markets, although in some countries the size of the agricultural sector of the economy has remained large compared with others. This has resulted in similar patterns to those in Britain of wage poverty and poverty resulting from unemployment, and also in similar family structures in which the impact of this poverty is experienced differently by men and women at different stages of their life cycle. As we shall see therefore statistical comparisons between countries reveal similar patterns of poverty, even though the extent and depth of it varies.

The development of welfare state regimes in all Western European countries has also resulted in a range of similar policies for preventing or relieving poverty. The notion of welfare state regimes has been discussed by Esping Andersen (1990) as a means of contrasting the similarities and differences in the structure of welfare provision in different countries. Drawing on this, Leibfried (1993) has identified four models of welfare state regime within Western Europe:

- The rudimentary (catholic) welfare state associated with the Latin rim countries.
- The institutional (corporatist) welfare state associated with the Bismarck regime in Germany.
- The residual (liberal) welfare state associated with Britain.
- The modern (social democratic) welfare state associated with the Scandinavian countries.

Esping-Andersen and Leibfried discuss welfare regimes at a very general level; however Mitchell (1991) has taken up their approach to investigate and compare income transfer policies across ten welfare states.

Of course these regimes are ideal types, summaries of features that are not replicated precisely in individual countries – for instance Britain does not have an exclusively residual welfare state. But they do represent approaches to social policy that provide for comparison between similar policy developments in different countries. This is particularly true of the original six EU nations, which all developed versions of corporatist welfare states with very similar social security and other antipoverty measures based on employment-related insurance benefits, with a range of limited safety net measures for those not covered by the main scheme. As will be discussed below, the development of EU policy and planning has led to increasing pressure for the coordination and harmonisation of social security and antipoverty policy between member states, and this is likely to lead to further convergence of policies in the future.

Despite the similarities in the development of welfare regimes, there are rather different traditions of poverty debate and poverty research in different European countries. As George and Lawson (1980) and Walker *et al.* (1984) discuss, in the past this has made direct comparisons between countries difficult, even where overall developments reveal similar trends. Obviously the Luxembourg Income Study will help to overcome some of these differences in the future. Already, however, the work of the EU, and in particular the central statistical department, Eurostat, has done much to develop a cross-national basis for comparisons of poverty and inequality within EU countries, as can be seen in the papers presented to the EU poverty statistics seminar in 1989 (Teekens and Van Praag, 1990).

In order to provide an empirical basis against which both national and community-wide antipoverty strategies can be assessed, Eurostat has attempted to produce measurements of poverty in EU member states that can be compared across national boundaries and over time (see EC, 1991; Atkinson, 1991a). Eurostat's most widely used poverty measure is the proportion of those receiving below 50 per cent of the national average income; and this measure has now been widely adopted in Britain (see Oppenheim and Harker, 1996, ch. 2). This permits cross-national comparisons to be made, whilst recognising the overall differences in standards of living between countries. To make a community-wide comparison between countries, of course, it would be necessary to adopt a community-wide measure, such as 50 per cent of the average income of the EU as a whole. This would give a rather different distribution of the proportion of Europe's poor in each of the member countries, accentuating the impact of the lower standards of some of the poorer countries. This can be seen in the comparison made in Figure 4.1. The comparison is based on 1985 information – the collection of international statistics proceeds very slowly – and so only covers the twelve member states then in the EU. However it reveals that a larger proportion of the poor live in countries such as Italy, Spain and Greece, and a smaller proportion in Germany, France and Britain. This is because the EU poverty line of 50 per cent of the average income is equivalent to two thirds of the national average in a country such as Spain (Atkinson, 1990b, p. 12). If the German national average were to be applied to Spain then this would create an even higher line, with the majority of people in Spain living in poverty, according to German standards.

The comparisons are made on relative measures, but the EU has been investigating the possibility of developing absolute measures of poverty for the purposes of international comparison. The aim here is to determine a European baseline level of living (EBL) using a measure of basic needs – European baseline needs (EBN). Although this is in principle an absolute measure, it is accepted that elements of relativity will need to be built into it to allow for gradual improvement over time as living standards rise (see EC, 1989).

Eurostat has also compared levels of poverty in European countries over time and looked at the impact of poverty on different sections of the population in different countries. These figures show an increase in the number experiencing poverty, using the 50 per cent of the national average income measure, in the then twelve countries of the EU from 38 million to 52 million between the mid 1970s and the late 1980s, or about 15 per cent of the total population (see Hantrais, 1995, p. 158). This is almost certainly a result of the impact of economic recession in all these countries, although the fluctuations between different nations is quite significant, with the rise in poverty being greatest in Britain, especially after 1980.

The changes in poverty in Europe also include a change in the composition of the poor, with a relative decline in the proportion of the elderly and an increase in the unemployed (especially the long-term unemployed), young people, single parents and migrant labourers. This is a similar pattern to the changes in the composition of the poor in Britain, and it has led European commentators to make the distinction between this 'new poverty' and previous life cycle experience of poverty

FIGURE 4.1   *The distribution of poverty in Europe, 1985*

(a) The distribution using national poverty lines

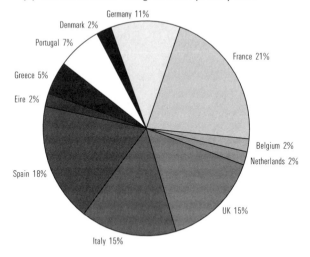

(b) The distribution using community-wide poverty lines

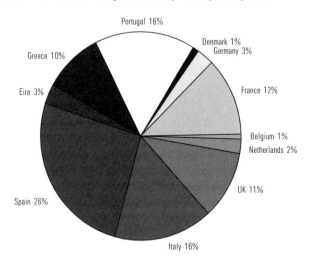

Note: Luxembourg is not shown separately.
Source: Atkinson, 1991a, p. 16.

(EC, 1991; Room *et al.*, 1990). This problem is accentuated by the fact that the new poor are generally excluded from the employment-related benefit protection that is provided by most corporatist welfare states, leading to a collapse in the comprehensive poverty prevention provided by such schemes and increasing reliance on inadequate and loosely structured assistance measures. In Germany for instance the proportion of unemployed people receiving insurance protection fell from 66 per cent in 1975 to 38 per cent in 1984 (EC, 1991, p. 10), and it has increased much more markedly since with the impact of reunification.

Evidence of the changing composition of Europe's poor is thus resulting in a reassessment of the effectiveness of antipoverty measures and a growth of fear about the potential marginalisation and social exclusion of the expanding group of new poor. The changing composition of Europe's poor also reveals spatial and racial dimensions. The higher proportion of poor people in the Latin Rim countries and other peripheral nations such as Ireland is creating a greater gap between these areas and the so-called 'Golden triangle' of Germany, France and Northern Italy, where industrial growth and well-paid employment are concentrated. A gap is also being created, even in these wealthier areas, between the indigenous labour in secure employment and migrant and immigrant labour, who are on the periphery of the labour market and are subject to poverty and exclusion in times of recession. The result of this is a tightening of migration and immigration policies within the EU, and a consequent growth of racist attitudes leading to divisions within the community. There is also a more general fear of what is referred to as 'social dumping', the drift of mobile capital around the community in search of low labour costs in poor areas, and the consequent fear of an overall reduction in the standard of wages and conditions in the longer term.

Policy debate and development within the EU is thus increasingly beginning to focus on the broader trends in the redistribution of wealth and deprivation throughout the community, which have been revealed by the improved availability and awareness of international comparisons of the experience of poverty. A general overview of developments in poverty and deprivation throughout the EU was provided in the early 1990s by the EU Observatory on National Policies to Combat Social Exclusion (see, for instance, Robbins *et al.*, 1994), although this was disbanded in 1994 with the winding-up of the third EU antipoverty programme, discussed below. Information on poverty in Europe has continued to be provided by the Commission, however; and it has been circulated by an independent agency funded by the EU to coordinate antipoverty action – the European Antipoverty Network (EAPN). The importance of developments in the European context of poverty was also discussed in recent pamphlet in Britain produced by the CPAG (Simpson and Walker, 1993).

European Antipoverty Policy

The EU started out primarily as an economic union, the European Economic Community, concerned with the development and regulation of trade rather than with the determination of economic or social policies within or across member states. Although this primary economic focus has remained of fundamental importance, in the latter part of the twentieth century the EU has become more and more concerned with attempts to intervene in national policy planning to develop community-wide initiatives to which all member states must subscribe. In the 1990s the establishment of the single European market in 1992 (Grahl and Teague, 1990) was followed by the creation of the European Union under the Treaty of Maastricht and the commitment of all the member states to work towards monetary union and the adoption of cross-national social policy standards – although Britain has been opposed to the latter two developments and at Maastricht reserved the right to opt out of them if it so decided.

This growing concern with social and economic policy planning has been reflected in particular in a range of policy initiatives that have sought to respond to the problems of poverty within the EU, both directly and indirectly. Set against the massive economic programmes of the EU these social programmes have been relatively small-scale and limited in their scope and effect. Nevertheless they have been important in moving the problem of poverty and antipoverty policy onto the European agenda.

In general terms social policy planning in the EU can be said to have passed through four broad phases:

- *Phase I*, from 1957–72, was primarily concerned with market development, and in particular with the promotion and regulation of labour mobility between EU countries.
- *Phase II*, from 1973–84, was primarily concerned with the harmonisation and upgrading of employment practices, and in particular the promotion of equal pay and equal treatment of men and women within the community.

- *Phase III*, from 1985–92, was concerned with attempts to be more proactive in the establishment of community-wide standards for citizens' or workers' rights through the development of social policy norms, called *L'Espace Sociale* by the then EU president, Jacques Delors, and encapsulated in the EU's Social Charter, to which we shall return shortly.

- *Phase IV*, 1993 onwards, has been characterised by the transition to European union and the creation of the single market, together with the plan for monetary union, a common defence policy and ultimately, perhaps, political federalism within a United Europe.

As each of these phases of development has passed over to the next the extent and breadth of European planning and intervention across both economic and social policy has increased. This has particularly been the case in the social policy field since the 1980s, and it is a development that has not been entirely welcomed by the government in Britain, as we shall return to discuss below. Nevertheless the growing emphasis on interventionist planning has been represented in a range of more specific initiatives undertaken under various organisational formats within the EU, and these have had an important impact on antipoverty policy in Britain.

One area of specific initiatives that have been important in responding to some aspects of deprivation and growing poverty within member nations is the distribution of EU structural funds. These are used to provide support for particular initiatives in those member states that come under the broad aegis of the fund. There have been three major structural funds: the European Social Fund (ESF), the European Regional Development Fund (ERDF) and the European Agricultural Guidance and Guarantee Fund (FEOGA) (see Teague, 1989), although these have now largely been amalgamated into one. FEOGA has been used to support rural development schemes such as promoting cottage industries and training displaced farm workers; the ERDF has mainly been used to improve the infrastructure of poorer regions in EU countries, in particular those affected by industrial decline and underinvestment.

It is the ESF, however, that has been most important in terms of direct antipoverty strategy. Initially its scope and size were limited and it was used mainly to subsidise small-scale project work and facilitate labour mobility by promoting the formalisation of bilateral agreements between countries to guarantee social security rights for workers from other EU countries. After the early 1970s and the onset of economic recession, however, the operation and direction of the fund were shifted onto a more interventionist footing, in particular in helping member states to combat unemployment by providing support for job creation and training schemes, especially in regions experiencing industrial or agricultural decline. The size of the ESF budget also grew dramatically between the 1970s and 1980s, although after this growth it still only represented about 6 per cent of the community's total budget, and generally the fund would only meet 50 per cent of the cost of individual initiatives or projects. The scope of ESF activities therefore should not be overestimated – even though Britain did relatively well in terms of ESF support in the 1980s, this money represented not much more than 10 per cent of the total spent on similar schemes by the government through national programmes for job creation and training (Teague, 1989, p. 48).

In addition to the more general initiatives arising from the operation of the structural funds there have been a series of specific initiatives designed to tackle directly the problem of poverty within the EU, generally referred to as the three EU poverty programmes. These have all been very small-scale initiatives, the third programme being the largest with a budget of 55 million ECUs (£38 million) over five years from 1989–94, less than the annual budget of a social services department or a university. Nevertheless they have been symbolically important in providing an example of community-wide action to combat poverty, and they have resulted in the development of some interesting new initiatives in project-based antipoverty strategy.

The first programme ran from 1975–80 and comprised a small number of pilot schemes and studies in community development (Dennett et al., 1982). After these were completed there were no further projects for a period of four years of 'evaluation and reflection' (EC, 1991, p. 15). Then a second programme was established to run for five years, from 1984–9, with a budget of 29 million ECUs. The second programme included 91 local action research projects throughout the twelve member states that were designed to build on the actual experience of local antipoverty work, with the results coordinated in academic institutions in Bath and Louvain (Room et al., 1993). This work was supplemented by statistical and attitudinal research carried out on a community-wide basis by Eurostat and the EU survey agency Eurobarometer (EC, 1990).

The third antipoverty programme directly followed the second and ran for five years, from 1989–94. The broad aim of the programme was to foster the economic and social integration of the economically and socially least privileged groups, echoing wider concerns about marginalisation and social exclusion. As in the previous programmes, this was to be achieved primarily by working *with* poor people in action research projects based on partnership principles. There were 39 projects across the then twelve member states, those in Britain being based in Belfast, Bristol, Edinburgh and Liverpool and coordinated by a unit at Warwick University.

Included in 'Poverty 3', as it was called, was the establishment in 1990 of more general research and evaluation work to be carried out by the EU Observatory on National Policies to Combat Social Exclusion. This included representatives of active poverty researchers from all the participating member states, and produced annual reports detailing both changes in national policies and developments in European poverty trends (for instance, Robbins *et al.*, 1994). In 1994 the Commission proposed replacing 'Poverty 3' with a fourth EU anti-poverty programme, but this was blocked by the representatives of the British and German governments. The EU antipoverty initiative therefore fell into abeyance and the Observatory was disbanded.

As can be seen, the poverty programmes were very small-scale initiatives by European-wide economic standards. By targeting limited resources onto a few local areas little could be done to combat the broader problems of poverty within the member states – this is a problem with all targeted antipoverty policies and we will discuss it in more detail in Chapter 15. However what the action research projects did provide were examples of initiatives to combat poverty and ways of working in partnership with poor people that could be utilised to develop more comprehensive strategies in the future, either at the national or the community level, and many of these lessons have been taken up and addressed to wider political audiences by other anti-poverty agencies, such as the EAPN.

The wider political message about the need to combat poverty at the EU level at the end of the twentieth century can also be seen in the developing commitment of member states to the adoption of European-wide social policy measures such as the Social Charter. The Community Charter of Fundamental Social Rights for Workers, to give it its full title, was developed by the Commission in the 1980s to provide a framework for primarily employment-based rights to be adopted by all member countries in order to guarantee minimum standards across the community. There was hostility to this from some countries, notably Britain, and as a result the original proposals were watered down somewhat in the final version, endorsed at the Maastricht Summit in 1991 – although even this was too much for Britain, which insisted on reserving the right to opt out of the charter when it was eventually introduced.

The focus on employment-based rights is symbolised in the use of the word 'workers' rather than 'citizens', and reflects the continuing dominance of economic and labour market concerns in EU social policy planning. However it also reflects a European tendency to identify employment and adequate wage levels as the major means of combating poverty within labour market economies. This is revealed in its most positive form in the aim of extending minimum wage guarantees throughout the community. Statutory minimum wages have existed for some time in countries such as France, the Netherlands and Luxembourg. More recently they have been developed in others, and it is Labour Party policy to introduce them in Britain. Together with measures to create jobs and provide training, especially for the long-term unemployed, minimum wages are seen in Europe as the major means of preventing poverty; and, coupled with employment-based insurance schemes for social security protection, these measures have continued to provide a basis for antipoverty policy planning in the 1990s, despite the growing recognition of the problem of 'new poverty'.

The other important development in EU antipoverty policy to come onto the policy agenda in the 1990s was the move towards the harmonisation, or 'concertation' as it is sometimes referred to, of social security provisions throughout the member states. Bilateral agreements between nations developed between the 1960s and 1970s have permitted workers moving between member states to receive protection under the different national schemes. However, with the greater integration of social and economic policies in the 1990s, discussion has begun on the possibility of creating community-wide social security protection. Despite broadly similar structures, however, the social security schemes of EU member states exhibit significant differences in practice, and harmonisation into one community-wide scheme seems unlikely for some considerable time. Recent discussion has therefore focused on the possibility of creating a separate EU scheme of social security protection, sometimes referred to as the 'thirteenth state' (now sixteenth state), under which the Commission would guarantee a particular set of social security rights for citizens moving from one country to another.

Such a community-wide social security protection would certainly provide a potentially powerful vehicle for the development of institutional structures to combat poverty that would go far beyond the limited initiatives of the structural funds and the antipoverty programmes. They would create pressure on both the Commission and national governments to contemplate further moves towards the harmonisation of policy planning, which may prove irresistible as the twentieth century draws to a close. Such pressure would make the European context of poverty and antipoverty policy much more important for all member states than it has been in the past. This is likely to have significant consequences for poverty in Britain, despite past British reluctance to embrace European policy planning.

Future EU policy development may also be influenced by the changes in Eastern Europe flowing from the collapse of communism in the Eastern Bloc. The reunification of East and West Germany has already led to the need for a significant redistribution of resources within the German economy, which has to some extent upset European economic planning. If EU support, and even EU membership, is extended to the restructuring of Eastern European countries, where high levels of unemployment and deprivation are being experienced, then this may limit the scope for rapid harmonisation across other nations and may put a premium on new economic and geographical priorities for EU structural initiatives.

The moves towards greater integration and harmonisation within the EU are also likely to have the effect of further segregating European countries from the wider international context. High standards of employment and wages in the EU countries are likely to be brought about at the expense of maintaining a high overall balance of trade with other countries throughout the world and of excluding from Europe large numbers of migrant or immigrant workers from low-wage, Third World countries. Integrated Europe, therefore, may also become 'Fortress Europe', providing relatively high standards for most of its citizens within an increasingly unequal wider international context of poverty and deprivation – although, as discussed above, this is part of a much broader debate on the global context of poverty, of which European protectionism is only one part.

Britain in Europe

Although Britain has been a member of the EU since membership was expanded from the original six nations in 1973, British commitment to and involvement in the idea of an integrated European community has always been somewhat contradictory. In 1975 the Labour government held a national referendum to confirm commitment to membership, and opposition to full participation in EU social and economic policy remained a prominent strand of Labour politics until the late 1980s. In the 1980s and 1990s members of the Conservative governments under Margaret Thatcher and John Major also revealed themselves to be reluctant Europeans. During this period Britain was frequently in a minority of one in discussions over both the pace and extent of European integration. In particular Britain refused to join the European currency control system, the Exchange Rate Mechanism (ERM), refused to support the development of a single European currency and, as we have seen, was unwilling to endorse the Social Charter of workers' rights.

British reluctance to embrace the European ideal can almost certainly be traced back to British imperialism and its commonwealth links with previous colonial nations, as well as to its geographical and cultural isolation from continental Europe, in particular the closely related original six EU member states. In some circles isolationism may also be based on belief of the alleged superiority of British economic and social policies following the construction of the postwar welfare state. Underlying all these views is an assumption that closer participation in Europe may lead to a threat to British economic development and a fall in British standards.

Whatever the historical basis of assumptions about British superiority in social and economic policy, it was clear by the 1990s that they had no contemporary foundation. As discussed above, poverty levels rose faster in Britain than in other European countries in the early 1980s, primarily because economic recession was being experienced more acutely in Britain; and British welfare policy has increasingly drifted away from Beveridge's comprehensive ideal towards a residual, means-tested, welfare regime, unlike the corporatist, institutional, welfare states of most of our European neighbours. The Conservative government's opposition to further European integration seemed to be based more and more on the dogma of nationalism and the supremacy of the British parliament than on any realistic assessment of future economic prospects; and during this period Labour switched from its opposition to European economic union to a recognition of the superiority of EU economic planning and social protection, and openly embraced a new future for Britain in Europe.

In the early 1990s economic pressures finally forced Britain to join the ERM, although the conflicts this produced in the Conservative

Party were enough to result in the resignation of Thatcher as prime minister. Her replacement, John Major, took a more positive stance on European cooperation and added Britain's signature to the Maastricht Treaty in 1991. In 1992, however, economic recession and pressure on the pound forced Britain to leave the ERM, and more vocal opposition to the Maastricht Treaty within the Conservative Party dampened some of the enthusiasm for a more rapid move towards European union.

Despite reluctance and procrastination, however, it is likely that closer integration of the EU countries will continue, and that in this process Britain will necessarily become more closely tied to its European neighbours. Following the establishment of the EU single European market in 1992 no British government is likely to contemplate abandoning EU membership, and thus the pressure on future governments to participate in monetary union and enter discussions on political union will mount as the need to compete within and influence the development of the European marketplace becomes essential to economic prosperity. Competition within the European market is also likely to require adherence to European social policy norms, and so for economic as well as social reasons acccptance of a gradually enhanced social charter seems inevitable. This will put pressure on future British governments to guarantee workers' rights – for instance to job security and equal pay – in conformity with European standards, and possibly even to introduce a community-based minimum wage.

In addition to this broad European social and economic context in which British governments will have to operate, there are a growing range of EU initiatives in social and economic policy that will affect all member states and from which Britain may benefit both directly and indirectly. As discussed above, EU social and economic policy initiatives have become more and more extensive and interventionist in scope. These trends are likely to continue towards the turn of the century.

Partly because of the severe impact of the recessions of the 1970s and 1980s in Britain, especially in the old industrial regions, this country has already been a major beneficiary of EU structural funds, in particular from the ERDF and ESF. Between 1981 and 1985 Britain was, after Italy, the biggest recipient of ESF money, amounting to 244 million ECUs in 1984 (Teague, 1989, p. 47). Although support from structural funds is often conditional on the provision of equivalent amounts of money from national or regional government in member states, the continued influx of such resources, targeted on areas experiencing economic decline and high levels of deprivation, has been of increased importance in attempts to combat poverty in Britain in the 1990s – not least because of the limited amount of public money that has been available from national funds for such developments. Britain's place in Europe is therefore likely to continue to make it subject to international pressure for social and economic reform within the country. The result of this may be a decline in the power and importance of the British parliament in determining significant aspects of welfare policy; but from the point of view of antipoverty initiatives and social security protection this may well result in improved provision for combating poverty. Of course this means that Britain will also increasingly be merely a part of Europe within the broader international stage, and international comparisons of poverty and antipoverty policy are likely to be restricted to some extent by this relatively limited focus; but even this limited international context will transform academic and political understanding of both the problem of poverty and its potential solution.

Part II

Definition and Measurement

5

Defining Poverty

The Need for Definition

This part of the book deals with the problems of defining and measuring poverty. This chapter and the next will concentrate on a discussion of attempts to define poverty and the ways in which these definitions have changed and developed over time. Arguably it is the issue of definition that lies at the heart of the task of understanding poverty. We must first know what poverty is before we can identify where and when it is occurring or attempt to measure it, and before we can begin to do anything to alleviate it.

As discussed in Part I, however, disagreements over the definition of poverty run deep and are closely associated with disagreements over both the causes of poverty and the solutions to it. In practice all these issues of definition, measurement, cause and solution are bound up together, and an understanding of poverty requires an appreciation of the interrelationship between them all. Nevertheless some logical distinctions can be made, and they will have to be if we are to make any progress in analysing the range of theoretical and empirical material these debates have produced.

The need for definition is in fact recognised by most of the major researchers and commentators on poverty issues. In his study of poverty in Britain in the 1960s and 1970s, Townsend opened the report with a definition of poverty that was crucial to his approach to the study and the findings it revealed, and which has been widely used by others since:

> Individuals, families and groups in the population can be said to be in poverty when they lack the resources to obtain the types of diet, participate in the activities and have the living conditions and amenities which are customary . . . in the societies to which they belong (Townsend, 1979, p. 31).

67

However debates in Britain about the appropriate way to define poverty go back at least to the end of the nineteenth century and to the work of the two pioneers of the study of poverty – Booth and Rowntree; and throughout much of this time this debate has focused particularly on the fundamental distinction that is alleged to exist between absolute and relative poverty.

Absolute poverty is claimed to be an objective, even a scientific definition, and it is based on the notion of subsistence. Subsistence is the minimum needed to sustain life, and so being below subsistence level is to be experiencing absolute poverty because one does not have enough to live on. On the face of it this is a contradiction in terms – how do those without enough to live on, live? The answer, according to absolute poverty theorists, is that they do not for long; and if they are not provided with enough for subsistence they will starve, or – perhaps more likely in a country such as Britain – in the winter they will freeze. Indeed every winter a significant number of elderly people in Britain do die of hypothermia because they cannot afford to heat their homes.

The definition of absolute poverty is thus associated with attempts to define subsistence. We need to work out what people need to have in order to survive; then, if we ensure that they are provided with this, we have removed the problem of poverty. This notion of absolute or subsistence poverty has often been associated with the early work of Booth (1889) and Rowntree (1901, 1941), although Spicker (1990) and Veit-Wilson (1986) respectively argue that these are mistaken or oversimplified judgements and that in practice both employed more complex, relative definitions in their studies. It is also often assumed that absolute poverty was removed by the welfare reforms introduced in Britain immediately after the Second World War, although this too has been subject to wide-ranging debate, as we shall see below.

In recent times there has been a return to the emphasis on absolute poverty as a result of the growing impact of the new right's contribution to social policy debate in Britain. An early example of this was the work of Joseph and Sumption, who claimed that 'An absolute standard means one defined by reference to the actual needs of the poor and not by reference to the expenditure of those who are not poor. A family is poor if it cannot afford to eat (1979, p. 27).

In 1989 the theme was taken up by John Moore, then secretary of state for social services, in the speech quoted at the beginning of Chapter 1. He called this speech 'The end of the line for poverty' and in it he castigated relative notions of poverty as 'bizarre', because they seemed to be suggesting that, as poverty was related to average standards of living, it would continue to exist no matter how wealthy a country became. Absolute poverty is thus contrasted with *relative* poverty. This is a more subjective or social standard in that it explicitly recognises that some element of judgement is involved in determining poverty levels, although as we shall see the question of whose judgement this should be is is a controversial one. Judgement is required because a relative definition of poverty is based on a comparison between the standard of living of the poor and the standard of living of other members of society who are not poor, usually involving some measure of the average standard of the whole of the society in which poverty is being studied.

Relative definition of poverty is associated in particular with the Fabian critics of the postwar achievements of the welfare state in eliminating poverty in Britain, most notably the work of Townsend (1954, 1979) and Abel Smith and Townsend (1965). Their argument was that although state benefits had provided enough to prevent subsistence poverty for most, in terms of their position relative to the average standard of living in society the poorest people were no better off in the 1950s and 1960s than they had been in the 1940s. Thus in a society growing in affluence, as was postwar Britain, remaining as far behind the average as before continued to constitute poverty. As Townsend put it in his 1979 definition, quoted above, relative poverty prevents people from participating in activities that are customary in the society in which they live.

This notion of participation is not only the product of postwar Fabian thinking however. Commentators as long ago and ideologically as far apart as Adam Smith and Karl Marx appeared to recognise and support it. According to Adam Smith:

> By necessaries, I understand not only the commodities which are indispensibly necessary for the support of life but whatever the custom of the country renders it indecent for creditable people, even of the lowest order, to be without. A linen shirt, for example, is strictly speaking not a necessity of life. . . . But in the present time . . . a creditable day labourer would be ashamed to appear in public without a linen shirt (Smith, 1776, p. 691).

Similary Marx wrote that 'Our desires and pleasures spring from society; we measure them, therefore, by society . . . they are of a relative nature' (Marx, 1952, p. 33).

Of course absolutist critics, such as Moore (1989), argue that these relative differences are merely inequalities, which will exist in any society, and that the relativist protagonists are using the notion of poverty illegitimately to redistribute wealth rather than to prevent want. This debate underlies much of the politics and policy of poverty prevention or alleviation in modern societies, and we shall discuss it in more detail shortly. Once we do examine what the supporters of both absolute and relative definitions of poverty mean, however, we will begin to realise that the distinction is in fact largely a false one. As mentioned, Veit-Wilson (1986) has demonstrated how Rowntree, often thought of as the architect of the absolute definition of poverty, in reality utilised relative measures. This is because the bald distinction between absolute and relative poverty is in practice an oversimplification of much more complex definitional problems.

Absolute and Relative Poverty

Absolute definitions do appear to have some sort of objective logic to them based around the notion of subsistence – having enough to sustain life. But this begs the question, what is life? What we require for life will in practice differ depending on place and time. For instance what is adequate shelter depends on the ambient climate and the availability of materials for construction – even the homeless poor living in London's 'Cardboard City' in the 1990s arguably are only able to survive because of the availability of cardboard. Adequate fuel for warmth also depends on the climate, the time of year, the condition of someone's dwelling and their state of health. Adequate diet depends on the availability of types of food, the ability to cook food, the nature of the work for which sustenance is required and – according to Rowntree, who allowed more in his basic diet for men than for women – on gender. Diet might also depend on taste – Rowntree included tea in his basic British diet, although it is of negligible nutritional value.

Thus different people need different things in different places according to differing circumstances. Differing individual needs will also be affected by the living or sharing arrangements they have with other individuals in families or households, an issue to which we will return in Chapter 7. What is more people's circumstances will in practice be determined by their ability to utilise the resources they do have in order to provide adequately for themselves. Although Rowntree attempted to use the independent judgement of nutritionists in order to determine a basic diet to act as a subsistence definition of poverty, he still distinguished between primary and secondary poverty. *Primary* poverty referred to those who did not have access to the resources to meet their subsistence needs; *secondary* poverty to those who seemingly did have the resources but were still unable to utilise these to raise themselves above the subsistence level – although Rowntree distinguished between these, he referred to both as poverty.

As mentioned, Rowntree included 'non-necessities' such as tea in his subsistence measure. In a second study in 1936 he also included the cost of a radio, a newspaper, presents for children and holidays. This was not only a recognition that absolute standards may not be the same thing as avoidance of starvation, but also that these standards change over time. In their review of definitions and measurements of poverty, Fiegehen *et al.* (1977) note that for all apparently absolute definitions there is a tendency to raise minimum levels as living standards improve. This was revealed starkly in an attempt by Stitt and Grant (1993) to use Rowntree's subsistence methodology to produce an absolute measure of poverty for the 1990s, which included significant weekly sums for swimming, trips to the cinema and other leisure activities – important needs perhaps, but certainly debatable as necessary for subsistence.

Of course Stitt and Grant were using their knowledge of cultural needs in the 1990s to determine the weekly budget upon which their research was based. As Veit-Wilson (1986) argued, Rowntree's studies of poverty also relied primarily on a similarly arbitrary assessment of lifestyle in York at the time of the surveys, drawn from the judgement of Rowntree and his interviewers. This is an inherent problem in the setting of budgets based on needs, to which we shall return shortly. However we cannot simply conclude from it that absolute definitions of poverty are wrong and relative ones right. There are problems with the relativist case too, and many of these were exposed by Sen (1983) in a persuasive attack on the orthodoxy of relativism.

If poverty levels change as society becomes more affluent, then it is not clear how the position of the poor can be distinguished from others who are merely less well-off in an unequal social order. This raises the question of where, and how, to draw a line between the poor and the rest. This was taken up in Piachaud's (1981a) critique of Townsend's 1979 study of relative poverty, which we discuss below. In essence the argument is that any cut-off line is arbitrary and merely involves the imposition of a subjective judgement of what is an acceptable minimum standard at any particular time.

Sen takes this further with the suggestion that if the relative position of the line remained the same, then during a period of recession in which overall standards drop there may be no increase in poverty, or conversely in a very wealthy society people would still be poor if, say, they could not afford a new motor car every year. This, he suggests, is clearly absurd, there must be some absolute measure against which relativities can be assessed. In searching for this Sen returns to Adam Smith's reference to the 'need' for a linen shirt. He argues that this provides a basis for an absolute, rather than a relative, definition of poverty, because Smith refers to the lack of the shirt as destroying a person's dignity – it is shameful.

It is this experience of shame or, as Sen later argues, the lack of capability that it exemplifies, that makes a person poor. The commodities needed to avoid this incapacity vary from society to society and within one society depending on the circumstances of individuals, but the *lack* is absolute and it is this that constitutes poverty. Thus poverty is a separate status that is different from simply being less well-off.

Of course Sen has trouble defining lack of capability. He attempts to base this on a Rawlsian notion of social justice, in which what we are prepared to argue is 'just' is the minimum state that we ourselves would accept as tolerable within the existing social order, so that those incapable of achieving such a standard experience social injustice and are therefore poor. But this is a rather abstract and philosophical approach to social values, and it has never been successfully applied to social policy debate or planning. Indeed such a notion of justice is essentially a matter of judgement or debate or political preference – and not an objective or scientific fact. For instance Sen implies that starvation is objectively recognisable as poverty, yet as discussed above attempts to arrive at a definition of an adequate diet to avoid starvation have been fraught with disagreements.

Thus absolute definitions of poverty necessarily involve relative judgements to apply them to any particular society; and relative definitions require some absolute core in order to distinguish them from broader inequalities. Both it seems have major disadvantages, and in pure terms neither is acceptable or workable as a definition of poverty. If we wish to retain poverty as a basis for analysis, measurement and ultimately political action, therefore, we need to avoid the disadvantages of both, or rather to capitalise on their advantages.

In practice most attempts to define and measure poverty do combine both, as Fiegehen *et al.* (1977) noted, usually by selecting a poverty standard, expressing it in income terms and then applying it to the income distribution of a particular society in order to reveal the proportion in poverty. The most frequently used of such measures in Britain has often been the level of basic assistance benefits (currently Income Support), as this is clearly an example of what the government regards as necessary at any particular time. It is a readily available definition, it is related to household size with equivalent amounts specified for different household members (see Chapter 7), and, as we shall see, fractions or multiples of it can be used to measure those below the level or just above it. Atkinson (1990a) has discussed the history of the minimum level implied by benefit scales in Britain, pointing out that they include a mixture of absolute and relative features.

However, as Veit-Wilson (1987) has pointed out, the use of benefit rates to define poverty is tautological. In political terms it cannot provide a definition upon which to act as it is already the product of political action. If there are those below it, and most studies of poverty find that there are, then they could be classed as poor; but this does not give a meaningful picture – either absolutely or relatively – of their poverty. Furthermore, as John Moore (1989) argued in his speech attacking relative definitions of poverty, it means that if the government were to raise the level of benefit in response to political pressure to alleviate poverty, then the extent of poverty might appear to increase; and if it were to lower the level as a result of a decision to reduce state support, then the number in poverty might be reduced. A logical definition ought to operate in exactly the reverse direction to this.

Thus there have been other attempts to define poverty that incorporate in differing degrees both absolute and relative features, but without the tautology associated with the use of benefit levels. These have been developed in Britain and a range of other countries, in particular the United States. They include 'budget standard' methods, drawing on the Rowntree absolutist tradition of a list of necessities, and 'deprivation indicator' methods, drawing on the Townsend relativist tradition of deprived lifestyle. There are also variations in between, aiming at some consensually based definition using income proxies or community-based deprivation indexes. There is also the attempt by R. Walker (1987) to combine all of these by using communities themselves to determine 'democratic' budget standards.

Budget Standards

Budget standards approaches to defining poverty are based on attempts to determine a list of necessities, the absence of which can then be used as a poverty line below which, presumably, people should not be permitted to fall. They are thus absolutist in structure; but, as Bradshaw *et al.* (1987) argue, budgets can also represent socially determined needs. Budget standards definitions are usually based on the notion of a (weekly) basket of goods. The idea was pioneered by Rowntree in his studies of poverty in York (1901, 1941; Rowntree and Lavers, 1951), where a weekly diet was constructed based on the advice of nutritionists.

Rowntree's was a long and detailed list of goods including, in the 1950 version, 10 ounces of rice at 5d, 6 pounds of swedes at 1s 3d, 1 egg at 3d and, of course, half a pound of tea at 1s 8d. Nevertheless it provided only for an extremely frugal standard of living, as he admitted in 1901:

A family living on the scale allowed for must never spend a penny on railway fare or omnibus. They must never go into the country unless they walk. They must never purchase a halfpenny newspaper or spend a penny to buy a ticket for a popular concert . . . and what is bought must be of the plainest and most economical description (Rowntree, 1901, p. 167).

The narrow-minded meanness of this basket-of-goods approach was expertly exposed in 1922 by Ernest Bevin, then leader of the dock-workers' trade union, in an incident described by Atkinson (1989, p. 27). During an enquiry into dockworkers' pay, evidence as to need had been presented in the form of a minimum basket of goods. Bevin had gone out and bought the recommended diet of scraps of bacon, fish and bread and then presented them to the researcher, asking whether he thought it sufficient for a man who had to carry heavy bags of grain all day.

Of course baskets of goods need not be so frugal, especially if they are explicitly based on an attempt to define a socially determined standard. There is a long tradition in the United States of attempts to define and cost the required living standard for a worker's family, going back to the Bureau of Labour Statistics' (BLS) work of the early twentieth century. The approach has been adapted and developed by other researchers utilising different standards, for instance by the New

York Community Council, which maintained a variant of the BLS budget. However there are inevitable problems associated with the use of baskets of goods determined by experts because this involves the imposition of arbitrary and, as Bevin demonstrated, often hopelessly unrealistic judgements by those who probably have no experience of living on them. They are thus unworkable in practice when compared with the expenditure patterns of real people, as Rowntree's researchers found out (see Veit-Wilson, 1986).

Since budget standards are supposed to represent required expenditure patterns therefore, surely it would be preferable to base them on actual patterns of expenditure rather than on hypothetical expert judgement? This is what the Watts Committee in the Unites States tried to do. Statistical evidence on expenditure patterns was used to draw up different levels of expenditure. There was a 'prevailing family standard', fixed at a median level, but also a 'social minimum standard' at 50 per cent below this and a 'social abundance standard' at 50 per cent above it. Bradshaw *et al.* (1987) compared these to British standards, using purchasing power parities to avoid exchange rate variations, and found similarities between the social minimum standard and assistance benefit levels in Britain.

Bradshaw has also undertaken other work in Britain using expenditure patterns and the weekly budgets of people living on assistance benefit (Bradshaw and Morgan, 1987) and those of benefit claimants in the north-east of England (Bradshaw and Holmes, 1989). These have demonstrated that weekly budgets derived from expenditure patterns provide inadequate resources for those living at these levels – for example leaving just 94p a week for a woman to spend on clothing, a diet deficient by 6500 calories and only enough money for one haircut a year (Bradshaw *et al.*, 1987, pp. 180–1). These studies provide a picture of the poverty of those living on benefit that avoids the tautology of the official definition based on the scale rate.

More recently Bradshaw has continued this budget standards research. In the early 1990s he established the Family Budget Unit, which used expert judgements and expenditure patterns to determine a range of different budgets for certain different family types, as in the BLS work in the United States. These included a 'modest but adequate' budget, based on average 'normal' living costs, and a scaled down 'low cost' budget, which could be taken as a kind of subsistence or poverty standard. However even the 'low cost' budget produced a weekly income figure for families with children that was about a third greater than the existing assistance benefit rate (Bradshaw, 1993a, 1993b).

Before this Piachaud had undertaken similar research to establish expenditure-based budgets for the cost of children (Piachaud, 1979). He then used this to measure the number of children in poverty (Piachaud, 1981b). These were politically important findings, especially for the CPAG, which published them. They were also repeated by the CPAG in the 1990s using Bradshaw's family budget approach (Oldfield and Yu, 1993). However their political appeal was still based on the assumption that it was possible, and desirable, to determine an objective standard of living against which the situation of real children could then be compared. This is perhaps more acceptable in the case of children, for whom we expect that others will determine their lifestyle, than it is for adults, who may legitimately have their own views about what is adequate for them.

Piachaud's and Bradshaw's implicit assumption is that anyone seeing the evidence of the inadequacy of the weekly budget will recognise the existence of poverty – as in Bevin's 'docker's breakfast'. But this is to assume a consensual standard based on average expenditure patterns – that is, merely a relative comparison – and thus to assume what is intended to be proved. It is still either a tautological definition or one based only on the judgements of experts (Bradshaw and Piachaud) or non-experts (their readers).

Such a definition also cannot escape Rowntree's primary and secondary poverty dilemma. Most if not all families spend some money on 'non-necessities' such as alcohol and tobacco (see Bradshaw and Morgan, 1987, p. 14). One way to avoid this dilemma may be to adopt what Veit-Wilson (1987, p. 201) calls a 'sociological' approach to budgets and accept that ordinary people's living patterns include non-necessary expenditure. Therefore the poverty level should be the income at which people, following their ordinary expenditure patterns, would have sufficient for necessities. This is effectively what Rowntree means by his notion of secondary poverty; and still it does not get round the problem of defining necessities, nor the relativities issue of how much non-necessary expenditure is acceptable as ordinary (keeping pets, running a car, pursuing a hobby). But it does suggest that some broader averaging out of expenditure patterns and weekly budgets may permit more 'consensual' definitions to be arrived at. This has been attempted in some more detail in income proxy measures.

Income Proxy Measures

When the Watts Committee in the United States based definitions of standards on the income levels necessary to maintain various weekly living norms, they were in effect moving towards the use of income levels as a proxy for budget standards or expenditure patterns. The seminal work of Orshanksy in 1965 in the US took this process further by preparing income thresholds for various family sizes to be used as the basis for future poverty research by the American Social Security Administration.

Following the nineteenth-century German researcher Engel, she compared the expenditure patterns of families at different income levels, and she found that lower-income families spent a greater proportion of their income on necessities. The proportion of income spent on necessities thus declined as income rose and more non-necessities were purchased. This is referred to as the 'Engel curve' (Figure 5.1).

Orshansky argued that average expenditure devoted to necessities could thus be used to determine the poverty level. She suggested that people were in poverty if more than 30 per cent of the household budget was spent on food (Orshansky, 1969; see Bradshaw *et al.*, 1987, p. 173). This provides an income proxy for poverty, based on the purchase of necessities. And of course the cut-off point need not necessarily be 30 per cent, or the measure need not only be expenditure on food. For instance in Canada a level of 62 per cent of spending on food, clothing and shelter has been used. However instead of fixing the

FIGURE 5.1 *The Engel curve*

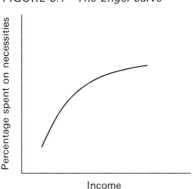

point arbitrarily it could be discerned from the Engel curve itself. Engel curves are not usually a simple curve, but are more of an 'S' shape, representing more complex changes in patterns of expenditure (Figure 5.2).

The inflection points, marked by the arrows, are where the marginal propensity to consume more of a particular type of good accelerates or slows down – the 'turn over point'. Above the first point, higher income makes a wider range of expenditures possible; later points are likely to represent stages where the variety of new expenditure is exhausted and the quality of goods bought becomes an issue in determining patterns. The turnover point therefore gives the level at which choice replaces need when determining expenditure – the poverty level. Bradshaw *et al.* (1987) claim that it is possible to derive such a point for most household types based on expenditure on food, clothing and fuel.

In practice this is similar in conception and operation to the poverty threshold derived by Townsend and others from the deprivation indicator approach discussed below. Like Townsend's method it is a *behaviourist* approach, constructed from evidence of behaviour patterns revealed in surveys of household or family expenditure. However it is still dependent on a judgement by experts as to what constitute the necessities against which expenditure is measured. Other income proxy researchers have sought to overcome this by developing a *consensual* definition of needs and the incomes required to meet them and thus avoid poverty, through asking respondents in the community to make judgements rather than merely surveying behaviour.

FIGURE 5.2   *Inflection points on the Engel curve*

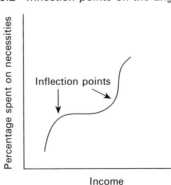

Of most significance here is the work of Van Praag and his colleagues at the University of Leyden in the Netherlands (Van Praag *et al.*, 1982). In a series of major social surveys conducted in a number of European countries, they asked the respondents what level of income they would need in order to make ends meet and avoid poverty. They also asked what cash income the respondents would attribute to various standards of living, described on a scale from very bad to very good. Fairly complex statistical analysis was then employed to derive poverty lines from the two sets of responses, based on what the respondents had said was necessary for an adequate standard – the 'Leyden poverty line' (see Veit-Wilson, 1987, pp. 190–1).

Thus here an income proxy is utilised to define a consensual poverty line, based on the notion of an adequate budget. This is a significant move beyond the arbitrary weekly minimum levels fixed by experts and nutritionists in earlier studies. However it is still dependent on judgements of adequacy used to fix lines derived from cash incomes specified in responses. This is based on an acceptable welfare function of income levels as applied to each society, and therefore it is, as Veit-Wilson (1987, p. 193) points out, a political choice – just like, of course, the levels for state benefits. Some have argued that this element of political choice when determining acceptable levels can be avoided by using deprivation indicators to define poverty.

Deprivation Indicators

Townsend, in his work on poverty in Britain in the 1960s, was the pioneer of the deprivation indicator method of poverty definition. As with his overall approach to poverty, it was drawn from the relativist critiques of the postwar complacency about the supposed removal of absolute poverty in Britain. In particular this complacency was based on Rowntree's third and final study of poverty in York (Rowntree and Lavers, 1951), which revealed a much lower level of poverty than the previous studies and appeared to confirm the view that welfare state reforms, based on the recommendations of Beveridge, together with growing affluence, meant that no one in Britain was any longer in need.

Townsend championed the idea that need, or rather deprivation, was relative, as is revealed in the quotation at the start of this chapter from the beginning of his 1979 report on poverty. However he believed that relative need, expressed as exclusion from everyday living patterns, was not a matter of mere arbitrary judgement but could be objectively determined and measured. This was to be done by drawing up a list of key indicators of standard of living, the lack of which would be evidence of deprivation.

In the survey upon which the 1979 study was based sixty such indicators, expressed as yes/no questions, were presented to over two thousand households. Around forty of these elicited yes/no answer patterns highly correlated with income. From these Townsend constructed a 'deprivation index' based on twelve indicators, such as the lack of a refrigerator, no holiday away from home in the last twelve months and the lack of a cooked breakfast most days of week, all of which correlated highly with low income (see Townsend, 1979, Table 6.3, p. 250).

The deprivation scores for different households, based on the index and summarised as the modal value for households in each income range, were then compared with the incomes of households, expressed as a proportion of the benefit entitlement for those households. These were then plotted onto a graph, using the logarithm of income as a percentage of benefit entitlement, and here they fell into two clear lines (Figure 5.3).

One line represented the changing position on the deprivation index of the bottom five income groups as income rose, the other represented the changing position of the top seven. The bottom five income groups were those with a household income below 140 per cent of Supplementary Benefit entitlement.

From this Townsend claimed that the point where the lines met, or to put it another way where the curve 'turned over', constituted a 'threshold of deprivation . . . that is, a point in descending the income scale below which deprivation increased disproportionately to the fall in income' (Townsend, 1979, p. 271). More generally, Townsend claimed, here was an objective definition of relative poverty; and the fact that the threshold, or poverty line, was at about 140 per cent of benefit entitlement confirmed previous claims by Townsend and others that those immediately above the benefit levels would still be in poverty in an affluent country such as Britain. What is more, of course, this also provided a powerful case for the introduction of an easy solution to the problem, at least in theory – raising the benefit levels by 40 per cent.

This was a ground-breaking step in the pursuit of a relative definition of poverty, but it was not without its problems, nor its critics. The most famous critique was that published by Piachaud in

FIGURE 4.3   *Deprivation by logarithm of income as a percentage of Supplementary Benefit rates*

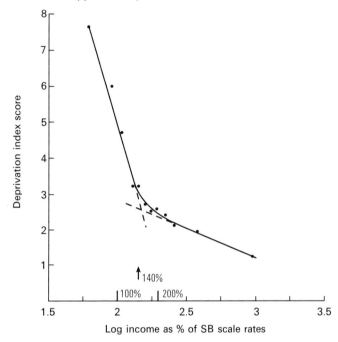

Source: Townsend, 1979, Figure 6.4, p. 261.

the journal *New Society* (Piachaud, 1981a; see also Desai, 1986). Piachaud criticised Townsend's list of deprivation indicators, which made it appear as though Townsend was setting himself up as an expert of what was an acceptable standard of life (for instance a cooked breakfast every day) and taking no account of taste as an explanation of the lack of particular indicators (for instance vegetarians will not want a joint of meat on Sunday, the lack of which Townsend saw as an indicator of deprivation). Piachaud also made a more technical criticism of the statistical technique, which had produced the threshold by the use of modal values, as this did not take account of variations around average points, which would have left the lines on the graph much less clear cut.

Desai discusses these criticisms in some depth, but he also demonstrates that a reanalysis of Townsend's data that takes them into account still produces the same threshold, thus apparently confirming the validity of Townsend's overall approach. However the approach and the threshold are at best a behavioural and not a consensual definition of the poverty line – as with the income proxy measures drawn from spending patterns. They also centrally involve the judgement of experts, in this case Townsend himself, in the determination of acceptable indicators of deprivation from which to derive the line.

These deficiencies, however, were taken into account in later studies that also used the deprivation indicator method – most notably those sponsored by London Weekend Television (LWT) for a television series called 'Breadline Britain'. The study was first carried out in 1983 and was subsequently published as a book (Mack and Lansley, 1985). It was repeated in 1990, using the same methodology, and screened as a second series of programmes (Frayman, 1992). These studies also used a list of indicators expressed as survey questions, but the development and the use of the list was much more sophisticated. The researchers asked their respondents whether or not they thought each potential indicator was necessary to avoid hardship; they then asked whether the respondents lacked those indicators and whether this lack was due to the lack of resources to purchase them.

From this a list of consensually agreed indicators, similar to but rather longer than Townsend's (Mack and Lansley, 1985, Table 4.1, p. 89), was drawn up to act as an index, which avoided the problems both of expert determination of acceptable indicators and of variations in the taste of respondents in choosing to go without. Although, as Veit-Wilson (1987, p. 200) pointed out, it is really a *majoritarian* rather than a consensual approach. In particular, for instance, it may still ignore the important cultural differences in living styles and living standards that might be experienced within a culturally diverse society such as modern Britain.

Just as in Townsend's study, however, the LWT data revealed a threshold between the bottom (four) and the top (eight) groups, although in their case the break occurred at around 135 per cent of the benefit entitlement level. Interestingly too, in the second survey the respondents' judgements as to the unacceptable lack of necessary items had slightly, but perceivably, changed to include such things as a decent state of decoration at home, an insurance policy and fresh fruit; confirming what Townsend had argued and Rowntree had conceded, that customary standards change as society develops. Rather depressingly the 1990 survey also revealed that a higher proportion of respondents were suffering from deprivation than in

1983 – an increase from 7.5 million to 11 million people who lacked three or more necessities.

These studies thus appear to strengthen the case that objective definitions of poverty lead to pressure for an increase in state benefit levels to alleviate the poverty revealed. They have also been widely used as a basis for other research into poverty standards and poverty levels within the country, for instance by local authorities seeking to investigate poverty in their area (Greenwich, 1994). However they utilise relatively simple surveys of opinions on poverty that require the respondents to address neither the consequences nor the context of any particular definition adopted.

Towards a Democratic Definition

In a discussion of poverty definition covering income proxy measures and deprivation indicator approaches, R. Walker (1987) argues that both are ultimately inadequate as they ignore the more important aspects of the purpose of defining poverty. The political context to poverty definition, as we have seen, is the need for action to eliminate it, but this seems to have been largely avoided in attempts to define poverty. In other words no attempt has been made to discover whether, and if so how much, people would be prepared to pay to eliminate what they define as poverty. Without this dimension, Walker argues, even consensual models are rather limited because they are rather hypothetical.

Perhaps inevitably the questions which are asked in surveys about income or deprivation are rather crude, and from an uninformed and unprepared public they are likely to elicit rather crude answers. To construct a fuller picture a more thorough process of public participation in determining poverty levels would be required – 'a democratisation of the budget standard approach' (R. Walker, 1987, p. 222) – based on in-depth interviews with individuals and groups. Such an approach would permit a mixture of income levels and deprivation indicators to be explored in the context of a discussion about the costs and benefits of differing definitions; and it has been attempted to an extent by Walker and his colleagues in a study of the cost of raising children in the 1990s, which reveals a wide range of diverse pressures on parents – and on children themselves (Middleton *et al.*, 1994).

Of course such studies are likely to produce highly complex and continually changing pictures of poverty, which appear as mixtures of various forms of deprivation rather than any clear and simple income line. As will be discussed in the next chapter, such a complex notion of deprivation is necessary in order to appreciate the various ways in which poor people are excluded or restricted in their lives within a complex, affluent society such as Britain. But this is not the definition of poverty that has traditionally been sought by researchers and politicians in order to measure its extent and develop policies to reduce or remove its effects.

Such a democratic process would also require, in theory at least, a political commitment to the removal of poverty thus discovered, which would be impossible to resist if the process were institutionalised. Such a commitment is unlikely to be forthcoming in the foreseeable future as governments have thus far seemed to believe that they have already embarked on the process of tackling poverty through the social security benefit systems and other antipoverty strategies, which will be discussed in Part IV.

These are already, of course, the product of democratic processes of one sort via the mandate of electoral democracy. Indeed in more general terms a democratically constructed and genuinely consensual definition of poverty is in effect a negation of the purpose of poverty definition in the first place. As we have seen in Part I, attempts to define poverty as a distinct social phenomenon have been developed in order to create political pressure for recognition that such levels of deprivation are problematic, and acceptance by politicians that something must be done about them.

It is this quest that gives the definition of poverty its social meaning, indeed arguably its *only* meaning. Once the political need to investigate the details of poverty in order to eliminate it is genuinely accepted, then the need for definition has gone and we are left with the multifaceted picture of the inequalities and inadequacies experienced in complex modern societies – and in less modern social orders too. We shall return to this more complex picture of deprivation and exclusion in the next chapter.

6

Deprivation and Social Exclusion

Relative Deprivation

The attempts to define poverty discussed in Chapter 5 all resort to use of a weekly budget or a fixed point on the income scale. As we shall see in Chapter 8, such a simple expression of poverty is essential if we are to measure its extent in a particular society at a particular time. However what this is in effect doing is basing the conception of the problem of poverty on a static monetary measure. It is reducing our understanding of poverty to concern with what we *have or do not have*.

However, as is implicitly recognised in the debates on the problem of definition, such simplified standards are really proxies for the more complex webs of inadequacy and disadvantage experienced by the poor or the less well-off – indeed in the case of income proxy measures they are self-confessedly so. In practice the experience of poor people extends beyond reliance simply on an inadequate income, it also includes a multifaceted combination of deprivations and unmet needs that prevent them from participating in society in the same ways that others do. The extent of these broader deprivations and their impact on individuals and households vary from place to place, person to person and time to time – and even at different times within one person's lifetime, a point to which we will return in Chapter 7.

Thus a full picture of the problem of poverty within a society needs to address these fine grains of the experiences of deprivation, which the simplified definitions and statistical measures necessarily overlook. This involves recognition of the many forms that deprivation can take in complex societies, and recognition of the extent to which this is a relative experience, the impact of which can vary between different people and different sections of society at different times. This in turn involves a focus not just on monetary poverty and on comparisons between income levels, but also analysis of the social and economic situations of individuals and families, and the extent to which these situations circumscribe the activities and life chances that people experience. This broader focus on deprivation thus requires the development of an appreciation of what we *do or do not do*.

Townsend has probably been the most articulate proponent of the notion of relative deprivation in Britain and beyond. In an article in the *Journal of Social Policy* (Townsend, 1987) he distinguished three different forms of relative deprivation:

- Lacking the diet, clothing and other facilities that are customary and approved in society.
- Falling below the majority or socially accepted standard of living.
- Falling below what could be the majority standard given a better redistribution or restructuring of society.

The first two direct attention towards access to social services – both public and private, which can affect our standard of living irrespective of our level of cash income – and also towards the use that is made of such services and the extent to which this means that people are able to do what is socially expected of them. The latter, he argued, is largely utilised in studies of developing countries, and suggests an attempt to impose relative standards that are not part of current custom and experience.

This raises the issue of the relationship between subjective and objective approaches to deprivation, which has also been the source of some debate. If relative deprivation is about perceptions of needs and lacks, then one implication might be that it only exists to the extent to which people perceive themselves to have needs that are not met, or are unable to do things they think they ought to be able to do. If you do not need or want such things, then in what sense can you be deprived of them?

This *subjective* dimension was explored in a seminal study by Runciman (1966), who examined different perceptions of deprivation. He found that many people did not perceive themselves as relatively deprived, over a quarter of his sample saying that there were no others who were better-off than themselves (ibid., p. 227). Even those who did experience relative deprivation often compared themselves to those not necessarily much better-off than themselves, for instance people with no children, people on shift work, university researchers or people able to let out a part of their home (ibid., p. 229). In an unequal society such as 1960s Britain therefore, people's sense of social justice was a rather limited one.

Of course this was hardly a surprising discovery. People's knowledge of the standards of others, especially of the luxuries of the rich, are fairly limited – not the least because the better-off do not frequently flaunt their wealth and may even, for a variety of obvious reasons, seek to disguise it. Furthermore we all have to live, and mainly do live, within our current circumstances – we learn to get by. Thus for many people, to maintain alongside such an accommodation a deep and burning grievance about what they are deprived of is neither comfortable nor healthy.

This point has led to the more general study of the strategies for coping with poverty in affluent societies, as explored by Coates and Silburn (1970) and incorporated into Lewis's theories of 'cultures of poverty', discussed in Chapter 2. However it should not be misinterpreted as implying support for a notion that deprivation and different standards are not serious problems. Townsend also explored subjective perceptions of poverty in his 1979 study and found that although a large number (over a half) of those 'living in poverty' did not feel poor, 'most of them none the less recognised in other ways that they were worse off than people with high or middle incomes, or than they had been themselves in previous life' (Townsend, 1979, p. 431). He also concluded that there was a strong correlation between such subjective perceptions and his measures of objective poverty.

What is more Townsend has consistently maintained that, in its focus on the conditions of life rather than on the distribution of resources, deprivation should be distinguished from the narrower concept of poverty; but this does not mean that it cannot be objectively defined and measured. He discusses criteria for the measurement of deprivation in the *Journal of Social Policy* article discussed above (Townsend, 1987). Here, as in his 1979 survey, he distinguishes between material and social deprivation – perhaps in implicit recognition of the absolute and relative dimensions of the phenomenon. He then went on to outline a list of indicators that could be used to determine and measure levels of deprivation, covering such things as diet, home circumstances, working conditions, family activity, community integration and social participation, deprivation of which could be used to derive scores for different individuals or groups. Of course the list of indicators is open to the same challenge of expert judgement as the list of indicators used to determine the poverty threshold discussed in Chapter 5. It is an objective measure, but not necessarily a consensual or even a behavioural one.

However the list demonstrates the potentially broader remit of the notion of relative deprivation. In complex and affluent societies necessities are not just food, clothing and shelter; and incomes or expenditure are not the only measures of standard of living. Where we live, where we work, how we work, how we spend our leisure time (if we have any), what services we have access to or receive – all these, and not merely our personal or household weekly budgets, affect our lives; and deprivation can extend into any or all of these broader aspects of lifestyle. Indeed it is this broader and richer (or poorer, for some) notion of 'lifestyle', rather than simply 'standard of living', with which discussion of deprivation has become associated. It is debatable whether lifestyle can be objectively defined and measured, but an understanding of how our lifestyles can alternatively be enriched or deprived is central to an understanding of poverty in affluent societies.

Deprivation at Home and Work

In his 1979 survey Townsend examined a number of the broader aspects of deprivation whilst undertaking his search for the poverty threshold. These included deprivation in housing, environment and workplace. Not having a decent home is obviously an important form of deprivation and one that is widespread, and seemingly chronic, in many affluent societies such as Britain. Townsend distinguishes three aspects of inadequate housing: structural defects rendering housing unfit, lack of basic amenities, and inadequate space or overcrowding. Clapham *et al.* (1990), in a textbook on housing policy, also discuss what they call 'housing disadvantage'. In Britain much of this is the product of the poor quality of the housing stock dating back to the last century.

Old houses inadequately maintained can and do decline in quality. Between 1971 and 1981 the number in serious disrepair in England increased by 21 per cent to over one million, and the number of 'unsatisfactory dwellings' rose to over 18 million (ibid., 1990, p. 63). In 1986 as much as 25 per cent of the stock was considered defective, and one and a half million homes were unfit for habitation or lacked basic amenities. Although, as Hills (1990, p. 13) has argued, these numbers have since begun to decline, they are still a significant element of deprivation for those who continue to live in unsafe, inadequate or overcrowded accommodation.

Many of the problems of poor quality housing are distributed across different housing tenures. But tenure differences can add to or accentuate housing deprivation. For private sector tenants there can be the added problem of legal insecurity, especially following the reforms removing Rent Act protection in the late 1980s. For council tenants there can be the stigma of occupying housing in a sector that has become increasingly residual and marginalised (Cole and Furbey, 1994). Housing expenditure subsidies from the state have not been used to remove or ameliorate housing disadvantage (see Hills, 1989), especially in the late 1980s, when increasing amounts of money were directed to tax relief on mortgage payments for relatively wealthy owner-occupiers.

Of course the most serious dimension of housing deprivation is homelessness – having no house at all. The number of homeless people has been a serious problem in Britain throughout most of the postwar period, despite the introduction of the welfare state and the development of public housing. The legislation on homelessness introduced in the 1970s gave a qualified right to a house to some homeless people if they had dependent children, although restrictions have been added since then. Yet the number of those registered as homeless under the law doubled in the decade after its introduction, rising from 50 000 to 100 000. For the large number of people not covered by the legislation, homelessness must be endured as a humiliating and debilitating deprivation. Countless thousands now sleep rough in Britain's major cities, with only cardboard boxes or plastic bags as a home. In London, where the number is greatest, this public manifestation of deprivation achieved the notoriety of a pseudonym, 'Cardboard City' – suggesting a permanence that the cardboard itself does not provide.

Such severe housing deprivation brings with it further disadvantages. Ill health is likely to result from sleeping on the streets. Employment is hard to find when no address can be given to prospective employers. Purchase of household and consumer goods is largely out of the question. Public or private services are mainly irrelevant – or even, as in the case of street cleaning, positively threatening. Homelessness is an obvious example of the problems of multiple deprivation, as Townsend and others have called this combination of needs and lacks; but multiple deprivation is not confined to those without homes.

Poor housing may be situated in a poor environment. Townsend also included environmental deprivation in his 1979 survey. Three indicators were chosen: no garden or yard around the house, no nearby safe place for children to play and a state of air pollution in the neighbourhood. Attention to the environmental context of our lives has increased considerably since Townsend's study. In cities in particular, litter, refuse and vandalism can add to the problems of pollution and safety, as can traffic volume. Lack of leisure space close to home is not the only indicator of this aspect of environmental deprivation – clearly the larger geographical context of lifestyle is also important. For instance life in a flat in a densely populated inner city is obviously environmentally poorer than life in a flat in a small town or suburban area with parks or open countryside within easy reach.

This broader geographical context of deprivation takes us into what Townsend refers to as the problem of 'poor areas' (Townsend, 1979, ch. 15). These are areas where multiple forms of deprivation are combined with large numbers of people living on low incomes. They are often found in inner city areas with poor housing, a low-quality environment and high levels of unemployment and benefit dependency. Many local authorities are well aware of such area-based deprivation in their localities and may seek to identify such areas in order to channel policy development towards them. Indeed in the early 1990s a large number of local authorities did begin to engage in attempts to map or profile the distribution of poverty in their areas, and used these to develop antipoverty initiatives and distribute certain forms of additional services and funding (Alcock *et al.*, 1995). Nevertheless areas of poverty should not be misunderstood as geographical proxies for other measures of the extent of poverty or deprivation. As we shall discuss in more detail in Chapter 15, some people living in such areas may not be deprived, and many people living outside them certainly will be.

Townsend also recognised that experience of deprivation was not restricted to where people live. Relative deprivation also extends to what we know or learn, for there are significant differences in the opportunities and experiences of the education we receive as children (Smith and Noble, 1995), and these differences can later result in differences in opportunities and experiences at work – at least for those who have paid employment. Some people work in conditions that are considerably more deprived than others, even though the pay differentials may not be that great. The working environments of miners and office clerks is an obvious comparison here, even though the former may earn more than the latter. Townsend identified four aspects of deprivation at work: the severity of the job itself (outdoors or indoors, standing or seated), the security of the job, the conditions and amenities of work, and the provision of welfare or fringe benefits.

Most of the problems of deprivation here are pretty obvious, although the issue of fringe benefits assumed much greater importance in recent years. Many jobs – often the more secure, pleasant and better paid ones – now include significant benefits, such as a long holiday entitlement, generous sick pay and maternity leave, occupational pensions, private health insurance, subsidised travel or even free accommodation (for instance No. 10 Downing Street, although here security may be a less significant feature!) Occupational welfare provisions such as pension schemes are particularly important for they continue the advantages – and the disadvantages – of differential employment situations beyond the period of the employment contract itself. As Mann and Anstee (1989) discuss, they are of increasing importance in the late twentieth century and contribute to the broader social divisions and deprivations that result from privileged or non-privileged access to the labour market. Those in secure positions in the *core* of the labour market are thus increasingly experiencing different standards from those on irregular and part-time contracts on the *periphery*.

Poor working conditions and poor housing conditions can both contribute to poor health. Clearly poor health is a significant form of deprivation within a lifestyle, and if it is serious it can affect the length and quality of life itself. There is a considerable body of evidence to suggest that poor health is associated with other aspects of poverty and inequality, notably the Black Report and the Health Divide Report, sponsored by the government but published privately by Penguin (Townsend *et al.*, 1988; see also Blackburn, 1991, ch. 2). These findings have been confirmed by more recent research on poverty and poor diet carried out as part of the Rowntree Inquiry into Income and Wealth in the early 1990s (Dobson *et al.*, 1994). The relationship between health and other forms of deprivation is, however, a complex one – causal links may operate in both directions. Certainly when poor health is serious enough to interfere with employability it is likely to lead to disadvantage in or exclusion from the labour market, and as we have seen this is closely associated with poverty and deprivation. Poor health may thus be compounded by other aspects of poverty.

It is nevertheless important to remember that poor health is a form of deprivation, whatever its association with other aspects of poverty and inequality of lifestyle. Chronic ill-health is debilitating and restricting, and it can reduce the enjoyment of even those pleasures that are still permitted by it, as diabetics and asthmatics know well. It can also exclude sufferers from a range of activities that others generally take for granted, although as mentioned exclusion is an aspect of deprivation that is not only associated with ill-health.

Social Exclusion

In the mid 1980s the contributors to a CPAG pamphlet called *Excluding the Poor* (Golding, 1986) drew attention to a range of new and broader aspects of deprivation that they argued were growing in importance in modern society. These included activities that had not traditionally been associated with either the experience or the definition of poverty, such as the issue of leisure. For instance, with reduced working time now a reality for all, albeit differentially distributed, what we do or do not do with our leisure time may be an important source of inequality and deprivation. The leisure industry, especially sport and culture or entertainment, is now a major feature of modern society – indeed it has been the main growth industry in Britain in the latter decades of the twentieth century. Yet access to and enjoyment of leisure facilities are subject to wide differences and deprivations.

Tomlinson (1986) quoted squash, a rapidly growing and yet expensive and inflexible sport, and Alton Towers, a vast but expensive and inaccessible leisure park now copied in many other places, as examples of restricted access to leisure. Leisure, therefore, is often associated with wealth, and thus the unemployed – although they apparently have extensive 'leisure time' – are in fact excluded from a large number of modern leisure activities. Enjoyment of leisure, especially sport, can also be associated with health, and thus restricted access to leisure can also contribute to inequalities in health.

Lack of access to our increasingly complex and interconnected communications network can also be a source of deprivation in modern Britain. Television, teletext, telephones and now fax machines and electronic mail have come more and more to dominate our lives – or rather the lives of some. For those without these modern inventions, for instance children with no television at home or lone parents with no telephone, they can be a source of social deprivation in the playground or material deprivation in the home.

Along with leisure and communications the other growth industry of the late twentieth century has been financial services – banking, investment, credit, insurance and so on. In particular the development of cheques, credit cards and direct debit cards has transformed the process of buying and selling. For those without access to these facilities therefore, deprivation can be significant – and there are many so deprived. Toporowski (1986) pointed out that only 69 per cent of adults had current bank accounts in 1985, and for those in social class E (the bottom) the proportion was 41 per cent. Exclusion from access to financial services can also exclude people from the advantages of borrowing and buying on credit, an important means of adding flexibility to consumption, and thus lifestyle, to avoid what might otherwise be significant short-term problems of deprivation.

However the disadvantages of credit can also lead to, or compound, deprivation. When credit can no longer be repaid it becomes debt, and the problems associated with debt have become more serious and widespread in late twentieth-century Britain. Parker (1988), Ford (1991) and Berthoud and Kempson (1992) discuss the problems associated with high levels of multiple debt among the less well-off. Such forms of debt are often combined with high rates of interest, thus they cost more; and when they are not repaid they can lead to pressure and threats from creditors and can cause insecurity and anxiety among debtors. Many debts, such as on owner-occupied housing, are secured against property that is also a home. When these debts cannot be repaid the house may be repossessed and sold to recover the loan. Such repossessions increased tenfold in the 1980s and doubled again to around 40 000 a year in the early 1990s. With the declining value of property at that time, after the sale of their houses many people still owed large sums of money – the problem of 'negative equity'. In circumstances such as these anxiety is acute, and well-founded; and the problem of debt can end in disaster.

Another form of hardship disproportionately experienced by the poor is the threat – or even the fear – of being a victim of crime. Having property stolen or damaged, or worse still being a victim of assault or attack, is a severe depletion of quality of life; and the threat of this happening again provides a nagging sense of insecurity that can only fully be appreciated by those who have suffered from it. Crime statistics, and more especially surveys asking victims about crime, for instance the Islington Crime Survey (see Young, 1986), have revealed that the highest levels of criminal activity and criminal threats are experienced amongst generally deprived groups living in deprived areas. In one council housing development in Killingworth near Newcastle on Tyne the problem became so great that the council decided to demolish a block of flats in an attempt to eliminate the problem, even though the recently built flats were structurally sound and there was no obvious local surplus of accommodation (see Cowan, 1988, p. 24).

The fear of crime has particular consequences for many of the most vulnerable groups in society. For instance older people, women and young children may be unwilling to venture outside in certain neighbourhoods at certain times of the day (or night) for fear of being attacked or robbed; this effectively excludes them from a significant part of their potential social activity. However such fear is not only experienced outside; violence in the home is also widespread and is largely directed at women, whose lives can be destroyed by it. Violence and harassment at home and in public are also frequently experienced by black and Asian people, for whom it provides a sharp accentuation of the broader deprivations resulting from racism, to which we will return in Chapter 10.

Ward's (1986) contribution to the CPAG pamphlet mentioned above discussed the political dimensions of deprivation in a democratic society. Taking an active part in political organisations may not be widely regarded as an essential part of lifestyle in twentieth-century Britain; but it is an essential element of any effective democracy. Those who are excluded from it by lack of money, time, knowledge or experience are deprived of the opportunity to participate in the democratic process. That such non-participation is significantly associated with those groups also disproportionately experiencing other aspects of deprivation – the unemployed, the low paid, women at home, the elderly and ethnic minority communities – suggests that the impact of this is a significant feature of deprivation, and one with a disturbing self-perpetuating potential.

The CPAG book in which this and the other contributions mentioned above appeared was called *Excluding the Poor* and in his contribution Williams (1986) focused on this wider aspect of deprivation as exclusion. He pointed out that this notion of deprivation as a form of social exclusion had in fact been discussed by a number of European commentators on the problem of poverty, particularly those associated with the EU's antipoverty programmes discussed in Chapter 4. Social exclusion was addressed as an issue in the second EU antipoverty programme in 1988 and was mentioned in the preamble to European Social Charter a year later (see Berghman, 1995, p. 11). The observatory established by the Commission as part of the third programme was explicitly directed at the monitoring of national policies to combat social exclusion (Room *et al.*, 1991; Robbins *et al.*, 1994). In the early 1990s the EU-sponsored international seminar on social exclusion attracted contributions from academics and politicians from a number of European countries (Room, 1995).

What the EU commentators were doing in their discussion of the problem of social exclusion was attempting to broaden the debate and research on poverty and deprivation beyond the confines of the circumstances and experiences of the poor to encompass the reaction to poverty by other social agencies and individuals throughout society. In this sense they argue that, rather than being a *state of affairs* – as poverty has often been conceived – social exclusion is really a *process* involving us all. Unlike poverty and deprivation, therefore, exclusion focuses our attention on what others *do to us*.

This emphasis on the conceptualisation of social exclusion as a process of division and disadvantage that affects not only the poor but the whole society can be seen clearly in some of the statements made by senior EU researchers on the subject. Tricart, a senior officer in the DGV, the section of the Commission responsible for social affairs, has argued that:

> Today, the concept of social exclusion is taking over from poverty, which is more static than dynamic and seen far more often as exclusively monetary poverty. . . . Social exclusion does not only mean insufficient income, and it even goes beyond participation in working life. . . . More generally, in stressing the rupture of the social link, it suggests something more than social inequality and therefore carries with it the risk of a two tier society, or the relegation to the status of a welfare dependent (Robbins, 1994, p. 12).

The danger of welfare dependency and the creation of a two-tier society were discussed in Chapter 2 with regard to the fears surrounding the creation of an underclass. There is clearly a risk here that a focus on exclusion could lead some people to argue that this is a product of changes in the attitudes and behaviour of those who have become excluded. However this is not the sense in which the concept has been used in European debate and research, which draws more directly on French research on social process. Here the focus is on *relations* between people rather than the *distribution* of resources (see

Room, 1995, p. 5). This can be seen in the comment of de Foucauld a French researcher from Lille working for the EU:

> It is the denial or absence of social contact which fundamentally distinguishes exclusion. The dignity of the individual derives from integration in a social network – or more precisely, into a system of exchange. An individual brings something to an exchange for the other person, acquires a kind of right, recovers his [or her] status as an equal. Social exchange is what provides both a social context and autonomy which are the two essential elements of the individual (Robbins, 1994, p. 8).

What is clear from this is the extent to which references to growing social exclusion are suggesting a breakdown in the entire social fabric. As individual human beings we live our lives in a social world; and this social world is based on the give and take of social relations, in which all of us as autonomous individuals must take part. Society is based on reciprocity – in order to take, we must able be also to give. In this sense social exclusion draws our attention to an even broader conceptualisation of the problem of poverty. Social exclusion also concerns what we can *do for others*.

Social Polarisation

The concept of social exclusion refers to a process, or a set of social relations, between poor people and the rest of the society in which their poverty is created and recreated. However the term itself still directs attention to the victims of this process, those who are excluded, and in so doing runs the risk of encouraging the kind of underclass analysis discussed above. If social exclusion is really a problem of, or for, the whole of society, then perhaps we should adopt a terminology that reflects this broader social context. Social polarisation may be such a concept, for it suggests not just exclusion at the bottom, but accentuating divisions throughout the whole of society.

There is certainly evidence to suggest that divisions throughout society have been growing at the end of the twentieth century and the problem of social exclusion is also part of a broader problem of social differentiation. One of the most consistent themes of the Rowntree research programme on income and wealth in Britain was the evidence it revealed of the increasing gap between rich and poor (Barclay, 1995;

Hills, 1995). However this gap is not just exemplified in the distribution of resources, it is also experienced in significant changes in the relations between rich and poor.

One of the Rowntree research projects (Green, 1994) examined the geographical aspects of the growing gaps within British society. This revealed that differences were growing at a general regional level between the richer and poorer parts of the country, but also that within regions or local areas the distribution of poverty and deprivation (and conversely of wealth) was becoming more concentrated. This theme was taken up in a CPAG pamphlet on the geography of poverty, which revealed similar problems (Philo, 1995). The greater concentration of poverty and deprivation in particular areas, and consequently among particular groups, is a disturbing example of increasing social polarisation. Concentration of poverty can reduce mobility and communication between places and people as some become trapped in deprived neighbourhoods – and others fear to enter them. It is also a phenomenon that can be found throughout society, and not only in the urban neighbourhoods often traditionally associated with 'pockets of deprivation'. Indeed in rural areas the experience of poverty as geographical isolation can frequently be even more accentuated as public and private services become more concentrated in distant town halls and hypermarkets (Cloke *et al.*, 1994).

Geographical isolation can also lead to cultural isolation, and in such a context the fears about disintegration of the social fabric referred to above become more understandable – and perhaps closer. It is no coincidence therefore that the EU's concern with social exclusion has led those involved to argue for the need for policy initiatives to reverse the processes of polarisation in society. EU antipoverty campaigners have therefore begun to talk about the need for action to promote social integration and encourage the development of social cohesion; and these were the themes that underlay the new Targeted Social and Economic Research programme initiated by the Commission in 1994.

Such concerns have also been important in motivating many of the locally based antipoverty initiatives that began to develop in Britain in the early 1990s. The local authorities that began to grow more aware of the increasing problem of poverty and deprivation in their areas quickly realised that it was also a problem of social exclusion and geographical polarisation, and they sought to respond to this by pursuing antipoverty strategies that focused on social regeneration and the recreation of social cohesion at the local level (*Local Economy*,

1994). Therefore just as the conceptualisation of poverty has moved beyond a focus on the mere lack of resources to encompass the broader fabric of social relations, so too have policies to combat poverty moved beyond the (re)distribution of resources to include the promotion of changes in social and economic structures. We shall discuss some of the implications of these changes in more detail in Part IV.

7

Households and Poverty Dynamics

Individuals and Households

The concepts of poverty and polarisation both address the problems experienced by individuals living in a society in which there are radically different standards of living; and in the complex definitional debates that accompany the discussion of these problems it is often easy to overlook the fact that it is individual people who are victims of deprivation and exclusion. Individual people experience poverty. However by and large individual people do not live all their lives as individuals – and even as individuals they do not remain in the same circumstances throughout their lives.

For a start most individuals live with other individuals in families or households, and in families or households they pool their resources to some extent and share their wealth, or their poverty, with other family or household members. Thus if we want to study the effect of poverty on individuals, and if we want to develop policies to ameliorate or remove these effects, then we must also study the household or family structure in which people live and in which resources are distributed and consumed. Secondly, individuals' circumstances do not remain the same throughout their lives. As we grow older we move from childhood to adulthood, perhaps to parenthood, and later into retirement. Our material circumstances and our chances of experiencing poverty or deprivation are naturally different at different times of our lives, in particular because this will affect our ability to provide resources for ourselves over time. Thus studies of poverty must also take account of such life-time changes and of the periods that different people may therefore spend in poverty – now called poverty dynamics.

Finally, our household and family structures of course will change over our lifetimes. Thus household structure and life-time changes are interrelated, and as we move from one household formation to another our chance of experiencing poverty and our experience of poverty itself will vary. So a weekly income of £100 means something rather different if it is received by a single man than if it is received by a couple with two young children; and measures of income that do not take account of this will not tell us much about the real experience poverty or deprivation.

Conversely many people in countries such as Britain may have no income of their own. Most children do not, but this does not automatically mean they are materially deprived since they may be members of households where the benefits of income are shared with them. How the incomes of different household formations and different members of households are defined and measured is therefore an important dimension of the problem of poverty and deprivation.

Household Size and Structure

In a collection of studies comparing the differing needs and resources of different household and family structures, Walker and Parker (1988) pointed out the importance of both differing household structure and life-cycle changes; and the various contributors to the book took up differing aspects of these issues. The question was also discussed by Townsend in his major poverty survey (Townsend, 1979, ch. 7). The most important initial issue raised by both is the need to distinguish between households and families, although on many occasions of course the two may overlap and the boundaries between them may not always be clear.

The logical (or sociological) distinction between the two is that unlike households, families consist of people with a more or less explicit commitment to joint living and sharing based on emotional as well as empirical, interdependency. Marriage is the most obvious symbolic representation of this, but the concept of family is not restricted to married couples it includes the dependent children of such couples and non-married partners (not necessarily heterosexual) who have made, or appear to have made, quasi-marital commitments. This narrow form of family is sometimes referred to as the 'nuclear family' to distinguish it from broader family and kinship ties between adult parents and children, or adult siblings.

The expectation is that members of families will pool and share resources and will expect, and welcome, interdependency; although, as will be discussed below, this is not always the case. This expectation is also enforced through the law, in particular in the rules covering entitlement to means-tested benefits in Britain, where those 'living together as husband and wife', together with their dependent children, are treated as an income unit and are paid at a lower (couple) rate than two separate individuals would be. The assumption is that two or more together can live more cheaply than one alone, and there is obviously some sense in this. For instance heating and cleaning costs will probably be commensurably reduced, although how these savings should be measured is a controversial issue to which we shall return shortly in a discussion of equivalence scales.

Reduced living costs such as these, however, will also be experienced by those sharing residential accommodation even if they share no family ties or commitments – hence the argument that households too constitute a basis for a presumed pooling of resources. Since households are not based on any explicit emotional commitment, then the equivalent of marriage or quasi-marriage cannot serve as a definitional guide, and what constitutes a household can vary enormously. For instance a household may consist of a family with adult children still living at home, or aged parents living with their adult sons or daughters – in effect forms of extended family. Alternatively a household could be made up of non-relatives living within one house and sharing some living accommodation for convenience, or more usually because of financial necessity, for example young single adults sharing a rented house.

Obviously there is a distinction to be drawn between family-based or household groupings. Arguably the former have made some interpersonal commitment to sharing resources, whereas the latter probably have not. Although of course the distinction between the extended family household and the single adults household confuses the difference considerably. The distinction is also important when attempting to compare the resources of different groups since households are generally a broader and larger category than families. This difference in size is likely to be significant. Having stated a preference for households as a basis for measurement, Beckerman and Clark (1982, p. 17) went on the show that, using the family unit, in 1975 3.2 per cent of the population were living below the basic assistance benefit level, compared with 2.3 per cent when the household unit was used. As Piachaud (1982a, p. 342) has argued, 'It is well known that the extent of poverty based on larger units is less than that based on smaller units since, for example, many poor individuals share households with better-off relatives'.

The importance of the distinction was demonstrated most markedly, however, in 1988 when the government introduced a change in the collection and presentation of official statistics covering low incomes. The change involved a switch from the previous basis of publishing the figures relating to low-income families (LIF), which were compared with Supplementary Benefit (now Income Support) entitlement levels and gave a measure of families in poverty according to this, to publishing the figures relating to households with below average incomes (HBAI), which were compared with incomes of other households in order to give a relative measure of income distribution.

The reasons behind the change were complex and controversial. They stemmed in part from the government's stated opposition to the use of benefit scales as a poverty benchmark, as argued by Moore (1989), but they also involved the more debatable claim that sharing within households was commonplace (DSS, 1988). Critics of the change were concerned not only with the principles behind this assumption, but also with the practical effect the changed basis for calculation would have on official statistical measures of poverty and inequality – especially as the government refused to publish the old data as a comparison.

In order to compare the changes resulting from the switch the Institute for Fiscal Studies (IFS) compared the figures under the new HBAI measure in 1988 with what these would have been under the old LIF (Johnson and Webb, 1990). Their analysis showed that the switch of basis from family to household reduced the percentage of people with low incomes and thus produced a measure that appeared to demonstrate reduced inequality, resulting from the assumption of greater levels of income sharing. They also discussed the other changes introduced in the 1988 measures, for instance the switch from normal to current income, which we shall discuss shortly. Nevertheless they concluded that the switch from family unit to household had 'by far the greatest effect' (ibid., p. 13).

Thus the difference between household and family measures is important, not just in the assumptions different measures make about how we organise our domestic lives – which of course can only be assumptions – but also in the consequences these have for the extent of poverty or inequality revealed by the different measures. For some time, therefore, researchers have tried to develop ways of including within statistical measures some mechanism for taking account of the reduced cost of pooled resources in families or households, so that comparisons can be made between the circumstances of those living in differing domestic arrangements. This has been done through the development of equivalence scales.

Equivalence Scales

Equivalence scales are an attempt to express in proportional terms the presumed costs-of-living reduction experienced by members of households sharing resources. They have been widely used in studies of poverty: for instance Rowntree's first 1899 survey (Rowntree, 1901) was based on an equivalence scale drawn from presumed dietary needs, under which the amount allowed for children in a household was estimated at between a third and a quarter of that for an adult. Thus a household containing one adult and one child would require an income that was between 1.25 and 1.33 times the income of a single adult household to achieve the same standard of living.

The most well-known and widely used equivalence scales today are the Income Support (IS) scale rates, where the lower rate for a couple compared with two single persons and the reduced rate for children produce an equivalence scale, using a base of 1.0 for a couple, 0.49 for a third additional adult in a household, 0.38 for a 16–17 year old, 0.32 for a child of 11–15 and 0.21 for a child under 11. These are of course arbitrary fractions based on the judgement of governments, which set the scales every year; but as established scales they at least give a consistent basis for comparative analysis.

Thus the change in the equivalence scales resulting from the move from the LIF to the HBAI basis for government statistical recording in 1988 aroused further controversy because of the change in equivalence values that accompanied it. The HBAI figures are based on a different and more complex equivalence scale than IS benefits, with finer gradations of changes for third and fourth adults and children with different ages. The more complex scale is not necessarily superior. It is debatable whether the marginal costs of additional household members and children with different ages can be so closely determined. However the main problem of the change was the lack of consistency it introduced, especially as the IS equivalence scales remained within the benefit system itself.

How to determine equivalence scales is a controversial issue. Fiegehen *et al.* (1977, ch. 7) discussed different models and the consequences of these. They used behaviourist measures, based on the 1971 FES, to determine the costs of different household members such as children. They then compared the scales based on these expenditure patterns to those assumed in the benefit rates and found that in practice there was little difference between the two.

Budget standard approaches have also been used to compare the needs of family members, especially children, with the resources implied in the equivalence scales incorporated into benefit rates. For instance Bradshaw's Family Budget Unit compared weekly budgets with benefit rates (Bradshaw, 1993a, 1993b; Oldfield and Yu, 1993), Roll (1986) focused on the cost of babies, and, most well-known, Piachaud (1979, 1981b) looked at the costs of children. All concluded that the costs are greater than the amounts allowed in the benefit rates. However Piachaud (1979) and Oldfield and Yu (1993) also found that the estimated cost of children varied with the age of the child, as did the benefit scales, suggesting that even if overall the rates were too low, the equivalence ratings themselves did reflect real variations in costs.

The great advantage of equivalence scales, as both Atkinson (1983, ch. 3.3) and Fiegehen *et al.* (1977, ch. 7) have argued, is that they permit households or families of different structures or sizes to be compared, in particular in terms of changes in expenditure patterns at different levels of income. Thus analysis utilising Engel curves, the points in income scales at which expenditure on necessary items changes, can be constructed and comparisons made between families of different types. Fiegehen *et al.* used this to show how Engel curves vary for households with and without dependent children, confirming our common-sense expectation that for households with children expenditure on necessities claims a higher proportion of income, especially at low income levels.

Intrahousehold Transfers

Different household and family formations therefore result in different needs and expenditure patterns, and as we shall see, these needs and patterns vary over time. Equivalence scales are a means of comparing different households or families by formalising assumptions about the reduced needs and expenditure that result from the sharing of resources within the household. However the comparisons based on reduced costs due to sharing in households are founded on two important assumptions, both of which can be subjected to critical debate. The first assumption is that sharing or the aggregation of resources does take place within households, and that this interdependency is non-problematic. The second is that two or more people can live less expensively than one and maintain the same standard.

The assumption of aggregation is a long-standing feature of both academic analysis and policy development; and it is obviously not without foundation. For instance, although most children have no income of their own we know that most parents expect to use a part of their income to provide for their children. Nevertheless it is far from clear whether all parents share all their resources with their children on an equal basis – and indeed common sense suggests that it is most unlikely that they do. When it comes to sharing between adults the assumption of equal sharing is even more questionable.

Obviously obtaining reliable information on the distribution of incomes within households is problematic, a point to which we shall return shortly, but recent studies that have attempted to do this suggest that unequal sharing is likely to be the norm. In 1982 Piachaud (1982b, p. 481) concluded that 'the distribution of incomes within families is highly unequal'. Later in the 1980s Pahl (1989) carried out research based on interviews with both husbands and wives to investigate in detail the different patterns of income distribution within families and found that patterns varied significantly – and frequently exhibited inequalities both in share of income and control over expenditure.

Given their relative exclusion from the labour market and their weaker position within it, it is usually women who are the less equal partners in such divisions, and as we shall see this is usually associated with women's greater responsibilities for caring work. One startling example of the depth of this inequality was Graham's (1986) finding that over a half of the women questioned in a survey of separated lone parents felt they were better off after separation – even though dependent on state benefit and living on the 'poverty line' – than they had been when they were sharing with partners with higher incomes – a finding that was confirmed in Pahl's (1989) work.

One of the reasons why the women in these families felt poor was because they did not control the resources – it was not their income that provided for the family and by and large they could not determine expenditure. This feeling of dependency is a central feature of inequality within households, and it is compounded by the assumptions about aggregation and sharing of living costs incorporated into benefit policy (see Esam and Berthoud, 1991). It is a social and an emotional as well as a material inequality, and it is a significant yet widely overlooked feature of poverty amid affluence to which we shall return in Chapter 9. Even when married women are in paid employment, family inequalities are not necessarily removed, for as Morris (1989) has shown, their income is generally lower and more likely to be spent on supplementing an inadequate housekeeping budget.

Of course poverty and inequality within households is not exclusively a female problem. The enforced dependency contained in policies that aggregate family and household incomes also has consequences for sick and disabled adults forced to rely on others at home, and for young unemployed adults, now up to the age of 25 under benefit regulations, assumed to be able to share their households with others.

The second assumption underlying the household basis for poverty measurement is that of the reduction in living costs that is associated with sharing. Again there is obviously some basis for this – heating can be shared, as can furniture and many other household items. However many of the reductions supposedly associated with shared living are indirect savings based on unpaid work performed within the household, usually by women. Piachaud (1987) contrasts the cost of oven-ready chips with home-prepared chips – the end result is more or less the same but one costs more to the household in terms of money and the other more in terms of time. For the high-flying executive we know that 'time is money', but this equation is equally valid for the housewife at home.

The standard of living of many households is maintained by, usually women's, unpaid labour at home cooking and cleaning. This is a substitute for a reduced family income, but at a cost to the family member performing the work. As Lister (1990) argued, this loss of time, 'time poverty', is a significant deprivation in the lives of many women and one that is disguised within the household measure of income and expenditure.

When unpaid work at home extends to caring for other dependants, such as children, the cost in time rises astronomically. In a well-publicised pamphlet Piachaud (1984) estimated that this averaged out at around fifty hours a week for the ordinary young child. This is more than the average working week in paid employment and a significant feature of a broader conceptualisation of the intrahousehold distribution of resources.

Both the direct cost (cash) and indirect costs (emotional dependency, loss of control and time poverty) of intrahousehold distribution have often been ignored in studies of poverty. Indeed it is only fairly recently that research has attempted to obtain information about such distributions. Although it hardly provides a justification, this may in part be due to recognition of the difficulties inherent in securing reliable data on such a potentially sensitive issue. Pahl's work was based on qualitative interviews with very small samples of households. The results were revealing, but they were not necessarily representative. Conducting large-scale quantitative research within households is likely to be difficult if not impossible to organise. However more detailed evidence of the distribution of resources within households and families is now very much a feature of research into the distribution of poverty and inequality, and this has been further encouraged by investigation into the distribution of such resources over time.

Poverty Dynamics

Because of the central role that earnings play in the distribution of resources within British society, the changes over time that people experience in their income patterns are largely a product of changes in employment prospects and earning capacity. With the changes in employment and earnings that have resulted from economic conditions in recent times these patterns can vary significantly. Nevertheless on average the pattern of income over a lifetime takes the form of an inverted U: earning capacity grows in early adulthood, reaches a plateau in middle age, and then declines with old age and retirement (Figure 7.1).

As we can see, the decline does not go completely back to zero in old age due to the effect of retirement pensions. Entitlement to a pension,

FIGURE 7.1 *Income over the life cycle*

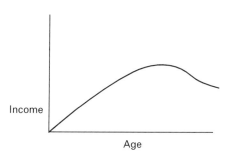

Income

Age

particularly a generous, earnings-related occupational pension, can significantly reduce the decline into poverty in old age. This means that the steepness of the decline will vary between different individuals depending on their employment status during adulthood, with non-manual workers generally experiencing a shallower decline as they get older due the retention of well-paid jobs with incremental salary scales and the enjoyment of occupational pensions.

It is clear from this that pensions, and other savings and investments, can be regarded as a form of 'deferred income'. Their impact on life-cycle wealth and poverty demonstrates the importance of regarding income as a resource over time, and not just when it is actually received. The ability to save and defer spending can operate to even out periods of relative poverty within the life cycle and therefore can mitigate to a considerable extent the deprivation associated with low income, if this is a temporary or a predictable event.

Saving for the metaphorical 'rainy day' in this way is a major feature of the balance between individual or family income and expenditure over time, and it can have a significant effect on the extent and the experience of poverty. The American academic Sherraden (1991) has even argued that saving and the acquisition of 'assets' is *more* important than income in determining and preventing poverty. This means that studies of poverty need to pay attention to the cumulative and lifetime effects of periods of low income or deprivation, rather than just utilising 'snapshot' measures of current circumstances. Atkinson (1983; 1989, ch. 1) has pointed out that studies of poverty based on a longer 'accounting period' – the period over which income is measured – are likely to reveal different rates of poverty, and this has been taken up in particular by R. Walker (1994) in research into these poverty dynamics.

The use of different accounting periods can operate either to lower or to raise poverty levels depending on how we perceive these. The longer the period over which overall income is measured, the lower the general level of poverty is likely to be, because over such a long period a significant number of people will move in and out of poverty – and thus will be able to spread the higher resources obtained during times out of poverty over the period as a whole. Such movement in and out of poverty is important and significant. Research from the British Household Panel Survey, which records the circumstances of a fixed sample of individuals and families over several years, has shown that around a half of the poorest tenth of the population move in or out of poverty within one year (Jarvis and Jenkins, 1995).

Panel studies such as this are valuable in avoiding the limitations of the snapshot surveys, which have more commonly dominated quantitative research into poverty. By measuring the experience of poverty over time (extending the 'window of observation') they permit different accounting periods to be adopted when measuring poverty. This can have the effect of reducing the overall number of those who are poor over time. However it can also reveal the more serious effects of longer periods of poverty for others; and for those who do remain in poverty for long periods of time these effects can significantly compound the deprivation that results from having to survive on a low income.

It is not just monetary savings or deferred income such as pensions, annuities and insurance policies that can operate to mitigate the effects of poverty over time. Spending and investment in consumer durables, especially housing, can also even out temporal inequalities. For instance a washing machine, a fridge or a freezer purchased in times of relative plenty can reduce problems of deprivation in times of need; and an owner-occupied house, especially once the mortgage has been paid off, can significantly improve a person's standard of living by removing the need to pay rent. Even when a mortgage is still in existence, however, owner occupation can provide additional resources: the declining real cost of the repayments when set against inflation can gradually reduce the actual cost, and the property can provide a capital asset against which further sums of money might be borrowed to meet future needs, although, of course, this depends on the gradual growth of the value of the property. Thus when this does not happen, as in the recession of the early 1990s, high mortgages on houses that are falling in value result in repossession and bankruptcy for some recent buyers, turning capital investment into future deprivation.

So although income and wealth can be spread by individuals throughout their lifetime to mitigate the problems associated with periods of deprivation, the success of such strategies is far from guaranteed – and conversely, the experience of periods of poverty can have a debilitating effect over time. Inability to save and invest now, or to buy durable goods for future use, means that resources are not there to be drawn on in the future. This can accentuate any deprivation due to long periods on a low income – a problem experienced by many older pensioners in Britain in the 1980s and 1990s, who did not have the benefit of the wide range of occupational and private pension schemes that have become available when they were working, even though they may have been earning enough to pay into one.

For individuals and families who encounter such longer periods of poverty the experience of deprivation is much deeper and more debilitating than for those moving in and out of a low income. Research by Kempson *et al.* (1994) into the circumstances of poor families – fittingly entitled *Hard Times* – confirmed that for most of them life was a constant struggle of seeking, and often failing, to make ends meet; and when debts were carried over from past times of hardship these often had the effect of dragging down families into further despair.

Increased awareness of the impact of different durations of poverty can thus provide evidence of reduced levels of poverty across the population as a whole. However measurement of the effects of poverty over time also reveals the debilitating experience of increased levels of deprivation among those unfortunate enough to remain poor over long periods. The message from poverty dynamics can therefore cut two ways.

Life-Cycle Changes

The differences in the extent and depth of poverty resulting from changes experienced by people over time in studies of poverty dynamics are one aspect of the temporal dimension of defining and measuring poverty. Panel research that follows individuals and families over a period of years can reveal the effects of changes over such periods, and the British Household Panel Survey will initially run for ten years. However most individuals live for much longer than ten years and over their lifetime they are likely to experience significant changes in their circumstances, which will operate to increase or reduce their risk of experiencing poverty. Changes experienced over the whole of the life cycle thus affect our understanding of the impact of poverty.

What is more the changes experienced over the life cycle are not the same for all individuals at all periods of time. Variations in demographic trends, shifts in the overall number of births and deaths, can significantly alter the life time experiences of different cohorts of the population. For instance a downturn in the birth rate will be represented fifteen or twenty years later by a reduced number of school leavers entering the employment market. This may well mean enhanced employment prospects, and hence reduced poverty prospects – for these young adults, irrespective of any individual effort or talent on their part or any policy changes introduced by the government. Conversely those born during the periods of so-called 'baby booms' may face greater difficulties in providing for themselves as they grow older as they will be part of a larger number of people reaching retirement age at more or less the same time.

Other demographic changes, such as changes in marriage and divorce rates and age at childbirth, will also affect individuals' earning capacity and income, and thus spending needs and spending and saving patterns. This raises the more general issue of changes in household and family structure over time, which is a long-established feature of discussion and analysis of poverty and inequality. As discussed above, differences in household structure will affect the circumstances of household members. However such structures are not static. Inevitably they change over time, and this family aspect of life cycle changes is crucial in influencing the impact of poverty and deprivation.

In his pioneering work on poverty, Rowntree (1901) identified five periods of alternating want and relative plenty through which a labourer would pass: childhood, early working adulthood, parenthood, working life after children had grown up and old age. In their discussion of such changes O'Higgins *et al.* (1988) identified ten life-cycle groups between which family structures vary in ways that are likely to impact on their standard of living. They then used FES data to compare the circumstances of a sample of different groups. They concluded that the principles behind Rowntree's model of alternating periods remained as relevant in the latter part of the twentieth century as at the beginning of it, although with changed economic and social circumstances the periods of differing resources and needs may have become more complex. For instance, with widespread owner-occupation families may rely on two incomes to pay for the cost of setting up a household during early adulthood, before any children are born, after which they will survive only one income while the children are young (see R. Walker, 1988).

O'Higgins *et al.* (1988) also included an eleventh group, lone parents, who are also now more likely to be poor. Townsend (1979, ch. 22) too identified lone parents as a group potentially experiencing deprivation; and as Millar (1989a) and Bradshaw and Millar (1991) have discussed, lone parents are predominantly mothers and most have become lone parent families following matrimonial breakdown.

Of course matrimonial breakdown is not a life-cycle event experienced by all, and it was certainly ignored in Rowntree's five periods of life-cycle need and plenty. However it is experienced by an increasing proportion of the population of Britain, with more than one in three marriages expected to end in divorce in the 1990s; and, as Millar (1988) has demonstrated, it is a life-cycle change with a significant impact on income and wealth. Townsend (1979, ch. 20) and Glendinning and Baldwin (1988) point out that this is also true of chronic sickness and disability – an issue to which we shall return in Chapter 12.

Unemployment too may have household and life-cycle consequences. For instance Cooke (1987) and Kell and Wright (1990) have shown that male unemployment can result in the wives of unemployed men withdrawing from paid work as well as their husbands. Given Walker's argument above about the importance of two incomes for families during certain periods of the household life cycle, this is likely to have an impact beyond the immediate period of lost income from wages.

One of the significant features of life-cycle periods of relative deprivation is that they are to a large extent predictable. They can thus be prepared for and the relative deprivation associated with them can be prevented or mitigated. This can be done at the individual level, for example through a private pension scheme, and private provision for the redistribution of household income over the lifetime is now widespread. However, and more significantly, it can be done at the social level by directing support from state benefits towards predictable periods of need.

This is the idea behind the notion of horizontal redistribution through social security championed by Beveridge (1942) and discussed in Chapter 14. The advantage of such collective protection from the 'cradle to the grave' is that it can provide for periods of need that may not be predictable at the individual level, including marital breakdown, although protection from this was excluded from the postwar national insurance scheme because of a government fear that it might encourage marriages to break up.

It is the needs of children and those who have retired, however, that have since Rowntree's day have remained the most important cases for horizontal redistribution through state support. Following Rowntree, Beveridge proposed the introduction of family allowances and retirement pensions to provide for these. Family allowances have now been replaced in Britain by Child Benefit, and pensions have been considerably extended and reformed. However both remain the most important and most widely claimed of social security benefits, confirming the link between our understanding of the experience and risk of poverty and the development of antipoverty policy.

8

Measuring Poverty

The Problem of Measurement

For most academics and researchers, as well as most politicians, the purpose of attempting to define poverty is to be able to measure its extent within or across societies, the implication being that where poverty is extensive it will be the focus of concern and policies may be developed to remove or ameliorate it. It is primarily because of this policy context that the task of defining poverty is, of course, so problematic. For the same reason the question of measuring poverty is fraught with difficulties and disagreements.

Fundamental to the debate on measurement, as in the debate on definitions, is the question of whether what is being measured is a separate category of poverty or merely a predetermined aspect of the broader measurement of levels of inequality, such as a line or threshold drawn towards the bottom of the income or wealth scale, below which inequality is argued to be, or presumed to be, unacceptable. We shall return shortly to the question of how to draw up a line to be measured. However the issue is further complicated, as Ringen (1988) has pointed out, by confusion over the use of both direct and indirect measures to draw the lines.

The emphasis on relative deprivation and standard of living when determining poverty levels, developed by Townsend (1979), Mack and Lansley (1985) and others, focuses attention on expenditure, or more accurately consumption, as a measure of poverty. But most studies of poverty, particularly those seeking to establish the number living below a given poverty line, including Townsend and Mack and Lansley, use income as a measure. Ringen's argument is that income cannot be used as a proxy for consumption since many aspects of consumption are not determined solely by income, notably the consumption of non-commodified welfare services – therefore if poverty is to be measured accurately, more sophisticated indicators will have to be developed.

This is an important point, and as conceded by Donnison (1988) in a reply to Ringen, crude attempts to equate cash inequalities with poverty are not acceptable in either academic or political circles. However, as discussed in Chapter 5, there have been some more sophisticated attempts to establish a link between income levels and consumption patterns, for instance via the notion of a threshold of deprivation. If the limitations of these are borne in mind, it may be feasible to use income measures to make some assessment of the number living in poverty according to certain definitions.

In fact the problems involved in the measurement of income and/or consumption extend well beyond the difficulties pointed out by Ringen. There are many other inconsistencies between different measures resulting from the means by which data is collected, analysed and presented, and we shall discuss some of these below. However these problems do not mean that, and should not be used to suggest that, we cannot arrive at any useful measures of poverty or inequality. As Atkinson in particular has consistently argued and demonstrated (for instance Atkinson, 1983, 1989), if care is taken to recognise the problems involved there is quite a lot we can say about the extent of poverty and inequality in Britain, and in other advanced industrial countries too.

Much of the work on measuring poverty has been quantitative in nature, using statistical techniques to count the number of people in poverty or to measure the extent of inequality. Indeed in Britain in particular this arithmetic tradition has a long and well-established history in academic circles and political debate, stemming from the seminal studies of Booth (1889) and Rowntree (1901) at the end of the nineteenth century.

However quantitative measures provide us with a rather limited picture of the extent of poverty and inequality in society. These limitations were graphically illustrated in 1920 in the interchange between Bowley, one of the British pioneers of poverty measurement, and Bevin, the trade union leader and later foreign secretary, over the 'docker's breakfast', discussed in Chapter 5. As Bevin's biographer pointed out, the trade union leader's (qualitative) measure of the meagre diet of bread, bacon and fish was worth 'volumes of statistics' in its effect on public opinion (Atkinson, 1989, p. 38). The qualitative measure tells us what a volume of statistics could never do – how poverty is measured in real life terms. Qualitative data is thus as important as statistical data analysis in the measurement of poverty, and we will return later to a brief discussion of the role of qualitative studies in poverty research.

Quantitative Measures

The great advantage of quantitative measures is their scale and their anonymity. A statistical survey, if it is large enough and if the sample of respondents providing the data is carefully chosen, can provide an objective and arguably scientific picture of the broader group or society from which it has been selected, particularly if standard measures of the statistical significance of the data have been reached. As suggested above therefore, quantitative measures have always been at the centre of poverty research and measurement in Britain. These can be based on existing statistical information collected by governmental or other agencies for different purposes, or they can be based on original data collected directly by researchers using survey methods to question a sample of the population. Both approaches have been widely utilised in poverty and inequality research in Britain.

Using Existing Data Sets

The main sources of existing data are government statistics, collected by government departments or the Central Statistical Office (CSO). In the past these used to include the 'Blue Books' – national income and expenditure blue books produced by the CSO from inland revenue data and other official sources, which provided a more or less consistent source of data on these from 1952 until the mid 1970s and were widely relied on by researchers and politicians. Since 1957 the government has also conducted a regular Family Expenditure Survey (FES) based on detailed information on the expenditure patterns of a relatively large sample of the population.

An early version of the FES was used by Abel Smith and Townsend (1965) in their famous study, *The Poor and the Poorest*, which demonstrated that high levels of poverty persisted in Britain despite the introduction of the welfare reforms of the postwar period. Extracts from it and other official sources also provide the basis of the annual statistical reports in *Social Trends* and *Economic Trends*. Since the 1970s the DHSS, later the DSS, has been utilising this data to publish the details of families with low incomes relative to state benefit, and now the HBAI figures discussed in Chapter 7. The most comprehensive official statistics dealing with incomes, including low incomes, however, were those produced by the Royal Commission on the Distribution of Income and Wealth, the Diamond Commission, which produced regular reports culminating in 1980 when they were discontinued by the Conservative government (Royal Commission, 1980); and it was partly to replace the income distribution data once provided by the Diamond Commission that the Rowntree Foundation established its Inquiry into Income and Wealth in the early 1990s (Barclay, 1995; Hills, 1995).

The great advantages of government statistics, of course, are that access to them is free and they carry the authority of their official status. They are thus used widely by academic researchers and political campaigners. The CPAG has a well-established national tradition of analysing and publicising official statistics on poverty and inequality in order to demonstrate, using the government's own figures, the limitations of policies aimed at reducing poverty (see Oppenheim and Harker, 1996; and Harker, 1996). And in the early 1990s a growing number of local authorities concerned about the increasing level of poverty and deprivation in their areas sought to analyse national and local statistical sources, such as the decennial census and the council's own Housing Benefit records, to develop profiles of local poverty (Smith, 1995; see also Alcock *et al.*, 1995, ch. 4).

Despite their apparent authority, however, there are limitations in the official statistics that need to be borne in mind in any attempt to utilise them as a poverty measure. For instance the FES sample is only about one in 2500, it covers only those in households (thus excluding the homeless or those in institutions), it has a roughly 30 per cent non-response rate, and, given the way the data is gathered, it is very likely to understate income. Thus not everyone or everything is covered, and poverty and low incomes in particular may be underrepresented in the figures.

Conducting Survey Research

It is partly because of limitations such as these, therefore, that some researchers have sought to collect their own quantitative data on poverty and deprivation, and original data also has the advantage of being able to cover a breadth and depth of detail not included in government and other official statistics. Some of the most significant studies of poverty have thus been based on surveys conducted by, or on behalf of, the investigators themselves. Rowntree (1901, 1941) and Townsend (1979) employed research workers to interview respondents and collect data. Mack and Lansley (1985), through London Weekend Television (LWT), used a contract research agency (MORI) to conduct a survey for them.

In a later study of poverty in London, Townsend (Townsend *et al.*, 1987) combined a survey of a sample of the population with cooperation and consultation with representative bodies in the local borough councils and the now abolished Greater London Council (GLC). Such locally based surveys of poverty grew dramatically in number in the early 1990s as local authorities used them to supplement existing data sources to profile the extent and distribution of poverty in their local area. Some local authorities adopted the methods used in national surveys such as the LWT research (Liverpool, 1991; Greenwich, 1994), whilst others developed a range of other means of collecting data (Griffiths, 1994).

Of course all the problems of sample size, non-response, and so on apply to the original data too. Nevertheless the control over the construction of questionnaires and the samples of respondents that original research provides permit a much greater range of data to be collected and analysed, as was demonstrated in Townsend's major 1960s and 1970s survey (Townsend, 1979). However collecting original data is costly, and Townsend's study in particular struggled with a budget that, though large by some research standards, was barely adequate for the task to which it was addressed.

Despite these problems some very useful and significant studies have managed to collect original data with relatively small budgets by using various opportunities arising from other activities. In the 1960s Coates and Silburn's (1970) classic study of poverty in an inner city area of Nottingham (St Ann's) was based on data collected by Workers Educational Association students and undergraduates at Nottingham University as part of their social studies curriculum.

Comparing Data

One of the broader limitations of original data, however, is its compatibility with data from other studies, either of different populations or at different times. One of reasons why Abel Smith and Townsend (1965) were able to discover higher levels of poverty in Britain in the 1950s than those revealed in Rowntree's final 1950 survey in York (Rowntree and Lavers, 1951) was because their work was based on a different and more extensive data source. Thus the difference was arguably as much to do with how the data relied on was collected as it was to do with different levels of poverty and inequality in British society. Over time this problem of comparability of data is indeed a large one, as Piachaud (1988) discusses, although, as he showed, adjustments can usually be made to the data to reveal some comparability if this is approached carefully.

If we want to make comparisons between levels of poverty and inequality in different countries, then the problem of comparability of data grows even greater, as mentioned in Chapter 4. Even in official statistics there are differences in policy over what information is collected, and differences in culture and convention over how this is done and how it is analysed and presented. At times this problem may have seemed insurmountable, but the increasing activity of the EU has led to a significant commitment to international comparability within Europe and to growing pressure within Europe for the collection of cross-national statistical information. For instance Eurostat, the Commission's statistical service, has launched a household panel survey looking at the movement of households in and out of poverty across the EU (Eurostat, 1993).

Currently there is also a major international collaborative venture to collect and analyse data on incomes – the Luxembourg Income Study (LIS), based in Luxembourg. This is a large and long-term commitment to establish and develop a database on income levels and poverty in a wide range of advanced industrial countries (see Smeeding *et al.*, 1990). Initially seven nations were involved across Europe and North America, but later others joined, extending the scope to forty datasets covering seventeen countries by the mid 1990s (de Tombeur and Ladewig, 1994). Data is provided for the LIS by each country, and this then is adapted by the research team to give comparable measures that can be accessed and reanalysed by researchers from all over the world.

The great advantage of the LIS, therefore, is that it provides a database that researchers can use and adapt for their own purposes. What makes this feasible now of course is the use of new technologies in information storage and retrieval on computers and microcomputers. The development of computer-based information technology has transformed and much enhanced the use of quantitative measures of poverty and inequality. Computerised data can be much more speedily collected and analysed, and even more importantly it can be readily transferred, adapted and reanalysed any number of times.

Users of the LIS can request data direct from the computer base using information links and then analyse the data as they wish, although obviously a fee is charged for this service. This accessibility and transferability of computer-based data is a trend that has been supported strongly in recent years by Atkinson, the leading British expert on quantitative measurement of poverty and inequality (for instance Atkinson, 1989, p. 38). As he argues, if such data can be made accessible to other researchers, then they can analyse it using their own poverty lines or poverty measures, thus avoiding the problems and disagreements over this discussed in Chapter 5.

With the assistance of Sutherland, Atkinson developed such a database as part of the LSE Welfare State Research Programme (TAXMOD), which could be used to measure the effects of potential changes in taxes and benefits on income distribution in Britain and could be adapted to respond to specific questions or assumptions made by different users (Atkinson and Sutherland, 1984). This was later extended to cover a larger range of income models and potential changes (POLIMOD), and it is now to be developed with EU support in a European basis (EUROMOD).

Adaptation and reanalysis of data, however, is constrained by the basic structure of the information available. As with all computer-based data, we can only get out what we have put in. This imposes obvious limitations on the international comparisons that can be made using datasets such as the LIS. In Chapter 7, for instance, we discussed the differences between the family and the household as a basis for measuring income. Although the LIS data includes family-based measures for all the initial countries in the study, it does not contain household data for all, so only limited comparisons can be made.

Problems of statistical comparability also extend to the question of whether comparison is being made between the *extent* or the *depth* of poverty – or to put it another way, between the number below the poverty line or the distance between those below the line and those above it. Counting the number of people, or households, below a poverty line is sometimes referred to as the 'head count' measure. It tells us how many are poor within a particular population, but it does not reveal the extent of poverty experienced by individuals or households because it does not tell us how far they are below the poverty line. Obviously there is a significant difference between say ten million people being just below the poverty line and five million people being more than 50 per cent below it. In the latter case fewer are 'in poverty', but their experience of poverty is much more serious – a point that is taken up by the poverty dynamics research discussed in Chapter 7.

Thus the depth as well as the breadth of poverty – or the 'poverty gap' as it is sometimes called – may also need to be measured in order to determine and compare levels of poverty. What is more, as Beckerman (1980) has argued, the distinction is not only of academic importance, it can also have an important effect on policy planning. The policies and resources required to lift a large number of people just a short distance above the poverty line would be rather different from those required to raise the incomes of a smaller number much higher. As we shall discuss in Chapter 14, social security policies in Britain have mainly been aimed at reducing the poverty gap, bringing people up to the poverty line; yet most quantitative studies of poverty are attempts to determine a head count of the number below the poverty line.

The importance of the poverty gap measure is that it can give us a clearer indication of the scale of relative poverty when compared with the broader distribution of resources within society. It is really a version of a measure of inequality, expressed in relation to a poverty line drawn within the overall income distribution. In practice of course, as we discussed in Chapter 5, this is what all definitions of poverty are, and thus all quantitative measures of poverty are primarily measures of inequality onto which definitions of poverty are mapped.

In order to do this definitions of poverty must be expressed in a form that can be applied as an indicator of poverty to a statistical database of income or expenditure. In most cases this takes the form of algebraic formulae, which can then be applied to the data to reveal the numbers and proportions of the poor. This use of indicators is a complex science, generally referred to as 'econometrics', and it requires an understanding of algebra that is likely to be beyond most social scientists. Atkinson is the most important and widely read exponent of econometric approaches to poverty measurement and he discusses some of the conceptual and practical issues involved in this in two famous papers reproduced in 1989 (Atkinson, 1989, chs 1, 2). The use of algebraic formulae permits us to make measurements of poverty, according to different definitions, from data on income or expenditure inequality and to compare these across countries or over time. Thus they can help to turn definitions into measures – although they cannot overcome the problem of disagreement over the definitions themselves.

Measuring Inequality

It is measures of inequality, therefore, that are at the heart of quantitative studies of poverty. Measuring inequality and changing patterns of income or expenditure distribution provides us with the broader picture of relativities of wealth and deprivation into which discussion about where to draw the poverty line can be introduced. Thus in order better to understand debates about poverty we need to spend a little time examining how measures of inequality operate and what kind of information they provide.

The most graphic demonstration of the power of inequality measures is Pen's famous 'Parade of Dwarfs' (Pen, 1971). In a fascinating popularisation of the distribution of income in British society, Pen characterised the spread of incomes as an hour-long parade of people whose height was symbolic of their relative place in the distribution of resources in society, with average income being represented by persons of average height. As the title of the paper suggests, under this representation the vast majority of people were dwarfs – only twelve minutes before the end of the hour did persons of average height appear. However after that, in the last ten minutes, heights grew dramatically, with doctors and accountants seven to eight yards high, and finally at the end a few people who were a mile high or more. Seen in this way the measurement of inequality is indeed staggering. Pen also presents it as a graph, which reveals in visual form the fact that so many are below the average, and that a few are far above it (Figure 8.1). The political importance of the relationship between inequality and poverty measures becomes much clearer when we recognise that the large majority of people receive below average resources.

The idea behind Pen's parade was taken up again in the 1990s in the presentation of the findings from the Rowntree Foundation's research on income and wealth. Hills (1995) produced an 'Income Parade' for the UK for 1990/91, which compared the incomes of various different ideal family types throughout the population, and revealed that average income was only exceeded by the top 30 per cent of households.

A more conventional, and adaptable, way of expressing the distribution described in Pen's parade is through the construction of what are called Lorenz curves. These are used to represent, in simple graphical form, the distribution of incomes in a particular country against what would be a hypothetical distribution of completely identical incomes. They are discussed by Atkinson (1983, pp. 15–17), who provides the following example based on the distribution of income in Britain in 1978–9 (Figure 8.2).

FIGURE 8.1 *Pen's 'Parade of Dwarfs'*

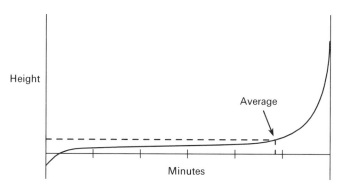

Source: Pen, 1971.

FIGURE 8.2 *The Lorenz curve*

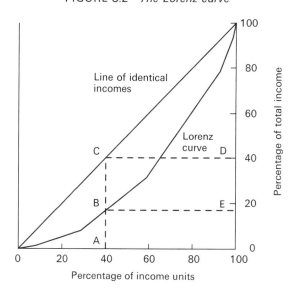

Source: Atkinson, 1983, Figure 2.2, p. 16.

The curve representing distribution in Britain lay below the straight line representing hypothetical identical income levels. Thus if all incomes had been equal, 40 per cent of income units would have received 40 per cent of total income – line ACD. In fact, however, distribution was not equal, it followed the curve below the line, and thus 40 per cent of people received below 20 per cent of income – line ABE. The trajectory of the curve below the line thus expresses the extent of inequality in society. The further away from the diagonal line the curve is, the greater the extent of inequality; thus a curve below that in Figure 8.2 would show 40 per cent of the population getting much less then 20 per cent of total income.

Lorenz curves not only have the advantage of expressing measures of inequality in a simple, visual form, they also allow comparisons to be made easily between different distributions (and thus inequalities) in different societies (see Atkinson, 1983, pp. 54–5). Thus if the United States has a Lorenz curve below that of Britain, then we can say that in general it is a more unequal society. This relationship can also be expressed in numerical form by calculating from a Lorenz curve a figure known as the Gini coefficient. This is the fraction that represents the relationship found in the graph between the area between the curve and the diagonal and the total area under the diagonal. Thus:

$$\text{Gini coefficient} = \frac{\text{area between Lorenz curve and diagonal}}{\text{total area under diagonal}}$$

This will always be a decimal fraction, for instance 0.4, because in all societies the curve will lie somewhere below the diagonal. But the closer to the diagonal the curve is, and thus the less the overall inequality, the smaller the fraction will be. Thus a society with a Gini coefficient of 0.4 generally has less inequality than one with a Gini coefficient of 0.6.

The Gini coefficient is a very simple comparative measure of inequality, but it is also a very crude one. In particular it cannot represent one potentially important feature of different distributions that can be represented by Lorenz curves, that is the spread of inequality. Atkinson (1983, p. 55) demonstrates this by comparing the Lorenz curves for Britain and West Germany (Figure 8.3).

As can be seen, here the curves are both below the line, but they intersect. The Gini coefficients for both countries may in fact be more or less the same, but the distribution of income in each is significantly different. Thus according to Atkinson there were more people in West

FIGURE 8.3   *Intersecting Lorenz curves*

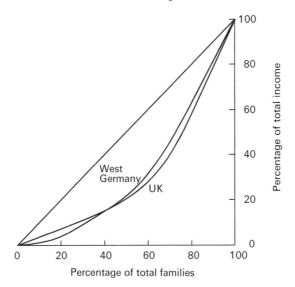

Percentage of total families

Source: Atkinson, 1983, Figure 3.2, p. 55.

Germany with low incomes than there were in Britain, but conversely those in the middle in West Germany enjoyed a comparatively higher relative position to those in the middle in Britain.

Measures of inequality therefore concern not just the relationship between those at the top and those at the bottom. They also tell us about the relationships between all those in between, and here patterns may and do vary significantly between different countries, as expressed by the intersection of comparative Lorenz curves. This is a similar distinction to that between the head count and poverty gap measures of poverty referred to above – both are important and may lead to important differences in policy to respond to the patterns they reveal. Of course distributions will also vary within one country over time, particularly if policy measures are introduced that aim to reduce, or increase, the extent of inequality. Measures of inequality compared over time can thus tell us something about the success or failure of such policies; and the recent increase in the level of poverty and inequality revealed by the Rowntree Foundation research (Hills,

1995), discussed in Chapter 1, suggest that recent policies in Britain have been far from successful in reducing these.

However, as suggested earlier, measuring poverty involves more than just the collection of statistics and the application of algebraic formulae; it must also encompass examination of what these dry figures mean for the real lives of real people. Therefore to gain a fuller understanding of poverty and inequality in Britain 1990s, or indeed in any country at any time, we need to use qualitative measures in addition to statistical surveys.

Qualitative Analysis

It is probably true to say that quantitative measures of poverty and the collection and analysis of statistics have dominated research and debate on poverty in Britain throughout much of the twentieth century. However the use of statistics has not prevented the development of a strong tradition of qualitative description and analysis of the experience of poverty that has sought to give life and meaning to the fairly dry tables and graphs of the arithmetic tradition.

Both Rowntree and Booth included descriptive material on the standard of living of the local people covered by their surveys, further underlining the mythical nature of claims that they were operating only with crude notions of absolute poverty. Townsend, in his major 1960s and 1970s survey of poverty in Britain, specifically focused part of his research, and a chapter of the book based on the study (Townsend, 1979, ch. 8), on what he called the impact of poverty. For instance here is an extract from a description of the impact of poverty on a young family suffering disability and with a handicapped child,

Mr and Mrs Nelson, 35 and 32, live with their three sons of 13, 9 and 6 in a four-roomed council flat in a poor district of Oldham, overlooked by a rubber factory belching smoke all day long and near a canal. They believe the flat is a danger to their health. 'One bedroom is so damp that it stripped itself'. The living room has a fire but they can only afford a one-bar electric fire to heat the bedrooms because they are terribly damp. The fire is taken from one room to the next. At Christmas the bedroom window was smashed by a brick. Because the family cannot afford new glass, the room gets too cold and the boys sleep in one bedroom (Townsend, 1979, p. 305).

More recently a review of the experience of poverty in the 1990s published by the CPAG, *Hardship Britain* (Cohen *et al.*, 1992), used interviews with people living in poverty to provide a depressing picture of the struggles in their lives. For instance,

> The family have no telephone, vacuum cleaner, electric kettle, or freezer and their fridge is in poor condition, as are all their other household goods. Although they try to give the children two hot meals a day, and often feel obliged to give them fruit and sweets (even though this stretches their budget), their lifestyle is in all other respects spartan. For example, the Chaudrys do not have a set of warm winter clothes or two pairs of all-weather shoes for everyone; the children get no treats and the family cannot afford to go and visit friends and relatives in other towns (ibid., p. 19).

As with this CPAG review of poverty in Britain in the 1990s, some of the most interesting and most significant qualitative analyses of poverty have been based largely or entirely on descriptive material. These include early works such as Mayhew's *London's Poor* and Orwell's *Road to Wigan Pier*, and more recent works such as Harrison's (1983) *Inside the Inner City* and Seabrook's (1984) *Landscapes of Poverty*. They also include a range of smaller studies published by organisations such as the CPAG and focusing on particular aspects of poverty, such as McClelland's (1982) *A Little Pride and Dignity* looking at child care costs, or on poverty in particular localities, such as Evason's (1980) *Ends That Won't Meet* examining poverty in Belfast. In the 1990s Kempson *et al.* (1994) produced a compelling analysis of the lives of families struggling to survive on state benefits, called *Hard Times*; and Kempson (1996) also published a review of qualitative research supported by the Rowntree Foundation, called *Life on a Low Income*. Qualitative studies generally seem to have more evocative titles than do statistical analyses.

Of course qualitative studies are generally not large scale, and the descriptions they offer cannot claim to be representative of poverty in any scientific sense. Despite their popular persuasive power they can therefore be more readily dismissed by critical academics or unsympathetic politicians, although in practice of course politicians may be influenced more by popular opinion, or by attempts to manipulate it, than they are by statistical rigour. However qualitative data can be linked directly to quantitative measures to harness the complementary strengths of measurement and description, as in Middleton *et al*s'. (1994) study of poor families, which revealed the sacrifices parents would make in order to minimise the deprivation experienced by their children. Such deprivation can be measured quantitatively, but an important part of what is being measured is lost in the process.

Like statistical analysis, qualitative description is also continually developing. The development of new information technologies has transformed qualitative representation of poverty as well as quantitative measurement of it. Here it is the development and growth of television and video that has been the powerful influence. Television and video descriptions of poverty, either real or fictional, can be seen and heard in the homes of a huge audience.

There have been a number of influential televised studies of poverty. Perhaps the most famous was the fictional 1960s drama on the homelessness and poverty of a young family, entitled 'Cathy Come Home'. However probably the most important example of this new genre of qualitative research presentation is the television series for which Mack and Lansley's important studies of relative poverty were undertaken in 1983 and 1990 (Mack and Lansley, 1985; Frayman, 1992). The studies were originally commissioned by London Weekend Television and were screened as a series of television programmes called 'Breadline Britain'. Like the survey itself, the programmes were largely based on interviews with respondents in their own homes. These were screened as a series of vignettes in which the people described their struggle to manage on the breadline. This made for harrowing viewing and presented to a wide audience the human costs of the statistical measures of poverty detailed in the survey, although, given the late night screening time the audience was probably not as large as it might have been earlier in the evening.

'Breadline Britain's' use of television to present the qualitative aspects of poverty research has since inspired other researchers to use video programmes as a supplement to, or even a replacement for, printed reports on poverty, inequality or social policy. For instance in 1990 members of the Social Security Research Consortium produced a video based on the findings of their research into the impact of the Social Fund on clients of rights and advice agencies, and this was presented to, among others, members of parliament in both the Commons and the Lords.

The use of television and video to enable poor people to describe their deprivation raises the broader issue of the role of poor people's determination of and control over the qualitative measurement of their poverty, and the presentation of this to the wider world. There is a strong element of paternalism in all academic studies of poverty and deprivation, which is most clearly revealed in qualitative descriptions or depictions of the lives of the poor. It has been argued by some, in particular by the one-time academic and now community worker in Glasgow's Easterhouse estate, Bob Holman, that the poor should be permitted, or encouraged, to speak for themselves about their experiences of poverty. Autobiography should replace biography, it is argued, not necessarily because it is a more accurate or convincing message, but because it places the power and control over the message in the hands of those experiencing the problem.

This raises a broader issue still, however, about the politics of poverty more generally – about whose problem poverty is and who should, or could, be expected to define it and determine how it is to be tackled. This issue has been taken up by Beresford and Croft (1995), and it is one to which we shall return in Chapter 13. In general, however, it is clear that self-description is, and should be, an important element of qualitative studies of poverty; and some studies, usually based within local community groups or campaigning organisations, have sought to present personal accounts of poverty to a wider audience. Beresford has continued to work with Lister and others (see Lister *et al.*, 1996) to establish a research project in Britain to harness poor people's experiences and perceptions of poverty; and the European Anti-Poverty Network (EAPN) is funded by the EU to provide a voice for the poor in European debate and policy development.

Part III

Social Divisions and Poverty

9

Gender and Poverty

The Feminisation of Poverty

Most attempts to measure poverty use household or family income or expenditure as the basis for counting or calculating the extent of poverty, as discussed in Chapter 7. Even when individual income is used, measurement tends to treat all individuals similarly as recipients of income without comparing their different circumstances or obligations. Insofar as this is explained or justified, and generally it is not, the assumption is that whilst income and expenditure are matters of public knowledge and concern, and thus amenable to public scrutiny and measurement, households and family circumstances and obligations are private matters that cannot and should not be the focus of public research.

We will return later to the significance of this alleged public/private divide in structuring our knowledge and perceptions of individual and family poverty. It is increasingly widely recognised, however, that differences in individual and family circumstances are crucial to determining the impact and extent of poverty, and that rather than being excluded or ignored they should be a central feature of any understanding of poverty. This is particularly true of the differences associated with gender.

The predominant focus on household and family income has obscured, or in Millar and Glendinning's (1989) words rendered 'invisible', the differences between men's and women's experiences of poverty – and differences in the extent and depth of poverty between men and women. The effect of this has most frequently been seen in the tendency to regard poor women as the wives or partners of poor (low-paid or unemployed) men rather than as the poor (low-paid or unemployed) wives or partners of men who may themselves be in well-paid employment. Even when women, as heads of households or breadwinners, are included, the particular problems that may be associated with their gender, for instance problems of discrimination or disadvantage within the labour market, are often ignored.

In recent years feminist critiques have begun to question and challenge this 'gender blindness' and to argue that focusing on the differences between men and women in research and policy analysis would reveal that women suffer poverty on a more widespread basis than men, and that their experience of poverty is quite different as a result of expectations about gender roles. Of particular importance here has been the work of Glendinning and Millar, especially the collection of papers published in their reader *Women and Poverty in Britain*, first published in 1987 and updated in 1992.

In recent discussions of gender and poverty there has sometimes even been talk of a 'feminisation of poverty'. As Millar (1989b) has discussed, this phrase was first used in the US, and it is a particularly ambiguous one. It could be taken to refer simply to the fact that as poverty levels increase more women are likely to experience poverty, or it could refer to a greater risk of poverty for women and thus a change in the balance between the genders, or indeed it could refer merely to an increased emphasis in research and policy on the poverty experienced by women. These have been alternatively analysed as the 'invisibility', 'gender balance' and 'reconceptualisation' theses in a critique of feminist approaches by Dey (1996). It is probably used in practice to mean all three of these, and the predominant evidence is that in societies such as the United States and Britain all three are to some extent true.

Certainly if poverty levels generally are increasing, which, as we have seen, they have been in Britain and the United States in the 1980s and 1990s, then this will affect women as well as men. There is also evidence that some of the changes associated with such recent increases have resulted in a greater proportion of this new poverty being experienced by women. Demographic changes resulting in greater numbers of single elderly, and marital breakdown resulting in lone parent households, have increased the number of households comprised predominantly of women and these are heavily overrepresented among the poor. Furthermore although there has been a general increase in women's participation in the labour market this has not led to equal status with male employees, and the growing impact of part-time and low-paid work, together with the increased levels of unemployment experienced over the last two decades, has affected female workers disproportionately (Pillinger, 1992; Lewis, 1993). Similarly changes introduced into social security policy have operated to restrict women's entitlement to benefits (see Oppenheim and Harker, 1996, pp. 109–10).

At a more general level still, the restrictions that have been introduced into public welfare services since the 1970s have had a disproportionate effect on women who, as Edgell and Duke (1983) pointed out, are the major beneficiaries of such services. The increase in private, voluntary and informal welfare has both excluded women from preferential treatment through the market, because of their position of economic disadvantage within it, and increased the burden on women at home to compensate for the gaps or inadequacies in other services. Changes in the welfare mix have thus contributed to a position of deepening deprivation for women.

The increased focus on the gender dimension of poverty in recent years has directed greater public attention towards the poverty experienced by women. However it should not be concluded from this that women's poverty is a recent phenomenon, nor that the disproportionate distribution of the experience of poverty between the genders is a result only of changes introduced in the 1980s. As Lewis and Piachaud (1992) pointed out, this maldistribution of poverty has been a feature of British society throughout the twentieth century. For instance at the start of the century 61 per cent of adults on poor relief were women and in the 1980s 60 per cent of adult dependants on state benefit were women – as the authors commented, '*plus ça change*' (ibid., p. 27).

This is partly due to the fact that households headed by women are more likely to be poor because of lower wages or a disproportionate dependence on benefits. However it is also due to the fact that, even in households comprising men and women with apparently adequate overall incomes, the distribution of resources within the household may be uneven, as we saw in Chapter 7, and may leave many, usually women, experiencing poverty. A study by Graham (1986) of women in families revealed that many experienced poverty, and over a half of those who then separated from their partners felt they were financially better off on their own, even when their only income was state benefit. One lone mother interviewed by Graham said:

I'm much better off. Definitely. I know where I am now, because I get our money each week and I can control what I spend. Oh, he was earning more than I get but I was worse off than I am now. I am not so poor on £43 supplementary benefit a week for everything for me and the two children as I was then. At least I know where the money's being spent and where it's not being spent. It might not last as long but at least it's being put into provisions for the home.

This is confirmed by Pahl's (1989) research, and by similar findings from studies of women entering refuges to escape domestic violence. (Binney *et al.*, 1981; Homer *et al.*, 1984) – although these were obviously cases where there was severe conflict within the household.

However it is not just the inequitable distribution of resources within households and families that contributes to women's experience of poverty. There is also the issue of who controls the resources and directs or determines expenditure, as revealed in the above extract. When the primary household income is acquired by men they can exercise control over how it is spent, and this may enhance the power they already hold within the household. Even when women in paid employment do bring their own resources into the household, the value of these is often not recognised and they are used to subsidise shortfalls in the housekeeping budget (Morris, 1989) or are targeted on particular additional goods or services (Piachaud, 1982b).

What is more, although it may frequently be the case that men control the resources, it is generally women who have to *manage* them, and who have to face the stark choice of determining priorities when living on a low income. This was revealed graphically in the findings of Kempson *et al*s'. (1994) study of families living on low incomes, which listed numerous examples of women having to make hard decisions on budgeting – and generally having to go without as a result. For instance one mother said:

> To be honest with you, the last time I bought for myself was for my husband's funeral. I don't buy anything at all for myself. My sister-in-law passes clothes on to me or they buy new things for my birthday . . . I've got nothing, but I don't go nowhere (ibid., p. 116).

This is one example of a number of instances of research evidence revealing the extent to which women will deny themselves even basic needs in order to cope with inadequate or reduced household budgets. Kempson *et al.* also found that women would eat smaller portions of food and go without meals, or hot meals, whilst at home alone during the day. In an earlier study Graham (1986) discovered that women may even go without heating, as the following quote from a mother in a low-income household reveals: 'I turn it off when I'm on my own and put a blanket on myself. Sometimes we both do in the evening but my husband doesn't like being cold and puts the heating back on'

(Graham, 1992, p. 220). As Land and Rose (1985, p. 86) once put it, 'self denial is still seen as women's special share of poverty'.

This self-denial includes the time women spend on unpaid work at home to supplement inadequate household budgets. Piachaud (1987) has pointed out that the amount of time spent on domestic work – for example preparing home-made as opposed to 'oven ready' chips – should be accounted for when assessing the real relative costs of different goods; and this time is usually women's unpaid labour at home. Much of women's time is expended in such work, and as Lister (1990) has argued, this can result in a significant experience of 'time poverty' for women who spend a large proportion of their lives trapped in monotonous and unrewarding domestic labour.

The extent of deprivation associated with domestic labour is not only the immediate loss of time and pleasure at home, however. There are also longer-term consequences for women's economic and social position that result in particular from the absence from the labour market associated with this, for instance in the loss of career advancement and the accumulation of occupational benefits or protection, as we shall discuss below.

In general terms therefore, women's poverty is not only greater and disproportionately more widespread than men's, it is in many ways a quite different experience – and thus in a sense it is a different problem. Poverty, as we have seen, is a political concept, and this political context extends to the politics of gender too. The feminist criticism of the gender blindness of much poverty research and analysis is not just that it has failed to measure or has underplayed the poverty experienced by women, but that it has ignored, and in practice concealed, the gendered experience of poverty and the different circumstances in which women are poor and deprived. This point is emphasised by Millar and Glendinning (1989) and is exemplified in much of the more recent research on women's poverty; however it has still to make much headway in the broader policy and political climate of antipoverty strategy. The importance of understanding the different experience of women's poverty cannot be overlooked, and we shall now discuss in more detail four of the main features of this difference.

Employment and Low Pay

Paid employment is the main source of income for the majority of people in modern British society, and it has been for well over a century. Thus access to the labour market and the wages received from it are crucial in determining resources for individuals and households, and for providing security and control over those resources. Women's position in the labour market is thus a central determinant of their wealth, or poverty; and research has consistently demonstrated that the position of women here is significantly different from that of men (see Dex, 1985; Beechey, 1987; Pillinger, 1992).

Although during the early period of industrialisation women were employed alongside men in the rapidly growing number of factories and workshops, there was a trend away from equal employment during the nineteenth century that involved the direct exclusion, via 'protective' legislation, of women from some forms of employment, such as coalmining, and the indirect discouragement of female labour by discriminatory employment practices, supported by male employees who in return demanded a 'family wage' sufficient to support a dependent wife and children.

The effect of these pressures was to exclude large numbers of, especially married, women from paid employment and to force them into dependency on men. They did not result, however, in the complete removal of women from paid employment. Many women continued to work, and for many families the male 'family wage' was not sufficient to provide for the household without the addition of women's supplementary earnings.

Nevertheless many women did leave the labour market, and by 1891 women's participation rate in paid employment was only 35 per cent compared with men's at 84 per cent (Lewis and Piachaud, 1992, p. 37). Furthermore women's employment came to be seen by employers, male employees and even women themselves as secondary employment operating to supplement male wages or provide minor household luxuries – 'pin money'. Thus women's wages were much lower than men's – for all industries they were 51.5 per cent of the average wage for a male manual worker in 1886 (ibid., p. 39). This created a vicious circle of secondary wage status that indirectly forced women into dependence, at least partially, on men, especially when they had children to support.

By the beginning of the twentieth century, therefore, women's separate and secondary position in the labour market was entrenched, reinforced and recreated by powerful ideological expectations about women's different responsibilities within the presumed family structure (see Gittins, 1993). During the twentieth century, however, and particularly since the Second World War, women's participation in the labour market has grown continuously (Wilson, 1994). Both married and single women are now much more likely than in the past to be in paid employment, with 66 per cent of working age women in employment in 1995 (DEE, 1996); and for those in employment there have also been some moves towards more equal pay and equal treatment at work, although this has been a long, slow and far from complete process.

Since 1975 legislation in the form of the Equal Pay Act and the Sex Discrimination Act has required equal pay and treatment for women at work, but despite this women's average hourly earnings have only risen to 77 per cent of that of their male counterparts (Lonsdale, 1992, p. 99). The reasons for the failure of the law requiring equal treatment are complex and multifaceted. In part they are a product of the nature of the legislation itself and the mechanisms for enforcing it (see Morris and Nott, 1991). However, more generally the failure reflects the fact that the broader structure of women's participation in the labour market, whilst it has grown overall, has remained quite different from that of men – and these differences remain a major cause of women's greater risk and different experience of poverty.

Therefore even though more women do now work, they tend to work in different jobs and under different conditions from men (Lonsdale, 1992; Wilson, 1994). Thus women are much more likely than men to be working part-time – 43 per cent of women are part-timers compared with 6 per cent of men (DEE, 1996) – and much of the growth in women's labour market participation can be accounted for by increased part-time working. Yet part-time work generally attracts lower rates of pay and gives rise to fewer contractual and statutory rights and protection. Women's part-time work also includes some of the worst-rewarded and yet most labour-intensive paid work in the form of 'home working', for example assembling clothing at home, processing mail orders or undertaking paid child care on a formal or informal basis.

What is more, even when they are in full-time work women are frequently engaged in different work and under different conditions from men. For instance female employees predominate in secretarial and clerical work, in nursing, in residential care and in primary school teaching. Indeed these jobs are sometimes referred to as 'women's work', and they are quite closely related to women's assumed domestic responsibilities. They are also generally low-status and lower-paid employment. In higher-status jobs in the same areas men tend to predominate, for instance as accountants, doctors, managers and lecturers. Within factory production women tend to work in different sectors from men, for example in clothing and hosiery production or food and drink preparation. Even within the same factory they are likely to be placed in different sections of the production process, for instance in the packing department; and again the jobs occupied by women are frequently those with lower status and lower pay (see Oppenheim and Harker, 1996, p. 103).

Of course all labour markets do exhibit significant elements of such segmentation and division. There are better, more secure and better rewarded jobs, and there are low-quality, insecure and poorly paid jobs, and there is generally little movement between the sectors. Barron and Norris (1976) once described this as a dual labour market with two sectors, primary and secondary, in which women tend to occupy the jobs in the secondary, poorer sector. In practice segmentation is probably more complex than division into two sectors only; but the overall point is still valid – within a segmented labour market women are generally employed in different and less desirable sectors than men.

Thus in the labour market on average women experience less security, worse conditions, lower status and lower pay than men. As Callender (1992) has discussed, this is likely to render them more susceptible to unemployment in times of recession, and to reduce the protection they may receive in such circumstances by way of redundancy pay, protection from unfair dismissal and entitlement to social security benefits. Furthermore their less secure and less consistent connection with the labour market is also likely to exclude them from many of the increasingly important occupational protections and benefits such as sickness pay, pensions schemes or share ownership schemes, all of which provide a cushion against poverty and deprivation beyond the period of employment.

A segmented labour market in which some employees can be kept in insecurity, on lower wages and without occupational protection and benefits is clearly beneficial to employers. Even when there may be no overt sexual discrimination therefore, the advantages of workers whose employment may be perceived by them, as well as by their employers, as secondary are advantages that employers are bound to exploit. Some have even argued, using neo-Marxist analysis, that this in effect means that women comprise a 'reserve army of labour' existing on the periphery of the securely employed, largely male, working class (see Beechey, 1978); although, as recent labour market changes have revealed, this insecure and reserve status is now one shared by many men too.

However the main point about women's secondary status in the labour market is that it is also related to more general ideological expectations about their responsibilities for domestic work, which remains strongly rooted in British society (Kiernan, 1991). As Morris (1991) has pointed out, the dual labour market is complemented by the dual roles that women also occupy as both paid worker and housewife. It is because women have to undertake a double shift of paid work and unpaid work that they more frequently work part-time and thus experience worse pay and conditions. Yet at the same time it is because they experience worse pay and conditions that there is so much pressure on married women to see their paid work as secondary to that of their husbands. This forces married women indirectly into dependence on their husbands. It is also a source of single women's greater risk of poverty, whether as single young women at work, divorced or separated single parents, or as single or widowed elderly pensioners with no occupational or earnings-related benefits. For many women therefore the experience may be one of being trapped in marriage or trapped in poverty – or both.

Social Security

Social security protection has always been based on support for the wage labour market and the use of benefits as a wage substitute, or a wage subsidy – an issue to which we shall return in Chapter 14. As a result of this the treatment of women within social security provision has in practice largely been determined by their treatment within, or outside, the labour market, and their presumed dependency on men. This could be seen in the nineteenth century Poor Law, where entry into the workhouse for unemployed women was reserved for those whose husbands would not provide for them, and better treatment was reserved for widows, for whom the alternative of family support did not exist.

When insurance-based benefits were developed in the early part of the twentieth century, the fact that they depended on contributions made whilst in paid employment effectively excluded most married women from protection. However even those women who were in paid work were treated differently from men, paying lower contributions and receiving lower benefits – generally around 80 per cent of the full rate. Even this reduced protection was challenged during the recession of the 1930s through the introduction of an Anomalies Act to prevent married women who were 'not really unemployed' from claiming unemployment benefit merely to enhance their married lives. The assumption of course, as in the case of the workhouse, was that married women did not need social security support because they could depend on their husbands. This assumption was reinforced in the means-tested Unemployment Assistance schemes that replaced the Poor Law in the 1930s, and it was extended to include dependence on other close family members, such as parents or children, with the result that single women too were effectively denied support in most circumstances.

The separate treatment and secondary status for women within social security provision became entrenched in social security after the reform of the system following the Second World War. The Beveridge Report, which underlay the reforms, made specific reference to the need for separate treatment for married women under the proposed insurance scheme on account of their responsibility for 'other duties' (Beveridge, 1942, p. 51). Beveridge's assumption was that married women would be engaged in unpaid work at home and thus would not need protection under the scheme other than through a dependants' benefit paid to their husbands. Only when a husband could no longer act as provider for his wife, in widowhood, would a payment (Widow's Benefit) be made directly to her. Beveridge had originally also suggested a payment to women after divorce, but this was not taken up by the postwar government for fear of encouraging marital breakdown. Thus although single women at work did pay contributions and could receive benefits in the same way as men, married women in employment could only make a reduced contribution in return for which no benefits were paid.

The means-tested assistance scheme that accompanied the introduction of insurance protection also continued the assumption of women's dependence on their husbands through the aggregation of family incomes as the basis for determining entitlement. If men had an income their wives could not independently claim benefit; and this presumed dependency was extended to single women living with men, to avoid a situation in which they might be treated more favourably than their married sisters – giving rise to the need for cohabitation tests and intrusive investigation into the lives of all single women claimants. Aggregation and dependence were restricted after the war to spouses or cohabitees, however, and did not extend, as the prewar scheme had, to other close family members.

What this implied was that for the purposes of safety-net support women were presumed to be dependent on male partners. Furthermore through the refusal or withdrawal of benefit for a woman presumed to be cohabiting with a man, the scheme in practice operated to enforce a particular model of family or household structure – a point to which we shall return shortly. Beveridge's intention had been that the assistance scheme would be of marginal and declining importance compared with the provision of benefit support through insurance. As we shall see in Chapter 14, however, this has not proved to be the case. Dependence on the means-tested assistance scheme has grown inexorably throughout the latter half of the century, and its coercive and intrusive reinforcement of family dependency has had particular consequences for women who, although they have constituted the majority of benefit dependants, were until the 1980s excluded from claiming in their own right unless they were single.

In the 1970s and 1980s changes were introduced into social security legislation to remove, at least formally, some of the discriminatory treatment experienced by women. In the 1970s insurance protection was reformed to permit married women to contribute and receive benefits on the same basis as men, although because of their past exclusion many women could still never establish full contribution records for long-term benefits such as pensions. In the 1980s, following a directive on 'equal treatment' for men and women from the EU, means-tested benefits were reformed to permit either men or women to act as the claimant and receive the family benefit, although aggregation and family dependency remained. Of course in most cases men remained as the nominated claimant, and as Millar (1989b) has pointed out, such moves towards formal equality of treatment within social security did nothing to address the broader problems of women's assumed dependency, which is such a central feature of the gender differences underlying the experience of poverty in Britain.

The expansion of benefit provision, in particular in the 1970s, to provide support for some of the additional costs of disability, also initially extended the unequal treatment and exclusion of women within social security. The non-contributory Invalidity Pension, a low-level, long-term benefit for people unable to work because of disability but with no entitlement to insurance protection, was not available to married women unless they could demonstrate that they were unable to perform normal household duties. The assumption behind this was that only in these circumstances would the family be in need, because domestic help would have to be employed rather than being provided by wives. This anomaly was only removed in 1984 following a restructuring of the benefit under threat of the impact of the EU directive on equal treatment.

In the case of the Invalid Care Allowance (ICA), however, the government resisted the directive until the eleventh hour. The ICA was a low-level, non-contributory benefit paid to those excluded from the labour market because they were undertaking substantial unpaid caring work for an adult at home. It was not payable to married or cohabiting women, who were assumed not to be in poverty as a result of such labour-market exclusion as they could rely on husbands or partners to support them. This was eventually challenged in the European Court in 1986, and it was only on the eve of the announcement of the success of this that the law was changed to permit all women to claim the benefit equally.

With the removal of the discriminatory exclusion from the ICA, the formal unequal treatment of men and women was more or less removed from social security provision. However in practice barriers to benefits remain. Woman are still less likely than men to have full contribution records, and are thus more likely to be dependent on lower, means-tested or non-contributory benefits (see Lister, 1992). This means that women claimants are more likely to experience the most stigmatising aspects of state social security protection.

Furthermore, in part because of women's secondary status in the labour market, they are also disproportionately excluded from participation in, and benefit from, the growing range of occupational and private social security provisions. In the last two decades there has been a rapid expansion of private and occupational provision for social security, for instance through the development of Statutory Sick Pay and Statutory Maternity Pay and the active promotion and subsidisation of private pensions. Exclusion from and disadvantage in employment has also excluded women from many of these new and more generous forms of support. Although some occupational and private social security schemes do sometimes provide payments for widows based on their husbands' contributions, this is an indirect support that continues the assumption of women's dependency, and it too can be lost if couples divorce (Groves, 1992).

Social security has been the main antipoverty policy measure in Britain throughout the last century or longer. However the benefits it provides, whether through insurance, means testing within state provision or various forms of private protection, have largely been predicated on and structured to support family units in which men and women occupy specific and distinct gender roles. The effect of this has been to exclude, either directly or indirectly, many women from receipt of social security benefits, and thus has increased their risk of poverty. This exclusion has often been associated with assumptions about women's caring responsibilities and their status as dependants.

The Costs of Caring

Women's secondary status in the labour market and the social security scheme is closely related to assumptions about gender roles within families, and in particular women's responsibility for caring work. There is a significant need for care in modern British society. Young children and adults with illnesses or disabilities need close and regular personal attention. However, although there is some limited public and private collective provision for such care, the majority of it is carried out in the home, and it is carried out by women. What is more, evidence suggests that this inequitable division of domestic labour is widely endorsed by public attitudes (Kiernan, 1991).

Indeed there is a widespread assumption that women are somehow uniquely equipped to undertake caring roles (see Henwood *et al.*, 1987), and this has largely dominated the development of support for such work. The papers in Finch and Groves' (1983) book – *A Labour of Love*, on caring for adults – discuss this gender stereotyping and point out that the expectation that women will provide care at home is inextricably linked to their emotional ties to their children or other family members. For women, therefore, caring *about* someone also means being willing to care *for* them, and this is an expectation that many women have even though they are aware of the heavy costs it involves.

These costs extend beyond the provision of support itself, however, for they also give rise to a greater risk of poverty for women. Those needing care themselves are obviously at risk of poverty, primarily because they are unable to secure support through paid employment or employment-related benefits. This is most clearly the case for children, who in most cases must be supported by their parents. However the women who are engaged in such caring work – especially when caring for young children or those with severe disabilities as this is effectively a full-time task – are similarly excluded from the labour market and hence they too are at risk of poverty. As Graham (1987, p. 223) remarked, 'Poverty and caring are for many women two sides of the same coin'.

Caring work at home is unpaid and so the link with poverty is obvious, unless women carers can be supported by another wage-earning family member such as a husband – and in the case of child care in particular the predominant assumption is that this will be the case. Even here, however, there is the problem of women's dependency on their husbands and the problem of inequities in intrahousehold transfers, discussed in Chapter 7. Plus, of course, there is the problem of the inadequacy of many men's wages to support a dependent family, especially a large one.

It was the potential inadequacy of men's wages to support a large family that was the prime economic pressure for the introduction of Family Allowances after the Second World War as a guaranteed form of state support towards the extra cost of child care in all families – although the expectation was that current wages should be sufficient to provide for one child and Family Allowances were only paid for second and subsequent children. When Child Benefit was introduced to replace Family Allowances in the 1970s, this was converted into a flat-rate payment for all children and was paid to the nominated carer, usually the mother. Partly because it is paid directly to the carer, Child Benefit has sometimes been regarded as an important contribution towards the cost of caring for children. It is important to note, however, that it is only a *partial* recognition of the cost of caring for a child. It does not cover all the cost involved in bringing up a child, for instance as calculated by Piachaud (1979) or as represented by the benefit rates for children; and it is not in any sense a recognition of, nor a protection from, poverty among carers. This is demonstrably the case for lone parents, most of whom are thus poor because they cannot rely on additional support from an employed partner.

For lone parents the cost of caring and the consequent exclusion from a labour market in which collective occupational provision for child care is very sparse collide to produce a high risk of – and a high level of – poverty (Millar, 1989a). The vast majority – around 90 per cent – of lone parents are women, and for them women's secondary labour market status compounds the more general problem of trying to balance caring responsibilities against paid employment to support a family. Millar has argued that gender is the crucial factor in lone parent poverty – 'it is precisely because lone mothers are women that they have a very high risk of poverty', she claims (1992, p. 149), and she points out that the relatively small number of lone fathers are less likely to be poor.

Lone parents, and in particular lone mothers, are therefore a significant and growing group among the poor. In 1994 over a million were dependent on Income Support (Oppenheim and Harker, 1996, p. 96). In 1993 the introduction of the Child Support Agency ostensibly provided a means of combating lone parent poverty by securing maintenance payments from the absent parent. In practice, however, the operation of the agency has been fraught with difficulties and setbacks – not least because of the pressure placed on it by the government to secure maintenance payments, which reduce social security dependence rather than increase parents' income (Garnham and Knights, 1994). Research on the work of the agency has also shown that up to a quarter of lone mothers have experienced considerable stress in their contacts with it, and that many more have suffered problems and delays in assessment and found payments unreliable and inaccurate (Clarke *et al.*, 1996). It has thus done little if anything to reduce the problem of lone parent poverty.

As already indicated, it is not only child care that may trap women in poverty. Adults with serious illnesses or disabilities also require care, and with growing longevity and improved medical standards this demand for care has been growing significantly at the end of the twentieth century. Indeed it is somewhat ironic that, as earlier child-bearing and smaller families have reduced the scale of the burden of child care for women, the growing demand for adult care has to some extent taken its place, resulting in what Roll (1989, p. 25) has called the development of a 'cycle of caring' for many women.

Adult care is also likely to remove women from the labour market and thus increase their risk of poverty. Since 1986 women engaged in full-time care have been able to claim ICA, but without another source of income this is no protection against poverty. In the 1990s the pressure on women to provide care for dependent adults has increased because of the government's policy to replace institutional care for dependent adults with 'community care'. In many cases the effect of community-based care has been to increase the risk of poverty for carers pressured into providing it, usually women – especially as adequate additional resources are often not available to support them in this.

It is not just low income that contributes to the poverty experienced by carers, however. As we have seen, the experience of deprivation and social exclusion covers a range of social and individual needs that people in certain circumstances may lack; and those involved in caring work frequently experience significant deprivation beyond the loss of adequate cash income. In particular they are likely to be trapped within the home for long periods of time and be engaged in monotonous, tiring and emotionally draining work with no obvious reward. This is especially the case for those caring for dependent adults – for whilst children will grow up and leave home, dependent adults are more likely to be in a deteriorating condition that will only be ended by their death, and a painful relief for their carers. The loss of control over their lives and time on a day-to-day basis is thus a significant feature of deprivation for carers. For them the notion of 'time poverty' may be particularly pertinent.

What is more, as Joshi (1992) has argued, the cost of caring does not just include those deprivations experienced at the time. Absence from the labour market, for mothers perhaps at a crucial point in their lives, is likely to lead to longer-term deprivation resulting from lost occupational benefits, lost training and career opportunities, and perhaps lost opportunities for saving and investment too. These are sometimes described as the 'opportunity costs' of caring work (Joshi, 1988) and they can add up to a significant loss, which women in general are likely to experience at some point in their lives. The assumption of course is that such costs can be borne because at such points women will be supported by their husbands. However this assumption of dependency is in reality more of a cause of women's poverty than a solution to it.

Dependency

At the heart of women's social and economic situation, and thus their greater risk of poverty, is their assumed position of dependency on men within the family. It is because it is assumed that women can depend on their husbands for material support that they have largely been excluded from full participation in the labour market and social security provision. Indeed in the case of the aggregation rulings for means-tested benefits such dependency has effectively been enforced on women.

As we have seen, however, the allocation of resources within households and families may not be equitable and may leave many women living below the standard enjoyed by their partners. Furthermore the incomes received by men may not be sufficient to provide adequately for a dependent wife (and children) and so in many cases women have to engage in paid work to supplement the family income and avoid poverty (Machin and Waldfogel, 1994). However because this is regarded as supplementary income it is frequently seen as less important than that of the male breadwinner and may not even be recognised as part of the family income by men (see Morris and Ruane, 1989). Consequently this secondary income status has the effect of reproducing and reinforcing women's lower wages, and their secondary employment status in the labour market.

The problem of dependency thus operates as a vicious circle for women who, when young and single, are pressured into marriage, in part at least because of the poor prospects of employment and pay, and once married (and especially after child bearing) are trapped into dependency on their husbands. Curiously enough there is evidence that this dependent status continues even when husbands are unable to support their wives, for instance because of unemployment (Davies *et al.*, 1994). In a study of unemployed men Cooke (1987) found that when men became unemployed their wives too tended to withdraw from paid work, thus continuing their dependency. There were sound financial reasons for this in many cases since, because of the rule that required earnings above £5 a week to be deducted from benefit entitlement, the wages women would have earned from part-time work would not in fact have increased the family income. However Cooke argues that the phenomenon was not purely a financial one, for its persistence appeared to outstrip financial logic and to be dependent on attitudes and social conventions.

Women's dependence on their husbands is of course an ideological and not merely an economic feature of gender stereotyping. It is closely tied to the broader ideology of family structure and family roles, which, as feminists have argued, involve clear differentiation and discrimination between men and women (see Gittins, 1993; Barrett and Macintosh, 1982). However, this differentiation, and the inequality and poverty that flow from it, is largely disguised from public view, and therefore from policy response by the ideological divide between the public and private faces of family life. What goes on inside the private world of the family, it has often been assumed, is of no concern to researchers or policy makers, and therefore, perhaps, is not problematic.

Important research such as Pahl's (1989) on household income distribution has now begun to penetrate this private world of the family, and feminist scholarship has begun to challenge the false nature of the public/private divide, in particular from the position of women at home for whom the private world of the home is also their public world. Research has revealed that dependency on a husband may conceal a poverty-level standard of living for some women (Graham, 1986), and in cases of conflict at home this income poverty can be compounded by other forms of deprivation. For instance, in the all too common case of domestic violence the lack of power and control that is an integral feature of dependency is starkly revealed, and it is clear that the price to be paid by those without such power and control can indeed be high. There cannot be a much poorer lifestyle than that experienced by a woman constantly in fear of violence from her partner.

However even when the issue of power and control does not develop into extremes of violence, the pervasive influence of dependency remains a central feature of the different experience of poverty for women and men. In a household where, because of an inadequate overall income, both partners are poor, the dependency and lack of control experienced by women can provide them with a different, and deeper, problem of deprivation. Lister (1990) has argued that this different experience can operate as a denial of 'citizenship' to women, who as a result are relegated to secondary status in the modern welfare capitalist state – and, as she points out, any challenge to this denial would involve 'radical changes' to the personal and domestic life in which it is situated.

10

Racism and Poverty

Racism and Ethnic Minority Inequality

Any understanding of the distribution of poverty and inequality in
society must pay attention to the impact of this on significant social
divisions and cultural differences. In modern British society this
involves recognising and analysing the impact of racism within the
social structure. In broad terms modern Britain is a racist society in
that there is significant evidence that black and other minority ethnic
communities experience discrimination and disadvantage on a disproportionate basis, and this cannot be explained merely as result of
chance or misfortune.

This does not make British society unique, nor in a sense is it all that
surprising. Discrimination and disadvantage for ethnic minority
groups is common in many if not most social structures, and certainly
there is overt evidence of racism similar to, and in some cases more
exaggerated than, that found in Britain in most other European and
Western capitalist countries. However widespread evidence of racism
elsewhere should not lead us to overlook the particular features and
particular causes of racism in British society, which have produced a
unique pattern of discrimination and disadvantage resulting in significant inequality and levels of poverty for certain groups within
society. Nor of course should the widespread experience of racism be
interpreted as suggesting its consequences are not a problem, or not a
problem amenable to analysis and policy response. Indeed it is because
'race' is such an important feature of the structure of poverty and
inequality that its impact must be included in understanding, and
tackled by, policy development.

What is meant by 'race' in this context, however, has been the
subject of some debate, both on terminology and on the use of terms
adopted. It is probably not a debate that can be entirely satisfactorily

resolved either because – as to some extent with the debates on the definition of poverty – meaning is inextricably linked to broader theoretical and political questions about the nature of the problem and the appropriate response to it. In the case of modern Britain this debate is founded in the country's imperial past, its subjugation of colonial populations and the assumption of 'white supremacy' that arose from this.

Thus in Britain 'race' is often taken to mean skin colour, and in particular the difference between white skin and black skin. This has been accentuated by the entry into Britain of a significant number of black ex-colonial residents, in particular after the Second World War. These immigrants and their offspring often vary in cultural backgrounds and skin colour. However they are all potential victims of discrimination or disadvantage based on skin colour, and thus are often generically referred to as 'black' when compared with the indigenous 'white' population.

Within Britain's black population there are a range of different communities with different cultural and religious traditions. These are sometimes referred to as 'ethnic minority communities', although they also include non-black communities such as Jews, Arabs, Eastern Europeans and others, all of whom may experience discrimination or disadvantage because of their culture, language or religion. Despite this, however, in modern Britain the racism experienced by the black population overlays their situation as minority ethnic communities. It is this racism of course, and not skin colour or cultural difference, that is the problem for black people in Britain; and it is this problem that is generally the focus of research and analysis of race and inequality in Britain. Thus it is racism and its consequences for poverty and inequality that we discuss here.

The racism faced by Britain's black population has a history as long as that of the population itself, certainly extending back to the early days of overseas trade and Britain's involvement in the slave trade during the growth of colonisation. Early black immigrants to Britain were generally associated with trading and seafaring activities, and tended to be concentrated in ports such as Cardiff, Liverpool and London. This geographical concentration was a trend that was followed by later groups of black immigrants to Britain, primarily as a result of discrimination in housing and employment markets, which forced the new residents into poor inner city areas that were less popular among the indigenous population. However such concentration may have compounded the problem of racism by appearing to minimise the wider integration of black people into other parts of British society, and as we shall see it has certainly contributed to the problems of poverty that have flowed from this.

In the early part of the twentieth century immigration by Jews and Eastern Europeans introduced new ethnic minority communities into Britain, and many of these faced discrimination and hostility from sections of the indigenous population. After the Second World War, however, and following the conversion of the British Empire into a commonwealth of independent countries with close links with Britain, larger numbers of black immigrants from the former colonies were encouraged to come to Britain, mainly in order to fill menial and poorly paid jobs that an indigenous population enjoying 'full employment' did not find attractive.

It was these immigrants in particular who experienced the discrimination and hostility that forced them into the poorer areas of London and large cities in the Midlands, Lancashire and Yorkshire. It was also they, because of their black skins and former colonial status, who became the focus of a new racism among the white community, which began to surface in the form of hostility, abuse, harassment and even violence in the late 1950s. By the 1960s this racism, allied to the weaker economic and geographical situation of the new black populations, was beginning to coalesce into a broader structure of discrimination and disadvantage based on race.

The hostility and racism faced by Britain's ethnic minority communities had not, however, been a feature of the academic and political debate that surrounded the introduction of the welfare state reforms of the postwar period (Williams, 1989). The welfare state was intended to challenge the 'evils' of prewar Britain, identified by Beveridge, through the development of universal state welfare services, as we shall discuss in Chapter 16. Racism was not recognised as an evil requiring state action however, although when black immigration began to increase during the early years after the war, racist reactions meant that black people did not experience equal access to universal welfare services such as council housing.

In fact the major period of black immigration into Britain was relatively short, and by the 1960s fears about unemployment and economic growth resulted in the imposition of immigration controls. Of course these controls applied to all potential immigrants into Britain (although not, after 1973, citizens of EU countries), but they were enforced with particular severity against black migrants (see Moore and Wallace, 1975). The effect of this was to compound the

hostility and suspicion experienced by the resident black population –
all of whom could thus be labelled as potential unwanted or illegal
immigrants

The pattern of immigration also means that the black population in
Britain shows some demographic differences from the indigenous
population, as revealed in research surveys carried out by the Policy
Studies Institute (PSI), the most recent being that of Jones (1993). The
most significant feature of the black population in Britain is the fact
that most are not immigrants at all, but were born here and have lived
here all their lives. There are proportionately fewer older people
among the black population, and a larger number of younger people.
This is due to the fact that family size is larger, especially among
Asians, and within this the number of lone parents is greater among
West Indians but lower among Asians.

As we have already mentioned, Britain's black population is not
geographically evenly spread throughout the country. Access to
(largely poorly paid) employment, discrimination in housing and
education, and more general racism have all resulted in black people
being concentrated in poor inner urban areas in a number of British
cities. As we have seen in Chapter 6, the geographical concentration of
poverty can compound the deprivation experienced by those living in
these areas – in the United States areas such as this with large black
populations are referred to as 'ghettos'. This ghetto existence is a
particular feature of the poverty and social exclusion experienced by
many black people in Britain, which may be compounded by racist
assumptions that even identify their presence as a 'cause' of local
deprivation.

In addition to geographical polarisation, black people in Britain
also experience isolation and exclusion from the indigenous white
population as a result of linguistic and cultural differences. Formal
communication in Britain, both written and verbal, relies on the use of
English. Those who do not speak or read English fluently are thus
unable to communicate adequately with formal agencies – if at all.
This is a significant problem for many black people, especially with
regard to the benefit system, as we shall see below. However linguistic
exclusion can also be compounded by cultural differences and by
cultural misunderstandings between black people and British institutions; for instance the assumption that large Asian families will
provide financial support for unemployed elderly or young relatives,
or that West Indian families are unstable and prone to separation.

Cultural exclusion also extends to a failure to take account of the particular, and different, needs of ethnic minority community members in the provision of universal services that have been geared to the needs of an indigenous culture – a problem that is sometimes unfortunately referred to as 'colour-blindness'. This includes, for instance, the health service's inability to respond to conditions to which black people are particularly or exclusively prone, such as the disease sickle cell anaemia; and the provision of standard services that do not recognise the religious or cultural preferences of some communities, such as school meals that do not include halal meat or school clothing stores that do not provide traditional dress for Muslim girls.

It is now increasingly widely recognised that there is a link between racism and poverty and exclusion in modern British society, for example the CPAG's poverty pamphlet contains a chapter on 'Race and Poverty' (Oppenheim and Harker, 1996, ch. 6). However it has not always been easy to establish a clear empirical link between poverty and race in Britain because most of the research on poverty and many of the statistical surveys, both government and independent, have not traditionally identified the skin colour or ethnic origin of respondents. This is not simply an oversight – a case of colour-blindness – it is in some cases also a response to a real, and reasonable, fear among the black population that attempts to identify 'race' in official statistics may be a real or potential, threat to the immigrant status of respondents, or that it may be used as ammunition for further racism against blacks.

It was partly as a result of such fears, for instance, that no questions about ethnic origin were included in the decennial census in 1981 and before, although a question was included in the 1991 version. Nor do the government's 'Households Below Average Income' figures include an ethnic breakdown, although the DSS Family Resources Survey does now provide data on income and benefits by ethnic origin. This can be contrasted with the situation in the United States, where debate and data on poverty and race are much more widespread (see Jennings, 1994). However some of the gaps have been filled in Britain by the publication by the CPAG of a pamphlet on poverty and race, which discusses the greater risk of poverty for ethnic minorities in Britain that is associated with employment and unemployment, housing and health, social security, and immigration policy (Amin and Oppenheim, 1992).

Employment, Unemployment and Race

In the employment field evidence of the disadvantaged position of black people comes in particular from the Labour Force Survey by Ethnic Origin and the PSI research (Jones, 1993) together with a range of other independent or local sources. In general these reveal that the occupational segregation that many black people experienced when they came to Britain in the 1950s has continued into more recent times. Black people coming to Britain were initially concentrated in low-paid, low-status, public-service manual work and in low-paid shift work in labour-intensive manufacturing processes such as textiles and hosiery. The PSI survey shows that black people were still disproportionately employed in distribution and particular sectors of manufacturing at the end of the 1980s (Jones, 1993). Amin and Oppenheim (1992, ch. 2) also reveal that black employees are more likely to be working shifts, Asian men are more likely than others to be self-employed, West Indian women are more likely than white or Asian women to be employed full time, and Asian women are more likely than others to be engaged in low-paid 'home working'.

The result of this is that average earnings are lower for black people than for white people. For instance the average hourly pay for all ethnic minority workers in 1993/94 was lower than that for whites – £6.82 compared with £7.44 (see Oppenheim and Harker, 1996, p. 118). The only significant exception here was the position of West Indian women, whose average rate was higher; although as Bruegel (1989) discusses, this is may be because their earnings were boosted by their greater likelihood of full-time employment. There are other differences within the black and ethnic minority populations, however, as Chinese and Indian workers often enjoy higher status and pay than West Indians, Pakistanis and Bangladeshis (Oppenheim and Harker, 1996, p. 124); but these do not outweigh the overall impact of inequality.

Lower wages obviously create a greater risk of poverty for black workers. This can be compounded by the larger average family size for some, especially Asian, workers to support, and the likelihood that wages will also be used to support family members outside the household. An earlier PSI survey found that 40 per cent of West Indian households and 30 per cent of Asian households sent money to dependants (Brown, 1984, p. 302). Of course low wages for families may be supplemented by means-tested benefits, but, as we will discuss below, there is evidence that black people are less likely than white people to be claiming these.

Black people's disadvantaged position in the labour market is also mirrored by their position outside it. Many of the low-status, labour-intensive jobs in manufacturing and public services into which black immigrant workers were recruited were those that were disproportionately affected by the impact of recession and public expenditure cuts in the 1970s and 1980s. This has led to higher levels of unemployment among black people throughout Britain, and this has been accentuated by the discrimination in recruitment experienced by black people seeking jobs, especially young, British-born blacks leaving education and unable to find any employment.

Thus the unemployment rates are higher for black people in Britain than for whites. In 1994 the unemployment rate for all ethnic minority men was 25 per cent, compared with 11 per cent for white men. This difference was exaggerated for young men under 24, and was much more serious for some particular ethnic groups, such as West Indian and African blacks (33 per cent) and Pakistanis and Bangladeshis (29 per cent). Similar patterns were also revealed for women within lower overall figures – 16 per cent ethnic minority and 7 per cent white (see Oppenheim and Harker, 1996, p. 116). There is also evidence that black people experience a longer duration of unemployment than whites, and again that this is more severe for the young unemployed (Amin and Oppenheim, 1992, p. 4).

Thus the labour market position of black people in Britain has remained significantly inferior to that of the indigenous white population, and as Amin and Oppenheim concluded, the restructuring of employment patterns that has taken place in recent times 'has affected ethnic minority communities particularly harshly' (1992, p. 41). This is a consequence of both direct discrimination and structural disadvantage in the labour market; and it has affected young British-born black people as well as their immigrant parents. It has exposed black people to a greater risk of poverty, and it has also resulted in higher levels of benefit dependency among black people. As will be discussed below, however, black people experience discrimination and disadvantage within the benefits system too.

Racism and the Benefits System

Because of their relative exclusion from the labour market black people in Britain experience disproportionate levels of dependency on the benefits system; and because of low levels of benefit, dependency is closely related to poverty and deprivation. Direct evidence of the number of black people dependent on benefits has in the past been difficult to obtain, however the Family Resources Survey (DSS, 1995b) now provides information on benefit receipt and ethnic origin. It also confirms previous evidence that within the state benefit system black claimants are likely to be disproportionately dependent on less-generous and lower-status means-tested benefits.

The reason for this segregation within benefits is because, as with much of the post-welfare state in Britain, the Beveridge social security system failed to recognise the ways in which its structures could operate to exclude certain groups of people. This is particularly true of insurance benefits, which are paid in return for contributions made during employment. Black people's relative exclusion from secure and well-paid employment is also likely to exclude them from insurance benefits, especially pensions (and more so earnings-related pensions), which are based on contributions made throughout a working life that could be broken by periods of absence abroad as well as unemployment.

Other apparently neutral qualifications for benefit entitlement may also operate against black people because of their immigrant status. This applies in particular to the residence tests that are applied to some of the non-contributory disability benefits, which we shall discuss in Chapter 12. These have now all been reduced to a period of six months residence in Britain prior to claiming, although in the past periods of up to ten years were required for some.

As a result of these factors black households are much more likely than white households to be in receipt of means-tested benefits such as Income Support and Housing Benefit; and much less likely to be in receipt of the National Insurance retirement pension (see Oppenheim and Harker, 1996, p. 120). These means-tested benefits are generally lower than those within the insurance scheme, and they are also subject to other restrictions that have a disproportionately disadvantageous impact on black claimants.

Means-tested benefits are only available to those ordinarily resident in Britain, and claimants are thus technically required to establish this when they make a claim. Normally speaking this is a formality, but as some recent immigrants are excluded from such entitlement evidence of resident status may be required. This has resulted on some occasions in the practice of checking the passports of all 'suspicious' black claimants in social security offices. Passport checking operates as an invidious disincentive to any black claimants to seek benefit support, whatever their residence status, and can lead to problems if passports are not readily obtainable. Benefits officers are instructed not to request passports routinely as proof of entitlement, but as Gordon and Newnham (1985, p. 24) found, the practice had become so widespread that 'many black claimants volunteer their passports believing it is only a matter of time before they are asked to produce them'. They quote one case where 'L, a 22 year old student, born in Britain, was asked for his passport four times in twelve months when he was claiming benefit in Manchester and Huddersfield' (ibid., p. 25).

The requirement to produce passports as evidence of entitlement acts as a particular disincentive for many black claimants because of its apparent link with immigration control. Immigrants who do not have a right to remain in the country may expose their status if they claim benefits in order to relieve poverty, because information provided to benefits offices may well be passed on to Home Office immigration control. Much more seriously however, fear of the Home Office connection may dissuade many perfectly legitimate black claimants from ever approaching the Benefits Agency because of misplaced uncertainty about their status in the country (see ibid., p. 29). Even for some of those who do have the right to reside in Britain, however, immigration status may affect potential benefit entitlement.

Most important here is the so-called 'no recourse to public funds rule'. Under this provision in the immigration rules, all dependants coming to join their families in Britain are prevented from claiming support from public funds. Public funds include all the major means-tested benefits, including Income Support, and housing for homeless families under housing law. The intention of the rule is to prevent immigrants from coming to Britain in order to claim state support, but its effect is to exclude from even minimum benefit protection a significant number of new entrants who may have no other practical source of support if the arrangements made on their entry fall through. Once again, however, the more disconcerting wider impact of the rule is its role as an indirect disincentive – based on a mistaken belief about exclusion from entitlement – for any black claimants, especially family dependants, to claim benefits, even insurance benefits to which they do have independent rights.

This problem is likely to be further compounded by the rules governing 'sponsorship', which require spouses, children or elderly dependants coming to Britain to be sponsored by someone in Britain who is willing to give a written undertaking to provide for them in circumstances of need. This is a particularly draconian requirement, although it is only legally enforceable in a minority of cases; and it effectively excludes people already on benefits from acting as sponsors and thus prevents their families from joining them. It also contributes to the problem of passport checking in benefit administration to identify potential sponsors for certain claimants, even when divorced or separated single parents may be seeking support many years after becoming legally resident in the country.

There are other groups of claimants who are excluded, in full or in part, from benefit entitlement because of their immigrant status. These include 'overstayers', people whose right to remain in Britain has technically expired and who may be threatened with deportation if they have to recourse to benefit, and those who are appealing against deportation or refusal of entry, who at best can only get urgent payments (see Gordon and Newnham, 1985, ch. 1). Refugees and asylum seekers are also only entitled to reduced levels of benefit support and in the late 1990s will be excluded entirely from protection – yet as the NACAB (1991, pp. 63–4) has pointed out, this is a group that frequently experiences acute deprivation.

All the rules on immigrant status and benefit entitlement of course apply equally to all immigrants, except those from EU countries who are free to travel within member states and to claim benefit support. However their effect within a racist social structure in which immigrant status is associated closely with skin colour is to exclude, either directly or indirectly, black people in Britain from free and equal access to the benefit system, and thus to increase significantly their risk of poverty. There are other reasons too, also related to immigration status, that may further disadvantage black claimants.

Those who have dependants or connections abroad may experience difficulty in providing for or maintaining these within the British benefits system, resulting in potential hardship for claimants here and for their relatives overseas. Children or other dependants abroad cannot be classed as part of a family for benefit purposes, thus even if payment is being made to support them in another country there is no benefit entitlement to cover this. The same is true for absences abroad to visit dependants, as benefits are generally only payable to those resident in Britain. However this exclusion can result in unwarranted hardship for dependants remaining in Britain during a visit abroad by a head of household, for they may fail to recognise the need to claim independently in their own right during the absence, especially when language barriers mean that leaflets and forms on entitlement, even if provided, are not understood. Conversely resources held abroad may be treated as available to claimants in Britain, thus reducing or removing entitlement to support, even when these cannot in practice be realised as assets.

In addition to the formal exclusion of black claimants from full benefit entitlement as a result of rules with discriminatory impact, there are also a number of informal ways in which black people can be excluded from receipt of full benefit support. A survey of black clients using Citizens' Advice Bureaux revealed many such practices, described by the NACAB (1991) as 'barriers to benefit'. These included delays in processing benefit claims while – unnecessary – checks were carried out to determine entitlement, and intrusive questioning to establish certain personal details such as marital status when marriages had been contracted abroad. They could also include direct racist discrimination against black claimants, as revealed in a PSI study of the administration of Supplementary Benefit in 1982. Part of the PSI study involved observation of officers in benefits offices, and it revealed disturbing examples of racism among some officers, one of whom was quoted as saying 'We get quite a few Pakis like that wandering in like lost sheep' (Cooper, 1985, p. 53).

Even when treatment is formally equal, however, black people may in practice be denied equal access to support because of the failure of the benefits system to address the particular problems they experience. Most important here is the language barrier. Social security benefits are administered in English. English is spoken in all offices, all forms are printed in English and must be completed in English, and, with one or two minor exceptions, all leaflets and publicity material on benefit entitlement are also printed in English. For those who do not speak or write English fluently, which is still quite common in some Asian communities, this can be a major barrier to receipt of support, as the NACAB (1991) survey again revealed. It is quite rare for benefits offices to be able to provide interpreter services for non-English speakers and thus those making claims may not be able to pursue their entitlement adequately. However it is equally likely that the absence of publicity and other literature in ethnic minority languages means that for many potential claimants even this point of contact is never reached. Cultural differences stemming from socialisation in different social structures may also lead people to fail to identify a right to state benefits as a potential source of support at times of deprivation (Cohen and Tarpey, 1986; Law *et al.*, 1994).

Thus, as we shall see in Chapter 14, although the problem of take-up of benefits is a significant one throughout the social security system, culture and language problems may make it a more serious one for black (non)claimants. A survey of claimants by National Opinion Polls for the National Audit Office revealed lower levels of take-up of means-tested education and health benefits among non-British/Irish respondents (see Amin and Oppenheim, 1992, pp. 54–5), and research in Leeds in 1993 revealed problems of take-up among Chinese and Bangladeshi communities (Law *et al.*, 1994). These differences are likely to represent a significant accentuation of benefit-related poverty for Britain's black population.

Racism and Social Exclusion

The problem of poverty is not just a problem of insecure or inadequate cash incomes. As we saw in Chapter 6, deprivation and social exclusion include a broader range of disadvantages, denials and powerlessness that can result in a reduced quality of life for some. For black people in Britain the existence of racism at all levels of the social structure means that many of these broader features of deprivation are also likely to affect them disproportionately – and racism itself adds a further burden to the problems with which they have to cope.

Housing is a significant source of inequality and deprivation, and housing conditions differ widely. After their entry into this country as immigrants in the 1950s and 1960s it was in trying to secure housing that many black people first encountered racism and exclusion. This included both the direct racism of private landlords and vendors who refused to rent or to sell to them, and the indirect racism of local authorities who put conditions on the allocation of council houses, such as residence tests, which black immigrants could not meet (Ginsburg, 1992). For those buying their own houses, a practice that is more common among some sections of the Asian community, restrictions in lending by building societies have also meant that purchasers have had to seek poorer properties in particular areas. As a result many black people have been forced to live in deprived inner city areas that are considered less desirable by the indigenous population and where the housing conditions are worst. For instance ethnic minority households are more likely than whites to be living in overcrowded accommodation, with 10 per cent having less than one room per person compared with only 1 per cent of white households – among Pakistani and Bangladeshi households the proportion is one-third (Amin and Oppenheim, 1992, p. 22).

Inequalities in health can also be associated with severe deprivation, and as recognised in the Black Report on health inequalities, racial differences can be detected here too (Townsend *et al.*, 1988, p. 58). Skellington and Morris (1992, ch. 5) reveal evidence of higher rates of mortality, including perinatal and infant mortality among sections of the black community. This is generally associated with poorer health, although black people also suffer specifically from some debilitating diseases that do not affect the indigenous population, such as sickle cell anaemia among people of black African descent. Inequalities in health can further be compounded by unequal use of health care and social services by black people; and there is evidence that major services such as community care do in practice operate disadvanta-geously for many ethnic minority communities (see Ahmad and Atkin, 1996).

Another state service within which black people do not receive equal treatment is education. As well as being a form of deprivation in itself, failure or underachievement in education is closely linked to poverty and inequality later in life. Poorer education is initially linked to the generally poorer services to be found in the inner city areas where large numbers of black people live. It is compounded both by direct discrimination within the education system, such as stereotyping black pupils as troublemakers or low achievers, and by the indirect exclusion that results from the ethnocentrism of the school curriculum. The Swann Report on the education of children from ethnic minority groups (Swann, 1985) laid much of the blame for inequalities within education on racism within the wider community, but Skellington and Morris (1992, ch. 9) provide evidence that black people's experience of education is structured by racism within the service and not just outside it.

Deprivation in housing, health and education add significantly to the financial inequality of black people in Britain, and they have remained important despite the introduction in the 1960s of race relations legislation designed to prevent direct and indirect discrimina-tion and promote equality of opportunity. However these indirect consequences may be compounded by some of the more direct scars of racism in ways that may severely deplete the quality of life enjoyed, or endured, by those who suffer under them. Racial harassment is part of a daily burden borne by most, it not all, black people in Britain. It is a burden that white people can never fully understand and many do not even recognise – although they may be contributing to it. Harassment ranges from being made to feel different and excluded, to being a victim of violence and disturbance in public or at home. This can discourage black people from sharing public spaces and can bring enduring fear and insecurity to the heart of their daily lives.

The experience of racial harassment is not of course confined to the poor inner city areas where large numbers of black people still live – and indeed the support and strength of black neighbours and friends in such areas may in part make such experiences a little easier to bear. Nevertheless the concentration of disadvantage and deprivation that black people experience throughout British society, especially when it is compounded by the fear and isolation produced by racial harassment, can contribute to an experience of poverty for our black population that is overlain by a feeling of exclusion and entrapment.

11

Ageing and Poverty

Poverty and Dependency in Old Age

Most of the studies of poverty that have paid attention to the age of
those who are poor have revealed that the risk and extent of poverty
varies with age. Indeed a major feature of Rowntree's (1901, 1941)
seminal studies of poverty in York was his notion of the 'life-cycle'
changes in the risk of poverty, as discussed in Chapter 7. Rowntree
identified three periods in the life cycle when there was an increased
risk of poverty: childhood, parenthood and old age; although, as
others have argued, changing life chances may in practice be more
complex than this for many. These periods of increased risk of poverty
can be contrasted with periods of relative plenty when income is higher
and/or demands are fewer. For manual workers this may be in early
adulthood when strength and fitness are at their peak; for white-collar
workers it may be towards the end of their careers when incrementally
based earnings are highest. In both cases, as we have seen, the effect of
distribution of income over lifetime is roughly 'U' shaped.

Rowntree's period of poverty risk associated with parenthood may
mitigate the enjoyment of relatively high earnings in early adulthood,
although this depends on household status and structure, and on the
success or otherwise of policies designed to provide support for
children and child rearers. What is consistent about all patterns of
life-cycle inequality, however, is the decline in income in old age; and
what many studies of poverty have revealed is that old age is closely
linked to risk of poverty.

As well as Rowntree's early recognition of life-cycle poverty in old
age, Booth's (1892, 1894) famous work on poverty in London at the
end of the nineteenth century revealed a much higher level of poverty
among the elderly than in the rest of the population. Similar conclusions about the extent of poverty in old age were reached by Townsend

165

(1979) in his major 1960s study of poverty in Britain. More recently Alan Walker (1980, 1993; Walker and Phillipson, 1986) has written widely on the link between old age and poverty and the reasons for this.

Townsend's research (1979, p. 787) found that a much higher proportion of elderly people (64 per cent) than non-elderly people (26 per cent) had an income that was less than 140 per cent of benefit entitlement, which was roughly equivalent to his definition of poverty. Since then, however, there has been growing poverty among younger unemployed and low-paid families, but as the Rowntree research in the early 1990s revealed, older people are still overrepresented in the poorest third of the population (Hills, 1995, ch. 2). Furthermore elderly people are likely to spend much longer periods in poverty, with four times as many living on benefits for longer than five years and seven times as many for longer than ten years (Walker, 1986, p. 186).

Elderly people's lower incomes and greater risk of poverty are obviously closely linked to their sources of income. In 1994/95 elderly people derived a much higher proportion (51 per cent) of their income from benefits than from earnings compared with the rest of the population (13 per cent) (Oppenheim and Harker, 1996, p. 61). This is a fundamental distinction that results from elderly people's systematic exclusion from the labour market, as we shall see below. However there are other factors that operate to reduce income in old age. Although in theory older people may be able to benefit from savings made over a lifetime, especially if they have insurance policies or private pensions that mature in later years, in practice only a few receive significant amounts from such sources. For the majority with relatively small savings the need to draw on these can rapidly deplete them, increasing the risk of poverty later on among the very elderly. Furthermore savings accrued and maintained over long periods of time can be severely affected by inflation, which reduces their real value – as many small investors have discovered in the last quarter of the twentieth century.

Despite the continuing evidence of lower incomes in old age, however, there have been some improvements in the absolute levels of income for elderly people. State pensions have increased more than benefits for the working population, notably in 1974; and the rising value of new earnings-related pensions has also benefited some. However these absolute increases in income for older people, together with the increasing number of younger people dependent on means-tested benefits (primarily as a result of increased unemployment) are sometimes used to present a picture of an apparent decline in the risk of poverty among older people. This is not true.

Certainly the proportion of persons dependent on means-tested benefits who were over pension age declined from almost 70 per cent in 1970 to around 36 per cent in the late 1980s (Falkingham and Victor, 1991, p. 6). However this was very largely accounted for by the increasing number of those below retirement age claiming these benefits, and the overall number of pensioner claimants has remained more or less constant. Furthermore, although the value of pensions has increased in comparison with the benefits received by people of working age, thus marginally improving the relative position of older people, this improvement has in no way matched the improvement in earnings for most working people – indeed the value of the single person's pension declined from 23.2 per cent of average earnings in 1979 to 17.5 per cent in 1994 (Oppenheim and Harker, 1996, p. 61). Given that earnings are still the main source of income for working-age people – but not for the elderly – this means that the poorer overall position of older people has remained, despite an accompanying decline in the fortunes of some younger people too.

Of course, as we have seen, inadequate income is not the only source of poverty – deprivation and social exclusion may result from factors other than low income. These broader problems disproportionately affect older people for a number of reasons. For instance older people spend a proportionately greater part of their weekly income on essentials such as food, fuel and clothing (Baldwin and Cooke, 1984, p. 45). This leaves less for luxury items, in particular consumer durables such as washing machines or telephones, which significantly enhance the quality of life. In addition to this older people's physical condition and the fact that more time is spent at home leads to a greater need for essential items such as fuel. Inability to afford such essentials can lead to severe deprivation – and even, as in the case of hypothermia in winter, death.

There is also evidence of significant inequality and deprivation in housing conditions for the elderly (Wheeler, 1986). Older people are much more likely to live in privately rented or local authority housing, where conditions are often poorer. Even if they are owner-occupiers, however, older people may experience poorer housing conditions, and with lower incomes they may be in less of a position to make improvements. Elderly owner-occupiers are more likely than others to live in houses without central heating, and they are much more likely (41 per cent compared with 22 per cent) to live in houses that are unfit or needing over £2500 of repairs (ibid., p. 219).

It is true that in many parts of the country there do exist concessionary schemes for free or reduced-cost access to some public services, such as transport and leisure facilities for older people. However the apparent benefits of these must be set against older people's generally lower incomes and reduced access to many private services. For instance the level of car ownership is lower among the elderly (Falkingham and Victor, 1991, p. 15).

Although there is some evidence that older people consume a greater proportion of some public services, such as health and social care, this is related to the greater need for such services among the elderly as a result of the disability and frailty that is sometimes associated with old age (McGlone, 1992). However, this association should not be overstated. The vast majority of elderly people (93 per cent) live in their own homes (Wheeler, 1986, p. 218), and the large majority of these (over 80 per cent) are not functionally impaired and can get around their home and go out on their own without difficulty (McGlone, 1992, p. 14). Furthermore, of those elderly people who do need care and support the vast majority receive it from members of their family (Qureshi and Walker, 1989, p. 122). Despite the real support needs of some disabled older people therefore, the notion that the elderly are dependant people requiring the support of the rest of society is largely a myth – a point to which we will return at the end of this chapter.

Retirement

In Britain, as in most other advanced industrial countries, earnings from employment are the main source of income for most households, and adequate earnings are the main means of avoiding poverty. For older people, however, earnings are not the main source of income, and the risk of poverty in old age is thus considerably greater. The reason why earnings constitute such a small proportion of the incomes of elderly people is that beyond a certain age people are systematically excluded from the labour market as a result of policies designed to encourage, or coerce, retirement from work.

The notion that people should retire from work at a certain age is a relatively recent one – it has only developed in advanced industrial countries over the last century alongside the development of pension payments for the retired. Although it is a notion that many, especially younger, people take for granted, it is in fact an extremely complex issue and one that has grown significantly in importance in the latter half of the twentieth century because of increased longevity following medical and health advances. At the same time the proportion of people, engaged in employment has reduced. The growing significance of retirement is also associated with the growth in the availability, and extent, of private pension protection under which workers can effectively save for their future retirement, as we shall see below.

Earlier in the twentieth century it was not common for older workers to retire automatically from employment. Indeed during the immediate postwar period – a time of 'full employment' – much store was placed in the value of older, experienced workers, and in 1951 around a third of men aged over 65 were still economically active (Phillipson, 1993). However since that time the number of older people in full-time employment has declined significantly, in particular because of the imposition of what is in effect a compulsory retirement age for most workers at the age at which state pension entitlement commences (currently 60 for women, 65 for men) – after this age workers are not protected by law from dismissal. In 1986 only one in fifteen men over the age of 65 were still in employment.

In practice, when older people do work they are not – unlike other marginalised groups such as women, black people or those with disabilities – concentrated in particular segments of the labour market, primarily of course because older people in employment did not enter it as older people, but have simply carried on with previous patterns of employment. The marginalisation of women, black people and others in employment is carried over into old age, and as we shall see these labour market inequalities also structure inequality and poverty in old age. However evidence is emerging that when older workers, even those below the pension age, do seek employment they experience discrimination and marginalisation (Harris, 1991) – a phenomenon that is part of the increasingly recognised problem of 'ageism' (see Bytheway and Johnson, 1990).

Ageism has also been experienced in the increased pressure that was first brought to bear on older workers during the economic recessions of the 1980s and 1990s to leave employment early to protect the jobs of younger people. Although many older workers, in particular those with significant personal pension entitlements, may welcome the opportunity to end their working life early, there are many others for whom such retirement is really a form of redundancy – and one with little prospect of further work (Harris, 1991). What is more this type of redundancy has begun to affect workers earlier and earlier in their working lives, with 'early retirement' schemes being offered to workers in their 50s and early 60s. As a result the economic activity rates among such people have begun to decline – between 1971 and 1991 the decline for 55–59 year olds was from 71 per cent to 67 per cent, and for 60–64 year olds from 54 per cent to 39 per cent (Phillipson, 1993, p. 1).

For those who have accrued significant savings over their lives and are entitled to a relatively substantial retirement pension, leaving work can be an opportunity to enjoy a relaxed and leisurely lifestyle. For those in unrewarding jobs that require strength and stamina rather than experience the opportunity to replace dependency on wages with dependency on pensions may also be attractive, and when illness, frailty or disability compound the problem of earning from work this may be particularly important.

However exclusion from the labour market can also have serious deleterious consequences that significantly reduce the quality of life of older people. For instance experience and knowledge are no longer valued – indeed they are usually ignored; contact with colleagues and friends at work is arbitrarily severed; and the status and respect that go with employment and productivity are taken away. As we have seen before, social exclusion is a significant feature of deprivation in modern societies. This is a problem that disproportionately affects older people through the experience of retirement; and for the large number of older people who do not have an adequate pension entitlement, absence from the labour market also means loss of an adequate income and thus a greatly increased risk of poverty and dependency

The concept of retirement, of course, only applies to paid employment. Unpaid work, especially that done in the home, continues after retirement or job release. In this context retirement is therefore something of a male notion, or perhaps more accurately a male problem. For older women, who are less likely than their younger sisters to be in full-time employment and more likely to be responsible for the bulk of home work, retirement is something that happens to their husbands. Indeed for some, unpaid work at home may frequently increase in old age because of the demands created by increased frailty and disability. Most of the elderly people needing care in their home receive it from family members, and in practice in many cases this work is done by other elderly persons in the family, usually a spouse

(McGlone, 1992). Exclusion from the labour market may therefore not mean increased access to leisure, and it may not mean cessation of work. Rather it may mean a transfer of work and leisure into the home – together with a reduction of income.

Pensions

In the nineteenth century, at a time when life expectancy was much shorter than today, no specific provision was made for income support in old age. Thus although some trade unions and friendly societies, and even some employers, provided limited pension protection for older members, the majority who reached old age had no right to financial support. If these people were unable to support themselves through employment, then the only alternative open to them was dependency on the Poor Law, and thus the workhouse. It was the poverty among older people that resulted from this that was highlighted by Booth (1892, 1894) in his surveys at the end of the century, and it led to some pressure on the government to provide directly for the elderly poor.

Following the example of Germany, therefore, pensions were introduced for certain older people in 1908. The original pension of 5 shillings a week, paid only to those over 70, was not based on contributions made during employment, and was subject to an income test – '5 shillings a week for cheating death', as one popular song put it. In 1911 a contributory social security scheme was introduced, and in 1925 pensions based on contributions were paid to those over 65.

Following the Beveridge Report (1942) on social security reform the postwar government introduced a supposedly comprehensive insurance-based pension scheme whereby all men over 65 and women over 60 were paid flat-rate pensions, with additions for dependants, based on their contribution records during their working lives. However because all current pensioners would have been automatically excluded from such a scheme because of their incomplete contribution record, the contribution conditions were effectively waived for them and full pensions were paid immediately, which, as we shall see in Chapter 14, prevented the scheme from ever operating from a funded insurance base.

In order to ensure that pensions were adequate to support the older people depending on them, Beveridge based his recommended rates on Rowntree's (1901 and 1941) nutritional guidelines for minimum subsistence. However to avoid a situation in which pensions might exceed earnings and thus discourage employment, and to encourage the development of additional private protection, which Beveridge saw as desirable, they were fixed at *only* this subsistence level. They were thus barely adequate and provided little protection against poverty. When Abel Smith and Townsend (1965) discovered large numbers of people living below the means-tested benefit poverty line in the 1950s and 1960s, the majority of these were pensioners living on state pensions that were not adequate to provide them even with the equivalent of this safety net income – although many of the pensioner claimants were not in receipt of the means-tested supplements to which they might have been entitled.

In absolute terms, however, the value of pensions increased in the 1950s and 1960s; and in the 1970s in particular pensions increased in relative terms when compared with benefits for the younger unemployed. In the late 1970s this gap began to widen because the basic insurance pension was increased in line with rises in prices or earnings, whichever was the higher, whilst other benefits were increased in line with prices only. After 1980, however, even the relative position of advantage against other claimants was removed when basic pension increases were restricted, like other benefits, to price inflation only. By 1995 this had lowered the weekly value of basic pensions by £20.30 a week for single persons and £33.05 for couples (Oppenheim and Harker, 1996, p. 61), with the result that around three million pensioners were receiving incomes at or below Income Support levels.

Throughout its history the basic pension has thus been kept at a relatively low level. This is in part because, like the benefits for those not in employment, it acts as a wage substitute and is kept below wage levels in order to deter voluntary departure from the labour market. However the link between pension entitlement and retirement, especially after the spread of early and compulsory retirement in the latter part of the twentieth century, has significantly undermined the logic of this unequal treatment. Pensioners who have been required to leave the labour market hardly require financial incentives to seek support through wages, and this may partly explain the relatively advantaged status that pensioners have enjoyed compared with other benefit claimants over this period.

The low level of pension payments was also a product of the basis on which the postwar social security scheme was established. By admitting all elderly claimants directly into the insurance scheme the financing was effectively based on a 'pay-as-you-go' basis, with current contributions being used to pay for current benefits, as opposed to being saved or invested as a deferred payment to existing contributors. Payment of current pensions out of current contributions thus created an inevitable pressure to keep pension levels down in order to keep the contribution levels for current contributors as low as possible. As the number of pensioners grew throughout the postwar period this pressure became stronger, a point to which we shall return below.

A low basic pension also acts as an important incentive for employed people to seek additional private financial protection for their old age. Beveridge (1942) had always hoped that state pensions would be supplemented by voluntary private insurance, and thus provided the basic pension levels were 'adequate' there need be no concern that they were below wage levels, since those in work could use their higher wages to purchase additional pension protection. Taken together with the pay-as-you-go basis of state insurance pensions, this meant that the notion of pensions as deferred earnings, rather than as a wage substitute for those no longer able to provide for themselves, was restricted to private-sector pension protection. This too has contributed to a 'public burden' myth about the effect of pension entitlement.

In practice occupational pensions – additional private protection provided by employers through contributions paid by employees into a separate pension scheme – did grow rapidly in the 1950s and 1960s as employers sought to attract workers by offering the advantages of pension protection through work. Sometimes referred to as 'superannuation', these early occupational pension schemes flourished mainly in private sector employment and the number of workers covered grew from 4.3 million in 1956 to 12.2 million in 1967 (Walker, 1986, p. 202). After that point the number of people covered began to decline, down to 5.5 million by 1983, although the number of public sector employees covered by such schemes was growing, rising from 4.1 million in 1967 to 5.4 million in 1983 (ibid., p. 203).

Many of the occupational pension schemes, especially those in the private sector, did not provide very generous protection after retirement, however; and most could not readily be transferred from one job to another – thus the rights accrued could be lost if employment changed. Also most pensions were not 'index linked' – that is, they did not rise with subsequent inflation, rendering payment levels increasingly inadequate during the high inflation climate of the late twentieth century. Furthermore occupational pension protection frequently assumed male career patterns of continuous contribution over a working life, with the final pension level being based on earnings at the end of the working life. This could seriously disadvantage women workers who had taken career breaks and any employees for whom final earnings were not the highest they had received.

The limitations on occupational pensions have thus meant that many of those contributing have not received significant financial returns from them. In some cases entitlement can amount to little more than a couple of pounds a week. This limited protection, together with the continued exclusion of many from even limited occupational provision, was one of the main reasons for the introduction of the State Earnings Related Pensions Scheme (SERPS) in 1978. SERPS is a complex extension of insurance pensions to provide a measure of additional pension income on top of the basic pension based on contributions made during the working life. This additional protection applies provisionally to all contributors, but in order not to undermine the protection provided by some occupational schemes, contributors to approved occupational schemes can 'opt out' of SERPS, paying reduced contributions and receiving only the basic state pension on retirement (see Atkinson, 1991b).

SERPS was introduced by the Labour government in the 1970s, but it had a measure of cross-party support because of its coalition with occupational protection. The state provision is not due to reach maturity until 1998 because only contributions paid after the starting date of 1978 are eligible for inclusion in the calculation of the earnings-related additional payment. This meant that the scheme was of little or no benefit to existing pensioners, and in the short to medium term it was able to do little to alleviate the risk of poverty in old age. It also contributed significantly to fears about the potentially high cost of future state pension payments, because like the original pension scheme, payments were made on a pay-as-you-go basis.

These fears became a government concern in the mid 1980s and were a major factor in the reviews of social security provision undertaken by the government prior to the reforms introduced in the 1986 Social Security Act. The original proposal in the Green Paper (1985) that preceded the legislation was to remove entirely the additional protection provided by SERPS because of the high costs that were expected to be incurred early in the twenty-first century. The proposal was opposed, however, by many employers and by the private pension industry, which did not welcome the burden of providing earnings-related pensions for all. What was eventually introduced therefore was a reduction in the amount of additional provision and a change in the basis of determining entitlement. Furthermore the reductions were not to take effect until after 1998, once maturity under the original scheme had been reached.

These changes did not allay the concerns in some circles that the increasing numbers of pensioners in the population at the beginning of the twenty-first century would continue to provide too great a demand on the state insurance pension scheme. In the 1990s both the government and the opposition parties, as well as a range of independent commentators, have sought to develop new proposals for the development of future pension provision that will reduce contribution costs either by transferring protection to the private occupational sector (see Field, 1995) or by targeting pensions onto those with low incomes on retirement (Borrie, 1994). No such measures have yet been introduced, however, and the need for them has been hotly disputed by some, such as Townsend and Walker (1995), who point out that the situation facing the financing of future pensions in Britain is in practice much less severe than that in many neighbouring welfare capitalist countries and could be contained within the existing insurance scheme.

The cuts made in SERPS entitlement will reduce the incomes of future pensioners, and may therefore contribute to a continuation of poverty and inequality in old age into the next century. They are also linked to the government's desire to encourage the development of private pension protection to supplement or replace state pensions. Private, as opposed to occupational, pension schemes developed little during the early postwar period, although they could have had the potential benefit of avoiding the limitations of occupational and employment-related schemes. In the 1980s, therefore, the government began to provide significant incentives for those investing in private pensions in the form of tax relief and investment bonuses, and after this private pension protection grew rapidly in scope and coverage.

Although still not as widespread as occupational provision, private pensions now provide a third area of pension protection, alongside occupational pensions and the state scheme. Some private schemes represent a more speculative investment than those in the occupational field, and in the early 1990s many of those investing in private pension schemes found that the risks they were exposing themselves to were much greater than they had initially been led to believe and that they would probably have been better off remaining in SERPS. Nevertheless private pensions do contribute to the possible improvement that future pensioners can now look forward to, and such provision may remove the fear of potential poverty in old age – for some.

However the improved prospects of some future pensioners will not remove the risk or the fear of poverty in old age for the many current and future pensioners who will not benefit significantly from such additional protection on retirement. Indeed what the existence of private and occupational pensions does in practice is to reproduce in old age many of the inequalities and deprivations associated with the inequities of the labour market earlier in life. As early as 1955 Titmuss referred to the fear that occupational protection could lead to the development of 'two nations' in retirement – one relatively affluent group enjoying the benefits of deferred earnings in the form of insurance payments and private pensions and one generally poor one dependent on the inadequate basic state pension.

This division between rich and poor in retirement has become more accentuated towards the end of the twentieth century, and has even led to the development of acronyms for the newer, wealthier pensioners, the most widespread being 'Woopies' (Well-off older persons). In practice both the size of this new group and the extent of their relative wealth have often been overstated (see Falkingham and Victor, 1991), but they do illustrate the growth of inequality in old age in the 1990s.

Inequality also results from the continuation into old age of the deprivations and exclusions experienced earlier in life. This means that class differences in income, housing, health and so on continue to divide people after retirement, as do gender differences and the dependence that family relationships frequently produce. As Britain's black population grows older differences arising from race and racism will be reproduced among the elderly. Thus poverty in old age, like poverty earlier in the life cycle, reflects broader social divisions.

Inequalities during working life, and particularly those that affect pension entitlement, also influenced overall life-cycle experiences of different cohorts of elderly people. As Atkinson and Sutherland (1991) have discussed, this means for instance that the generation of elderly people whose working lives were affected by the depression of the 1930s and the Second World War have had very different preretirement opportunities from subsequent generations, who have experienced relatively high levels of unbroken employment since the war. The former group thus experience lower incomes and a greater risk of poverty in old age.

As such groups grow older still their circumstances may worsen further, as any savings become depleted and possessions grow older and cannot be replaced. This problem is more generally reflected in differences and divisions between the 'young old' and the 'old old', where the risk of poverty and the experience of deprivation are more acute among the latter at a time when their need for support and care may be at its greatest. Thus class, gender, race and age structure the risk and the experience of poverty in old age, and these divisions have been heightened rather than reduced by developments in pension provision.

The Social Construction of Dependency

As discussed earlier, the association between ageing – and in particular old age – and poverty is closely linked to the notion of life-cycle changes in social status and economic circumstances. However this association is frequently misperceived, or misrepresented, as a kind of 'iron law' of determination, which can also be misunderstood as an assumption that old age is in some way a cause of poverty. Social circumstances cannot be causes of poverty, even though they may be associated with a higher risk of it for a range of other reasons. What is more, as the increasing evidence of relative wealth for some in old age demonstrates, this risk does not apply inevitably or evenly to all.

Nevertheless the link between old age and risk of poverty is a well-established one in Britain, and this pattern is reproduced in most other advanced industrial countries (Walker, 1993). Of course the motivation, in part at least, for Rowntree's and others' exposure of the phenomenon of life-cycle poverty risks was to encourage the development of policies to relieve or prevent the emergence of poverty in such circumstances. Family Allowances and Child Benefit are examples of policies designed to prevent poverty associated with child rearing. In the case of old age, however, policy developments have not in general prevented, or even challenged, the risk of poverty – indeed in many ways policies designed for the elderly have operated both to create and to reproduce poverty and dependency.

This has led Walker (1980) in particular to argue that the risk of poverty in old age is 'socially constructed'. Of course this is true, as we know, of poverty in all situations; but in the case of poverty among the elderly we can identify clear policy assumptions and policy developments that have contributed specifically to the higher risk of poverty faced by many old people. Assumptions are made about the circumstances or the needs of elderly people that are frequently unjustified and inaccurate, and policies are developed to respond to these assumptions, which may compound the problems faced by some people – or may even create new problems.

Perhaps the most pervasive and most long-standing assumption about elderly people is that because of their age they are no longer able to contribute to society and may even be unable to care for themselves. This may be presented sympathetically as a justification for support from the rest of society as a 'reward' for their previous contribution. However it is a contradictory notion that may also be interpreted as implying that elderly people are a burden on society, which willingly or unwillingly the rest of us have to bear. As we shall see shortly, this interpretation has gained increasing prominence in the late twentieth century as the number of elderly people relative to the rest of the population has started gradually to rise, and as life expectancy has increased.

In practice only a small proportion of elderly people do need care and support in order to remain independent, and many if not most are quite able to contribute to society if they are provided with the opportunity to do so. However some of the policies designed to provide care for the elderly operate to accentuate their dependent status rather than reduce it, in particular the denial of autonomy and control in many residential establishments and the inadequate provision of genuine support services to assist people to survive in the community. Minor disability can thus result in dependency and poverty in old age, when alternative policy initiatives could have prevented it (McGlone, 1992).

What prevents most elderly people from contributing to society, in particular contributing through productive work, however, are the policies that encourage or coerce retirement. Retirement moves older people into a situation of dependency on benefits, or on savings or pension protection of their own, and because these are frequently inadequate, this also leads to a greater risk of poverty among the elderly.

One of the main reasons for the low level of state pensions has been the desire by governments to minimise the cost of pension provision incurred by current insurance contributors and taxpayers because of the pay-as-you-go nature of state pension funding. This was compounded in the 1980s when the introduction of SERPS extended the scope of state protection. Thus although the growth in private pension protection has to some extent reduced the potential costs of the state scheme, there have been, as we have seen, cuts in the relative level of the basic pension, and also plans to cut SERPS and develop other means of reducing future pension costs.

Much of the concern about the growing cost of pension protection is based on an awareness that the projected numbers of pensioners relative to the rest of the population will increase in the early twenty-first century, and fears about the consequences of this. The demographic evidence of this is sometimes referred to as the 'gerontic ratio', and this ratio has been changing over a long period of time. In fact the proportion of elderly persons in the population has been increasing throughout the twentieth century. It rose from 12 per 1000 in 1901 to 34 per 1000 in 1981, and is projected to reach 38 per 1000 by 2021 (Falkingham, 1989, p. 218). The future changes will therefore not be so enormous, and in practice they are likely to be less than those anticipated in many other welfare capitalist countries with much higher levels of state pension protection (see Walker, 1993).

Furthermore the simplistic link between demography and dependency ignores a wide range of other factors that may or may not result in a need to redistribute resources towards elderly people. These include overall levels of productivity and the ability of older people to provide for themselves, both of which factors changed significantly in the early part of the twentieth century, when the gerontic ratio changed more dramatically than it will over the next few decades. They also include the ability and willingness of younger generations to continue to contribute to the state pension scheme in the anticipation that they too will benefit from this in the future.

Current debates about the balance between private pension protection and state support can sometimes operate to confuse the issue of who will pay for future pensions. They also contribute to the continued development of the problem of 'two nations' in retirement, in which the advantages of private protection and the risks of poverty are not shared equally by all, but in practice mirror disadvantages and deprivation experienced earlier in the life cycle. Nevertheless it is far from clear that the concern of politicians and policy makers with the impending burden of pension dependency is in fact shared by all sections of the population – and indeed, if it were, it could be seen as a curious example of shortsighted self-interest.

It is therefore *assumptions* that have been made about the needs and resources of elderly persons and the ability and willingness of society to prepare for future retirement that have operated to create and recreate the apparent problem of the burden of dependency in old age. As Walker (1980, p. 73) put it, 'So it is not *chronological age* that is significant in causing poverty and dependency . . . but the relationship

between the *social construction* of age and the social division of labour'
(emphasis in original). Throughout most of the twentieth century this
has resulted in an increased risk of poverty and exclusion in old age,
and as we approach the twenty-first century there is little evidence that
this picture is changing.

12

Disability and Poverty

The Costs of Disability

Disability is an umbrella term used to cover a wide range of physical conditions and social circumstances in which people may experience difficulties or problems in providing for themselves or participating in social activity. Of course loss or impairment of physical functions can be problematic: people who cannot see, hear, walk or clothe themselves obviously have to learn to adapt to their limited capabilities. However physical conditions such as these need not necessarily lead to social problems or social exclusion, and indeed they do not always do so. When assistance or support can be purchased or provided disabled people can and do participate fully in modern society. If they do not participate, and if they experience poverty and exclusion, it is because of their need to survive within structures that assume people are 'able-bodied' and that provide no support for those who are not – or may even directly exclude them. It is thus discrimination, rather than disability itself, which as the heart of the exclusion experienced by disabled people – and at the same time of their greater risk of poverty. For as Groves (1988, p. 171) put it, 'Poverty is disability's close companion'.

The problems arising from disability, both directly and indirectly, vary widely however, because so too does the nature of disability itself. Disabilities can include the loss or impairment of physical functions such as mobility, sensory deprivation such as blindness or deafness, or mental disabilities such as learning difficulties. These different disabilities lead to very different social needs and social problems. They have also resulted in much academic and political debate about how to define disability – and this debate remains largely unresolved and controversial.

In the 1960s a government-sponsored survey of disability carried out by the OPCS sought to distinguish three different conditions (see Oliver, 1991a):

- *Impairment* – meaning loss of function.
- *Disability* – meaning restriction of activity.
- *Handicap* – meaning a physical disadvantage that limits individual fulfilment.

In his major study of poverty in the 1960s Townsend (1979, ch. 20) went further than this and included chronic sickness in his discussion of the poverty and deprivation associated with disability. In the mid 1980s the OPCS (Martin *et al.*, 1988; Martin and White, 1988) carried out another survey of disability in which they developed a scale of severity of disability ranging from one (the lowest level of impairment) to ten (the highest level). This was a more sophisticated approach, although it obviously included in the lower categories people who might not be regarded by some as having a disability.

Different studies of the links between poverty and disability may therefore be using different definitions of disability – and perhaps different definitions of poverty too – making comparisons between findings problematic. The OPCS ten-point scale provides both the broadest and the most sophisticated approach, however, and it has been largely taken up in most of the recent discussions on the issue. Using the scale, the OPCS found that there were over 6.5 million people with disabilities in Britain in 1985, ranging from 1.2 million in category one to 240 000 in category ten (see Dalley, 1991, pp. 7–8).

The link between poverty and disability is not new of course, indeed it goes back to the nineteenth century and in particular to the growth of urbanisation (see Topliss, 1979). It was also recognised by Townsend in his survey of poverty in the 1960s (Townsend, 1979, ch. 20). In the 1990s, however, the OPCS data has been used to calculate that 47 per cent of disabled adults are living in poverty (Berthoud *et al.*, 1993). This is particularly because, unlike the rest of the population, most disabled people (78 per cent) rely on state benefits as their main source of income, with 27 per cent of households containing a sick or disabled person receiving all their income from benefits (see Oppenheim and Harker, 1996, p. 58).

Low income and benefit dependency are, as we know, major causes of poverty. For people with disabilities, however, low income is frequently compounded by the extra costs associated with living with a disability. These include the purchase of physical aids or adaptations to the home, the cost of medicines or ointments, the need to consume more fuel in order to heat the home full-time, and perhaps the need to pay for care or support within the home. Without additional income to cover such extra costs the standard of living of people with disabilities surviving on low incomes is likely to be further reduced.

There has been something of a heated debate on the extent of the extra costs associated with disability (see Berthoud, 1991). The OPCS survey included questions about additional needs and concluded that the average extra cost was around £6.10 a week. However this figure has been disputed by the Disablement Income Group (DIG), which on the basis of a more in-depth survey of people with more severe disabilities (Thompson *et al.*, 1990) put the figure at £69.92 – a significant difference.

Both these surveys were based on the direct questioning of people with disabilities. Berthoud compares these approaches with those that look at what people actually spend in a weekly budget, similar to some of the budget standards studies of poverty discussed in Chapter 5. These demonstrate extra expenditure on some items, such as fuel, durables and tobacco, and reduced expenditure on others, such as transport and clothing. As Berthoud (1991, pp. 77–8) points out however, these different expenditure patterns conceal a generally lower standard of living for people with disabilities because extra expenditure on some items leads to overall reductions elsewhere within a generally lower total weekly income. This greater risk of deprivation is confirmed by a DSS survey of income and expenditure patterns using the FES, which concludes 'that at similar income levels disabled people are more constrained and experience a lower standard of living than their able-bodied counterparts' (Matthews and Truscott, 1990, p. ix).

Extra expenditure on certain goods, particularly capital expenditure, is also likely to produce a greater risk of debt for disabled people. Research has revealed problems of indebtedness due to additional expenditure among people with disabilities, as well as particular needs for help and support in coping with their disabilities (Grant, 1995). However, as discussed earlier, poverty is not just a function of low cash income and financial restrictions. There are also broader features of deprivation and exclusion that disproportionately affect people with disabilities. Townsend's (1979, ch. 20) study revealed that people with disabilities experience poorer housing conditions and are less likely to have regular holidays. Disability is also frequently associated with ill-health, both as a cause and a consequence. Furthermore participation in social activities and leisure pursuits may be restricted by reduced mobility or sensory deprivation, leading to an overall reduction in the quality of life of people with disabilities compared with most able-bodied people.

The poverty and exclusion experienced by people with disabilities is frequently visited on other members of their household. As we shall discuss below, this is particularly the case for those who care for such people, including parents caring for children with disabilities. But the lower income and additional expenditure associated with disability mean that in general all household members are subject to a greater risk of poverty (see Glendinning and Baldwin, 1988).

Exclusion from Work

Exclusion from the labour market means exclusion from receipt of wages, which are the main source of income in modern industrial societies and thus the main means of avoiding poverty. Disabled people's greater reliance on benefits as a source of income, referred to above, is a direct consequence of their relative exclusion from the labour market. For the nearly 50 per cent of people with disabilities who have passed the retirement age, exclusion from work may be as much a function of age as it is of disability. However for younger people of working age there is considerable evidence that those with disabilities are at greater risk of unemployment and inactivity than the rest of the population.

The OPCS survey revealed that only 31 per cent of people with disabilities were in work, as opposed to 69 per cent of the general population (Martin and White, 1988), and from this it was calculated that the unemployment rate among 'economically active' persons with disabilities was around 27 per cent for men and 20 per cent for women compared with 11 per cent and 9 per cent respectively for the population as a whole (Martin *et al.*, 1989). More recent research has shown that disabled people are up to three times more likely than other adults to be unemployed (Berthoud *et al.*, 1993).

Disadvantage in the labour market not only involves exclusion, however. There is also evidence that those who are engaged in paid employment receive lower pay, with pay levels falling with increasing severity of disability (Lonsdale and Walker, 1984). Disabled people are more likely to be in low-paid, low-status employment, for example 31 per cent are in manual employment compared with 21 per cent of non-disabled workers (Oppenheim and Harker, 1996, p. 58), and they are more likely to lack formal qualifications (Prescott-Clarke, 1990).

Exclusion from the labour market is in part the result of direct discrimination by employers against people with disabilities, who they believe to be unsuitable for many kinds of work and possibly unreliable on health grounds. However this is compounded by other, potentially more important structural barriers to employment, in particular the failure of employers to adapt workplaces or work practices to permit the participation of people with disabilities. People with physical or sensory disabilities are perfectly capable of working within the limitations of their condition, and yet because of the structure of many working environments they are excluded from realising their potential to do this.

As a result of this there is considerable evidence that disabled people experience discrimination and marginalisation in the labour market (Smith, 1992; RADAR 1993). Such discrimination has been recognised in legislation that has sought to protect and promote the concerns of disabled people at work, although with relatively little overall success (Floyd, 1991).

The first and potentially most important measure is the quota scheme introduced in the Disabled Persons Act of 1944. The intention of the scheme was to ensure that at least 3 per cent of the workforce of organisations with more than twenty employees are people registered as disabled, although government departments are excluded from this, as are some other major national employers such as the health service. However the scheme has been ineffective in overcoming the exclusion of people with disabilities. Many such people are not registered under the act, the quota system is inadequately enforced, and the average proportion of disabled employees in organisations within the scheme is nearer to 1 per cent (Floyd, 1991, p. 216).

Until the 1990s there was no legislation to prevent discrimination against disabled people, unlike the areas of gender and race. Disability campaign groups have for some time lobbied hard for the introduction of such legislation, and in the mid 1990s the government introduced some limited measures aimed at making unlawful some acts of discrimination against people with disabilities. To some extent these were modelled on the civil remedies contained in other antidiscrimination legislation, and they may suffer many of the problems of enforcement already associated with these.

The 1990s also saw the introduction of a social security benefit aimed directly at improving the labour market participation of disabled people – the Disability Working Allowance (DWA). The DWA is closely modelled on Family Credit and it provides a supplement to the low wages of those who are defined as disabled according to certain criteria. Like Family Credit, in a sense it operates to encourage the payment of low wages to people with disabilities, and to trap them on these low wages because they will lose their benefit if their wages rise. As well as the poverty trap the DWA also creates something of a 'disability trap', for in order to benefit people must in effect be defined, and therefore labelled, as disabled. This may discourage those seeking to establish a 'normal' lifestyle from seeking support – as indeed seems to have been the case during the early years of the DWA, with only around 2000 people a year claiming the benefit and only a few hundred of these moving into employment as a result of such support (Rowlingson and Berthoud, 1994).

People with disabilities thus remain in low-status, low-paid employment, or are excluded from the labour market altogether. This exclusion not only prevents them from receiving the financial benefits of reasonable wages, it also effectively excludes them from the increasingly important indirect advantages of employment in the form of fringe benefits, occupational pensions and insurance, and participation in the state insurance scheme. The result of this exclusion is to carry labour market disadvantage outside the sphere of employment into the area of support available in retirement or other periods of unemployment. Thus here too people with disabilities are likely to receive lower incomes and be at greater risk of poverty.

Benefits and Dependency

Because of their relative exclusion from the labour market, the majority of people with disabilities (over 75 per cent) have to rely on benefits as their main source of income. In addition to this, people with disabilities are also likely to depend on benefits for longer periods of time than other claimants, thus compounding the problem of dependency and contributing to the downward spiral of poverty dynamics discussed in Chapter 7. Benefit provision for people with disabilities is therefore a potentially important element in reducing their risk of poverty, but in practice it has not been at all effective in doing this.

Benefit provision for people with disabilities has had a fairly chequered history in Britain. The policy has been one of piecemeal reform and *ad hoc* adaptation rather than consistent development, and it has resulted in the growth of significant anomalies between the way people with disabilities and others are treated, and even between the different treatment accorded to different groups among the disabled themselves (see Walker and Walker, 1991). People with disabilities who meet the criteria for ordinary benefits can of course claim these in the same way as other people. Indeed such benefits as the retirement pension or Income Support are the main source of income for a large number of people with disabilities who are not entitled to separate or additional provision as a result of their disability. However, following the Workmen's Compensation Act at the end of the nineteenth century, separate and additional benefits have been provided for some people, depending on the cause of their disability.

Thus in the past more generous benefit provision was made for people suffering disability as a result of industrial accidents or injuries sustained in war. In part the logic behind this was to provide a measure of compensation for the victims of such unfortunate events. The effect, however, was to secure for such people much higher levels of benefit entitlement than others with much the same disabilities but acquired in different circumstances. The differences here could be quite large, ranging in 1990 from £287.55 a week for someone on the war disablement scheme to £63.80 a week for someone not entitled to insurance benefit or the Severe Disablement Allowance (SDA) (Disability Alliance, 1990). However during the 1990s many of the more generous aspects of employment-based provision have been removed or reduced, and provision for disabled people has been made more equitable – albeit largely as a result of a levelling down to the protection enjoyed by the least well-off.

The postwar Beveridge insurance scheme made no specific provision for people with disabilities. Since the 1970s, however, a number of alterations and additions to aspects of benefit provision have been made to provide some support for some recognised extra needs resulting from disability. These included initially a higher national insurance benefit (Invalidity Benefit) for those unable to work due to illness or disability for over six months, and a lower, flat-rate, non-contributory benefit (Non-Contributory Invalidity Pension, or NCIP) for those not entitled to this because of their inadequate contribution record.

In the 1990s, however, the number of people claiming Invalidity Benefit began to grow and in 1995 the government replaced it with a less generous, national insurance-based provision (Incapacity Benefit), which was also subject to more stringent tests of ability, or inability, to work. It was expected that this would lead to many disabled people being forced onto unemployment benefit (the Jobseekers' Allowance) or taking up employment, although the statistical evidence from the DSS during the early years of the new benefit suggested that this was not in fact the case.

The NCIP was a discriminatory benefit and was not paid to married women unless they could demonstrate they were unable to undertake household duties as well as being excluded from paid work. It was therefore in breach of EU directives on equal treatment, and in 1984 it was replaced by the Severe Disablement Allowance (SDA), which was available equally to both men and women. Both benefits were fixed at a very low level, initially equivalent to 60 per cent of the national insurance benefit level. As a consequence those who had no independent means of support also had to resort to means-tested state benefit, and this has been the case for a large number of disabled people for long periods of time.

In the 1970s benefits designed to provide a contribution towards the extra costs of disability were also introduced. The Attendance Allowance (AA) was intended as a contribution towards the additional costs incurred by those who needed someone to care for them during the day or the night, or both. The Mobility Allowance (MA) was intended as a contribution towards the cost of basic mobility for those unable or virtually unable to walk. Both benefits were flat rate and were paid in addition to any other income, but neither of them were very generous and were unlikely to meet the full costs of those with severe disabilities. They were also subject to stringent medical tests, which meant that many people with minor disabilities were excluded from receiving them.

In addition to this formal exclusion, ignorance of the availability of these benefits or fear of the process of medical and legal assessment meant that many of those who were probably entitled to such benefits did not take-up their entitlement. The OPCS survey discovered that only 9 per cent of disabled pensioners received the Attendance Allowance in 1985 (Martin and White, 1988, p. 22) and only 3 per cent received the Mobility Allowance (Martin *et al.*, 1988). Furthermore, 45 per cent of all adults with disabilities who were not receiving these benefits said that they had not heard of either of them (Martin and White, 1988).

Following a government review of these disability benefits (White Paper, 1990), some minor amendments were made to the existing benefits, and for those under pension age a new benefit, the Disability

Living Allowance (DLA), was introduced to replace the AA and MA. The DLA took up the 'care' and 'mobility' components of the AA and MA, but it also introduced a payment for less severely disabled people, at a lower rate, extending coverage to around 300 000 (see Hadjipateras, 1992). However the exclusion of those over pension age from this extended protection introduced a severe form of age discrimination into disability benefit provision, and in practice excluded the majority of disabled adults from the improved protection (McGlone, 1992). There is also evidence that the take-up problems associated with the AA and MA continued with the DLA (Hadjipateras and Howard, 1993).

Finally support for some of the extra costs associated with disability was also provided from the 1970s for claimants of means-tested Supplementary Benefit by additions to the basic rate covering special needs. Although these additions had to be specifically claimed, and thus in many cases were probably not taken up by potential beneficiaries, they could provide a significantly increased weekly income for the many people with disabilities who were dependent on the basic means-tested scheme. When the reformed Income Support scheme was introduced in 1988, however, these additional payments were abolished and replaced with flat-rate weekly premiums paid on top of the basic benefit to certain people with disabilities. Although these premiums were easier to claim, they were not as generous as many of the former additional payments and thus a large number of people with disabilities lost significant benefit entitlement as a result of the change.

Despite the development over the last two decades of a number of new benefits for people with disabilities therefore, social security protection has not prevented a large number of disabled from experiencing a life of poverty on benefits. Disability campaigners continue to call for further and more radical reform of disability benefits, in particular the provision of a comprehensive disability income for all disabled people (Disability Alliance, 1992). Extending benefit provision rather than providing real opportunities for employment and services at work and at home to permit people to provide for themselves may, however, operate to trap people in disability – and therefore perhaps poverty – rather than free them to participate fully in society. This problem (to which we shall return in the final section) does not just affect people with disabilities, it is also visited on those who remain at home to care for them and may find that they too are trapped in their role.

Poverty for Carers

Disability, as we have seen, is a wide-ranging concept covering a number of serious and not so serious physical or mental debilities. Taking the wider definition employed by the OPCS in the 1980s, many of those who may be classed as having a disability are quite able to look after themselves, to get about unaided and to work productively. Nevertheless there are a significant number of people whose disability means they need help in performing sometimes quite basic bodily tasks. In order to survive therefore they need, at least for some of the time, the care provided by another person. The dependency that frequently accompanies this can severely reduce the quality of life of disabled people – however it can also have deleterious consequences for those providing the care.

State care of people with disabilities is provided in residential institutions designed specifically for the purpose, and in severe cases this will mean a hospital bed. However very few people require such intensive care; and very few get it. The OPCS survey found that only 7 per cent of all adults with disabilities lived in residential institutions (Martin *et al.*, 1988). For the vast majority of people care is provided in the community, or more accurately in the private home where both carer and cared for usually live. Carers in the home are normally family members – spouses, daughters or sons – and more often than not they are women (see Parker, 1990; McLaughlin, 1992). In 1985 the General Household Survey (Green, 1988) revealed that a total of around six million adults were providing care in the home, of which 1.2 million were heavily involved in caring work. The OPCS survey identified around one million 'main carers' within a total of 3.9 million providing help at home.

For those heavily involved in caring work, their responsibilities generally mean that they have to withdraw from the labour market. Even those who are able to remain in employment, however, may find that their work is limited in terms of time, place, career opportunities and suchlike. The effect of this is that carers are less active in the labour market and generally have a lower income than the population at large (Baldwin and Parker, 1991; Glendinning, 1990). Thus caring for disability, as well as disability itself, is associated with a higher risk of poverty.

The risk of poverty for carers is obviously closely linked to the poverty associated with disability itself. In practice both are likely to live in the same household and experience the harsh consequences of reduced household income. In such situations the dependency of one party on the other is likely to accentuate the problems arising from reduced income. When the carer is working the person with the disability is likely to be the dependant party; but when the carer is not in paid employment it is often they who are dependent on the person for whom they are caring because the household income, probably social security benefits, is likely to be determined primarily by the extent and cause of the disability.

As Glendinning (1990) has discussed, the development of benefit support for carers has been based on criteria for entitlement that depend on the benefit status of the cared for person. This is particularly the case for the main carers' benefit, Invalid Care Allowance (ICA), which can only be received by those of working age who are not in paid employment and are caring for someone in receipt of AA or the care component of DLA. These conditions also apply for receipt of the carer's premium addition to IS, and for the home responsibility exemption from National Insurance contributions.

Like the other specialist benefits for people with disabilities, the ICA was introduced in the 1970s. Like the NCIP, it was not initially paid to married or cohabiting women providing the care and was only extended to them in 1986 – resulting in a sixfold increase in the number of claimants (McLaughlin, 1992). It too is fixed at just 60 per cent of the long-term insurance benefit rate. It is thus below the level of Income Support and therefore insufficient to provide an adequate income for those with no other means of support.

Despite the extension of entitlement in 1986, however, it is quite possible that many carers are not even receiving the meagre benefits of the ICA. For a start it is only payable to those under pension age, and yet a large number of people with disabilities, and their carers, are over pension age. Furthermore its dependence on receipt of the DLA means that the take-up problems associated with this benefit are transferred in addition to the ICA and they are likely to be compounded by ignorance among carers of potential entitlement, especially those trying to survive on low part-time wages. Conversely the requirement that recipients should not be in paid employment also constitutes something of a caring trap for those in receipt of the ICA who would like to enter or return to full-time work but could not afford to lose this benefit.

Whether in receipt of benefits or not therefore, carers' incomes, along with the incomes of those they care for, are likely to be low, resulting in a greater risk of poverty and deprivation. It is not only this type of financial deprivation that is associated with caring responsibilities however. There are other costs of caring. Leaving paid employment in order to care not only results in an immediate drop in income, it also results in the broader 'opportunity costs' of lost promotion prospects and occupational benefits (Joshi, 1992). Carers may also experience costs of caring that result from the extra expenditure needed on fuel, laundry or other consequences of sharing a household with a person with a disability (see Glendinning and Baldwin, 1988). In addition to this are the less quantifiable costs of the anxiety of care, worries over the provision of the correct medicines and ointments for instance, and the self-sacrifice that home-based caring work inevitably involves.

In general terms the quality of life enjoyed by someone engaged in significant caring responsibilities within the home is likely to be almost as constrained, and constraining, as that of the disabled person. The work is hard, monotonous and demanding. It leads to anxiety, distress and perhaps conflict; and yet it is also frequently bound up with dependency – both financial and emotional. Caring for adults with disabilities can also be profoundly unrewarding – unlike children they will not grow up and become independent, indeed their condition is more likely to deteriorate than to improve.

Reproducing Deprivation in Disability

As we have seen, both persons with disabilities and those who provide care and support for them are at greater risk of poverty and are more likely to experience the deprivation and exclusion associated with a reduced standard of living in our modern society than other people. For persons with disabilities and their carers this may be experienced as a 'dependency trap' – reinforced by exclusion from the labour market, reliance on inadequate benefits and the problem of struggling to cope with the additional costs of being disabled in an able-bodied world.

The problem of disability can thus become a problem of deprivation too. As with age-related poverty, however, there is danger of perceiving a false causal link here. Disabilities may restrict the capabilities of those who suffer from them and may even reduce their quality of life because of this; but they are not the cause of poverty. Deprivation and exclusion are socially created problems, and if they are disproportionately associated with the experience of disability, it is because the social reaction, or non-reaction, to disability has created this link. In the case of disability it is very much a case of non-reaction leading to problems for persons with disabilities. Modern industrial societies, and even modern welfare states, have largely been constructed on the basis that the people who inhabit them, who produce and reproduce them and benefit from them, are able-bodied. This is true of workplaces, public and private buildings, transport systems, information and communication networks, retail outlets – indeed almost all venues for social interaction. In some places attempts have been made to provide for or accommodate persons with some disabilities, but these are generally the exception rather than the rule.

What is more, benefit provision targeted to meet some of the additional costs of disabilities has not been able to overcome these failings in more general support for social participation by disabled people, because it has focused on the symptom rather than the cause of the problem. It is because of the failure to provide directly for the needs of persons with disabilities that these people experience additional costs, and benefits to meet these will always be inadequate substitutes for more general social and physical restructuring. This inadequacy is compounded by the low levels at which such cost-related benefits are set, and the inevitable problems of non-take-up associated with them. Furthermore, in extending the scope of dependency on the benefits system, such targeted benefits can do more in practice to accentuate the problems of poverty and deprivation than to prevent them.

As radical disability campaigners have pointed out therefore (see Oliver, 1990), most of the problems associated with disability are created, and recreated, by the failure of social and physical policy planning to recognise or take account of the practical needs experienced by people with disabilities. The poverty and dependency associated with disability is the consequence, both directly and indirectly, of the failure to respond directly to these basic needs, and the effect of this has been to prevent disabled people from providing for themselves within the broader social and economic structure.

Part IV

The Policy Framework

13

The Politics of Poverty

The Arithmetic Tradition

Poverty, as we saw in Chapter 1, is a political concept. Thus academic interest in defining and measuring poverty, and academic research into the extent of poverty, have always been closely related to attempts to utilise such academic work to influence policy development or reform. Moreover political debate on poverty and antipoverty policy has always been a contested and even a conflictual arena. Thus the problem of poverty has produced political activity, and this has been true for at least the last 150–200 years of industrial society in Britain and elsewhere. Indeed the political activity generated by the problem of poverty has been growing gradually, although with increasing rapidity, over the last century or two. It is also becoming more organised and more varied, and increasingly the debate has focused not just on whether to politicise poverty, or what poverty to politicise, but also on how to organise political activity and who should be involved in this. We shall look at these issues in a little more detail shortly.

The pioneers of modern poverty research at the end of the nineteenth century, Booth and Rowntree, engaged in quite detailed calculations of the extent and distribution of poverty in the expectation that their evidence of the existence of the problem would create pressure on the government to develop policies to remove it. In the early twentieth century this strategy of using empirical evidence to influence political opinion was developed into a more organised form of political pressure through the work of reformers such as Sydney and Beatrice Webb, who consciously set out to combine academic work with political activity. The Webbs were instrumental in the establishment of the Fabian Society, a political group committed to working for welfare reform through political influence, in particular on the emerging Labour Party. They were also involved in the founding of the London School of Economics (LSE), an academic institution with a focus on research and education in social and economic planning.

Through the work of the Webbs and the Fabian Society therefore, the link between academic debate and political activity became established within British institutional structures. Their aim was to use evidence of poverty and social deprivation to expose the failure of the capitalist economic system and to challenge the political domination of the classical liberal tradition of political thought and its emphasis on the non-involvement and non-responsibility of government in economic and social reform. The growth in power of the labour movement and the Labour Party, where Fabian influence was primarily directed, and the gradual expansion of research activity and the number of research workers, as a product of the educational influence of the LSE, extended this challenge both quantitatively, in terms of the empirical evidence produced, and qualitatively, in terms of its impact on political and especially government thinking. Commentators have come to refer to this development as the 'arithmetic tradition' (see Alcock, 1996a, ch. 1).

With the introduction of the welfare state reforms of the postwar period by the Labour government of the late 1940s, it appeared that this tradition had finally become the decisive influence on economic and social planning. Beveridge's proposals for insurance benefits to prevent poverty drew heavily on Rowntree's research into the nature and extent of poverty. It also appeared that these reforms were successful in removing poverty, as the Fabians had argued they would be. Further research by Rowntree (Rowntree and Lavers, 1951), carried out after the introduction of the welfare changes, suggested that the number of people in poverty was very small compared with the numbers cited in earlier studies.

This belief in the achievements of the postwar welfare reforms was challenged in the 1960s by the evidence that poverty still existed and had been 'rediscovered' in affluent Britain. The evidence of the continuation of poverty was the product of research carried out by Abel Smith and Townsend (1965) and other academics at the LSE. It was based on a reassessment of the definition of poverty and a revitalisation of the tradition of empirical research to measure its extent and provide pressure on government to respond to it. It was thus a continuation of the arithmetic tradition of the Fabian Society, albeit with a more sophisticated approach that was directed not so much at the politics of classical liberalism, but rather at the complacency of the postwar 'consensus' that welfare reforms could be, and indeed had been, successful in removing poverty (Alcock, 1996b).

The expectation of the postwar Fabians was that those governments and opposition parties that supported the role of welfare in industrial capitalist society would readily respond to evidence that welfare reforms had failed to eliminate poverty, and that they would be prepared to adjust or develop policies in order to achieve greater success. Initially this strategy appeared to be successful, at least in extracting from the Labour opposition of the early 1960s promises to introduce significant policy reforms if the party was returned to power.

Labour was returned to power in 1964, but the promised reforms never materialised in the form anticipated by the Fabians. Whether the failure to make significant changes was primarily the product of changed economic circumstances or merely lack of political will, will obviously remain a matter of debate. However it led the Fabian academics to continue their efforts to utilise further evidence of continuing poverty to maintain and extend the pressure for reform. This pressure included, as it had in the past, political influence as well as academic research, for instance from Labour cabinet minister Margaret Herbison, who resigned in protest when the promised welfare reforms were abandoned by the government in the mid 1960s. It also included pressure from newly formed campaigning organisations such as the CPAG, as we shall see below.

It was through the CPAG that the frustration of Abel Smith, Townsend and other Fabian academics increasingly came to be expressed, in particular through the publication in 1970 of a CPAG pamphlet entitled *Poverty and the Labour Government*, which produced evidence that the 'poor had got poorer' under Labour. This was a more outspoken criticism of Labour politics than any previously levelled by the Fabians, who had generally regarded Labour as an ally in securing welfare reforms. It was received with hostility in some government circles, and was even blamed by some for contributing to the party's election defeat in 1970.

Following the fall from power of the Labour government the Fabian Society published a critical review of its achievements in the social policy field, edited by Townsend and Bosanquet (1972). The book was written in the spirit of informed academic criticism, but clearly underlying it was frustration at the perceived limitations of Labour's record on social policy reform. Similar frustration was felt by many after the end of the Labour administration of 1974–9, and a similar critique was published (Bosanquet and Townsend, 1980).

The assumption underlying both critiques, and indeed underlying the whole arithmetic tradition of Fabian political influence, was a belief that governments of welfare states should utilise the machinery of the state to resolve, or at least relieve, social problems such as poverty – in other words that there should be political consensus on the role of the state in the prevention of poverty. This was linked to a constitutionalist assumption about the desirability and viability of a strategy based on exerting pressure on parliament and government departments to persuade them of the need for reform. In the 1980s both these assumptions came openly into question.

The Thatcher governments of the 1980s were openly critical of the postwar consensus of the role of the state in welfare reform, and in particular of the dangers of continual pressure for extensions of social policy at the expense of support for the private market and the capitalist economy. They challenged the idea that welfare reforms would benefit poorer people, and argued that seeking support for extensions of state expenditure, ostensibly in order to achieve further welfare benefits, was merely an attempt to 'buy votes' (see Green, 1990). In his famous speech on poverty in 1989 the secretary of state for social services, John Moore, openly attacked the claim that there was still a large number of poor people in Britain. He rejected the relative notion of poverty utilised by Fabian academics and criticised them for their attempts to discredit the achievements of British economic development.

In addition to the changed attitude of government ministers in the 1980s there was also a change in the climate of political influence on government. The evidence and arguments of Fabian academics and antipoverty organisations such as the CPAG were challenged by academics and organisations seeking to use the same channels of academic debate and political argument to press the case for quite different policy priorities and policy changes. These organisations were arguing for a reduction in state welfare and a return to the classical liberal politics of which the old Fabians had been so critical. Although these were not new arguments, they attracted for their protagonists the label of the 'new right' (see Levitas, 1986). New right organisations included the Institute of Economic Affairs (IEA), founded in 1957 but revitalised in the 1980s, the Centre for Policy Studies, established by Keith Joseph and Margaret Thatcher, and the Adam Smith Institute (ASI), which produced a range of proposals for the radical reform of social security provision (ASI, 1984, 1989).

Faced with such a challenge from the right and with a largely unsympathetic and unyielding government, adherents to the Fabian arithmetic tradition experienced a significant setback in the 1980s in their strategy to prevent poverty. Their arguments were challenged and their influence severely reduced. As a result of this the politics of poverty in Britain underwent a major transformation during this period. No longer was it possible to assume that poverty and deprivation were problems recognisable by all in British society, and that the government was under an obligation to respond to evidence that such problems continued to exist in the midst of growing affluence.

Right-wing proponents inside and outside government argued that such evidence was bogus, and that state obligations extended only to the relief of proven destitution through targeted (means-tested) state benefits fixed at basic minimum levels, whereas left-wing critics continued to claim that poverty had to be understood as a problem of deprivation and inequality, and that only state intervention to redistribute resources across society would be able to alleviate this. In other words the debate was no longer about what *could* be done, but rather what *should* be done, and in this climate detailed empirical research was not such an important factor in the argument.

Thus by the end of the 1980s the arithmetic tradition, which had dominated the politics of poverty throughout most of the earlier part of the twentieth century, was under challenge within a changed political climate. However this did not lead to the abandonment of the Fabian strategy. Academic research into the definition and extent of poverty continued, and in the early 1990s was given new impetus by the work of the researchers on the Rowntree Inquiry into Income and Wealth (Barclay 1995; Hills, 1995). The work of EU researchers and commentators also began to have an increasing influence on political debate in Britain, in particular debate on the new problems of social exclusion and social polarisation (Room, 1995), and political debate on antipoverty policy was inspired by the work of the Commission on Social Justice (Borrie, 1994). In the late 1990s the politics of poverty thus remains an important element of academic and political debate, and a continued focus for political campaigning.

The Poverty Lobby

Central to the Fabian strategy of utilising academic argument and academic research to secure change and development in government policy was an attempt to foster close and influential relationships with government ministers and departments; and particularly during the periods of Labour government in the 1960s and 1970s this was a relatively successful strategy. In the 1960s and 1970s Abel Smith was an adviser to the secretary of state for social services, and Piachaud was a member of the prime minister's political unit. During this time Donnison was appointed as chair of the Supplementary Benefits Commission. Prominent Fabians also entered parliament directly as elected members, most notably the entry in 1979 of Frank Field – previously director of the CPAG and later chair of the House of Commons Select Committee on Social Security.

However gaining direct political influence by entering the corridors and committee rooms of power has been supplemented in the politics of poverty by the indirect pressure exerted by campaigning activity outside the exclusive worlds of Westminster and Whitehall. Indeed throughout the twentieth century, in addition to the research and formal political influence of the arithmetic tradition, academics have combined with political activists and members of various organisations representing different special interests and demands to establish independent groups to campaign for a range of policy changes. Such groups have sometimes been referred to by political scientists as pressure groups.

An early example of such pressure group activity was the 1917 Committee, later renamed the Family Endowment Committee, which was established by Eleanor Rathbone and others to campaign for the introduction of family allowances to reduce poverty among families and children (Macnicol, 1980). The committee was wound up in the 1940s after its eventual success in persuading the government to institute a family allowance scheme, although the scheme was not quite in the form the campaigners had wanted, nor was it entirely the product of their campaigning efforts.

After the 'rediscovery of poverty' in the 1960s, however, and the revitalisation of the arithmetic tradition, Fabian academics began to look again at the possibility of establishing independent campaigning organisations to carry the message of reform outside the narrow confines of academic debate and political influence. Their aim was to establish vehicles outside government and the civil service, and outside academic institutions, to voice opinions on the need for reform and policy development that were informed by academic argument and research, but not limited by the need to appease narrow political interests. This, it was hoped, would get poverty, and the need for antipoverty policy, onto the political agenda and provide a voice for proposing policy reforms that were not necessarily currently accepted within government or opposition political circles.

Abel Smith and Townsend, the authors of the influential book on the persistence of poverty in affluent Britain (1965), were involved in the establishment of a group to campaign for improved support for poor families and children. The group was initially called the Family Poverty Group, but was shortly renamed the Child Poverty Action Group (CPAG) (McCarthy, 1986). From these modest but influential roots the CPAG grew fairly rapidly into a well-informed, well-respected campaigning organisation. It had active and effective leaders in Tony Lynes and his successor Frank Field and was successful both in attracting the recognition of politicians and civil servants and in helping to put the problem of poverty onto the political agenda (see Whiteley and Winyard, 1983). By 1981 MacGregor (pp. 141–2) was writing that the CPAG had become 'part of the fabric of British politics'.

Getting poverty onto the political agenda was just one of the aims of the CPAG however, and arguably not the most important one. They were also concerned to bring about genuine policy change to reduce or remove poverty, especially among children and families. This of course was a more difficult task, especially after the mid 1960s when the increasing pressure of economic recession gave governments little room, they claimed, to increase welfare provision. Nevertheless some important policy changes were introduced, especially during the 1970s, for which the CPAG could claim a fair measure of indirect responsibility. In particular these included the ending of the wage-stop (a means of restricting the benefit entitlement of some unemployed claimants) and the introduction of Child Benefit. The latter was a hard-fought battle indeed, in which cabinet leaks and trade union influence were orchestrated by the CPAG to maintain the pressure for reform on a government that was seriously considering abandoning its promises to implement the scheme (Field, 1982).

The CPAG is perhaps the most important and most widely respected (Whiteley and Winyard, 1983, p. 18) group campaigning for reform in the poverty field. But it is not the only group – there are many others representing different special interests or promoting various policy reforms. These include Age Concern, the Disablement Income Group (DIG), the National Council for One Parent Families (NCOPF), the Low Pay Unit (LPU) and Shelter, which campaigns against homelessness. In their discussion of these campaign groups Whiteley and Winyard distinguish between *promotional* groups, comprising professionals or volunteers campaigning for reform on behalf of others, and *representational* groups, representatives of those experiencing poverty or deprivation who are campaigning to improve provision for all those like them. They point out that both forms of organisation can be found campaigning in the poverty field and that both have their advantages and their disadvantages in the political arena. As a whole, however, by the 1970s these groups had begun to develop a collective identity forged out of their shared concern for policy reform and had come to be called the 'poverty lobby'.

The poverty lobby did not just share a common concern for certain policy reforms however. When their concerns were sufficiently close, various organisations combined to form joint campaigning organisations to publicise particular shared interests or press for particular policy reforms. Such 'umbrella' organisations included the Child Benefit Now campaign of the 1970s and the Social Security Consortium of the 1980s. In the mid 1980s, when the government's review of social security threatened to lead to restructuring and reductions in benefit provision, poverty lobby organisations also combined with trade unions representing employees in the Department of Social Security (described by Whiteley and Winyard, 1983, as 'producer' groups) in an organisation called Action for Benefits to campaign against what they regarded as undesirable benefit reforms.

The campaigning work of the poverty lobby groups includes a wide range of activities aimed at securing maximum publicity and maximum influence for the groups' ideas. The CPAG, for instance, conducts its own research and publishes this together with other research findings in a series of high-profile policy texts (Becker, 1991; Oppenheim 1994; Harker, 1996). The group also regularly submits evidence and memoranda directly to government departments and ministers, organises meetings and conferences to discuss and publicise proposals at both national and local level, and attempts to utilise the established media – the press, radio and television – to present ideas to a wider audience.

The power of public expression through the media has become of increasing importance to all political campaigners in the latter half of the twentieth century. The media operate both to publicise ideas and to shape them, and their influence in defining the problem and the politics of poverty cannot be ignored. Poverty lobby organisations therefore regularly provide press releases to publicise their work and respond to requests for interviews on radio or television. However journalists and broadcasters can themselves initiate influential political debate by reporting evidence of deprivation or even using the problem of poverty as a theme in fictional dramas. Throughout the 1960s and 1970s the magazine *New Society* was an important forum for evidence from poverty research. During the same period there were a few highly influential television dramas focusing on the problems of poverty in Britain, notably 'Cathy Come Home' and 'The Spongers'; and in the 1980s and 1990s the televised presentation of important new research on poverty by London Weekend Television in the 'Breadline Britain' programmes took sophisticated arguments on the definition and measurement of poverty to a potentially mass audience.

In their assessment of the influence and achievements of the poverty lobby, Whiteley and Winyard (1983) point out that the success of campaigning work depends on a number of factors, not all of which are within the control of campaigning groups. They highlight in particular the political environment within which they are operating, the strategies they choose to promote their ideas and the resources they have to support their work. These influences vary from group to group and over time. The resources supporting the CPAG have enabled it to survive as an influential campaign group for over thirty years, and its broadly based strategies have permitted it to maintain pressure for reform across a range of fronts. However the changed political climate of the 1980s restricted the influence of the CPAG, as it did the influence of the Fabian academics, who have always worked so closely with it.

Despite this hostile climate however, the poverty lobby has continued to grow and develop, incorporating an increasingly wide range of specialist groups and umbrella organisations. Most however are mainly composed of professional campaigners employed to carry out the campaigning aims of the various groups. They are campaigners *for* the poor rather than campaigners *from* the poor. The politics of poverty also includes the political activities of those who are poor themselves, and it is to this issue that we shall now turn.

Campaigning by the Poor

Having made a distinction between promotional and representational groups, Whiteley and Winyard (1983) conclude that most organisations within the poverty lobby are promotional. That is, they are neither composed of nor representative of poor people or benefit claimants. The major poverty campaign group, the CPAG, is a promotional organisation: its National Executive Committee is primarily composed of professionals elected at the open Annual General Meeting, and the daily work of the organisation is carried out by full-time salaried workers.

However the CPAG also has a structure of local branches that meet regularly in cities and towns up and down the country. They also get together annually to elect branch representatives to the national executive. Many of these local branches do include claimants and other poor people, which in the 1990s would include higher-education students, who are often active participants in local campaigning work. The involvement of such people in the broader activities of the CPAG has posed the question for this organisation of how far such people should be involved and encouraged in policy development within the group. It also raises the more general question of whether the poverty lobby should not be more actively representative of poor people themselves.

This issue of campaigning *by* the poor, as opposed to *for* the poor, is an important one in any discussion of the politics of poverty, and it has been a controversial one in some debates among concerned parties – both poor and not poor. One influential protagonist of the case for prioritising campaigning by the poor in the promotion of antipoverty policies has been Holman, one-time professor of social policy, author of an earlier textbook on poverty (Holman, 1978) and later community worker on a large housing estate in Easterhouse Glasgow. In numerous articles in publications such as the *Guardian* newspaper Holman has argued that poverty campaigning should concentrate on 'letting the poor speak'. His argument is that only those who experience poverty can know what it is like, and tell it like it is; and therefore that their testimony is both the most authentic and the most effective evidence of the problems that need to be addressed. Furthermore if poverty campaigning is seeking to promote the cause of policy reform to address such problems, then the nature of the reforms promoted should be determined not by academics and politicians, even though they may be sympathetic to the poor, but by those who know through experience what they need.

In fact the issue of campaigns by rather than for the poor is not a new one. In the nineteenth century the government and reformers alike feared the collective action of the disaffected 'residuum' (see Stedman Jones, 1971). In the twentieth century, between the wars unemployed claimants organised themselves into the National Unemployed Workers' Movement and sought to join or to cooperate with the trade unions representing employed workers in the TUC. There was much tension and distrust in this liaison, although it produced some important and influential campaigning activity, most notably the 'hunger marches' and the Jarrow crusade (see Vincent, 1991, pp. 56ff).

In the 1970s and 1980s unemployed claimants again established membership organisations, now called 'claimants' unions', which attempted to develop political links with other labour organisations and poverty lobby groups and were coordinated for a time by an umbrella organisation called the National Federation of Claimants Unions. The great strengths of the claimants' unions – their basis in the spontaneous collective spirit of the unemployed and a membership made up exclusively of benefit claimants – were also their major weaknesses however, at least in organisational terms. Active membership was difficult to sustain over long periods of time and in the face of little prospect of significant improvement in the circumstances of most unemployed people – unless they became employed, at which point they would become ineligible for membership. Individual claimants' unions were usually temporary phenomena therefore, and the national umbrella organisation was unable to maintain a permanent profile in the political arena.

What the organisational difficulties experienced by the claimants' unions reveal are the genuine problems involved in sustained and coordinated campaigning by poor people. For a variety of reasons related both to the financial deprivation with which they must constantly struggle and to the social isolation that frequently results from this, poor people do not find it easy to engage in organised political activity, and organised political groups have not found it easy to involve poor people. Some of these problems were discussed at a forum on 'Working Together Against Poverty' in York in 1990 (Lister and Beresford, 1991) at which academics and professional poverty campaigners met with representatives of poor people. Financial hardship, limited knowledge, the experience of stigma and lack of energy and confidence were all identified as factors inhibiting poor people from involvement in campaigning activity. As one participant at the forum put it, 'We may not feel we've got much energy left for anything else. We don't want to speak out when we are unsure of a good response' (ibid., p. 7).

Ward (1986) has discussed more generally the debilitating consequences of poverty and deprivation have on participation in political activity. These include the direct costs of participation, such as membership fees, transport, socialising and keeping up to date, and the indirect consequences of poor health, poor environment and lack of time, which inhibit involvement in any organised, active pursuits.

Perhaps most important of all, however, are the political contradictions at the heart of poverty campaigning by the poor. As already discussed, poverty is a political concept. As such it is a problem, an undesirable state of affairs about which something should be done but is not being done. To identify oneself as poor, therefore, is to identify oneself as having a problem and being in need of help. This is a negative categorisation, which poor people desperately trying to survive, perhaps with dignity, in a hostile world may not willingly and openly wish to adopt. As another participant at the York forum put it, 'Nobody wants to be poor. It's not something we want everyone to know. Some people don't want to tell others they are poor or even admit it to themselves' (Lister and Beresford, 1991, p. 10).

In this context it is easy to see how the experience of poverty and the exclusion of the poor act to reproduce each other in a kind of vicious circle. However this is neither a reason for the denial of a place for the poor in campaigning against poverty nor an excuse for not continuing with efforts to find ways in which their concerns and experiences might be harnessed into political activity. Beresford and Lister are continuing to seek to develop opportunities for poverty research and poverty debate to incorporate more directly the views and participation of poor people themselves (Lister *et al.*, 1996).

Important though the issue of the involvement of poor people in political campaigning is, however, there is a problem with any implicit assumption that only poor people can act as advocates of the cause of antipoverty. Clearly poverty and the experience of deprivation is an issue for poor people, but it is *not* only an issue for poor people. As we have seen in Chapter 1, there are problems in adopting a purely subjective definition of poverty, that is, identifying poverty only with the experiences and perceptions of those who are poor. Poverty campaigning that is limited to the experiences and initiatives of poor people runs the risk of being similarly self-defeating, for the reasons just discussed.

Identifying the politics of poverty only with the politics of the poor also ignores the fact that poverty is also a problem for others in society too – both in particular, in terms of self-interest because those not poor now may become poor in the future, and in general because the existence of poverty in society may be unacceptable to those who wish to be part of a social order in which others do not suffer deprivation and exclusion. This issue has become much clearer and starker with the increasing availability of evidence of the social polarisation of British society in the 1990s.

Indeed it is to a shared belief in greater social justice that poverty campaigners must appeal if they are to secure support for policy changes to remove poverty; and this cannot be achieved if poverty is perceived and presented as a problem only for the poor. Thus the involvement of poor people in campaigning against poverty can be a supplement to the more general activities of academics, politicians and professionals – but it cannot be a substitute for them.

14

Social Security Policy

The Principles of Social Security

Defining and identifying of poverty in advanced industrial societies involves an implicit argument that state policy should be developed to remove poverty or prevent it from occurring. The politics of poverty, therefore, is effectively the politics of antipoverty policy; and just as the politics of poverty can be traced back to the development of industrial society, so too can antipoverty policy. What such a historical review reveals is that throughout this period the major focus of antipoverty policy in Britain and all other industrial societies has been social security policy.

The idea behind social security policy is the use of support, collected in the form of contributions or taxes from those in employment, to provide an income for those who cannot secure an adequate income for themselves and thus are at risk of poverty. Social security is therefore a form of redistribution of resources from those who have more than sufficient to provide for themselves to those who do not have enough. By and large this redistribution has been organised by state, but state benefits have always been accompanied (for some) by separate private protection. The resources redistributed are generally cash, in the form of taxes and benefits, but they can and sometimes do include support in kind, for instance the provision of free school meals to the children of poor parents.

The aim of social security payments therefore is to combat poverty, and as a result it could perhaps be assumed that the amount of benefit provided should be sufficient to prevent benefit claimants from experiencing poverty. However social security benefits have not always operated as such a simple poverty prevention measure. The fixing of benefit levels has in practice been subject to a number of factors other than the determination of a national minimum income (see Atkinson, 1990a).

For a start there has been concern to ensure that benefit levels can be afforded in redistributional terms from the taxes that must pay for them, and to ensure that state benefit levels do not interfere with the setting of wage levels in the labour market. For some, therefore, benefit support may provide only a contribution towards an income that is sufficient to prevent the experience of poverty. For others, however, social security protection may provide more income than is needed merely to prevent poverty. This is because some benefits have been designed to provide an income in retirement or unemployment that is linked to the income received whilst in paid work. Such 'earnings-related' benefits are a common feature of private social security protection and are incorporated into the state scheme in Britain for some pensioners through SERPS; they are also frequently found in social insurance protection in other European countries. The assumption that benefit levels represent an income sufficient to prevent poverty is therefore an oversimplistic one – some benefits do not provide enough to keep some claimants out of poverty and others aim to secure incomes much higher than any basic minimum poverty line.

The fixing of benefit levels has also resulted in conflict and confusion in debates by academics and politicians on the definition and measurement of poverty. As we have seen there is much disagreement about how to define poverty and how to express this in terms of a weekly income. The state benefit level, in particular the level of assistance benefits, is therefore sometimes taken as a proxy definition or measure of poverty approved by the government. Yet this provides a logical contradiction with the role of such benefits in preventing poverty, and as government spokespersons have sometimes pointed out, it could result in an increase in antipoverty measures, such as raising of the benefit level, leading to an apparent *increase* in the number in poverty.

Overall therefore, although the central aim of social security policy remains the redistribution of resources to tackle the problem of poverty, there is no guarantee that there will be consistency or agreement on how such support should be provided – or whether in practice it will be effective. Inconsistency and disagreement here has focused in particular on whether the aim of social security should be to *prevent* poverty, through the provision of an income sufficient to lift recipients above the poverty level, or merely to *relieve* poverty, through the provision of a contribution towards those falling below a defined poverty level. As we shall see, British social security has at different times fluctuated between the pursuit of these two differing aims, at some times appearing to pursue both simultaneously. Another major disagreement concerns the issue of horizontal versus vertical redistribution in social security.

- *Horizontal* redistribution is primarily concerned to tackle the life-cycle poverty identified by Rowntree through the provision of benefits to people during periods of need, such as retirement, financed by contributions collected from them at times of relative sufficiency, such as employment. Within such a scheme all are potential contributors and potential beneficiaries, and resources are redistributed within society across people at different stages of the life cycle.
- *Vertical* redistribution operates according to quite different principles. Here the concern is to redirect resources from those with sufficient to those in need without any expectation of a link between payment and receipt. With such a scheme those in need may never even be in a position to contribute and may require support at any time – and for long periods of time. What is more those who pay may not expect to benefit from their contributions.

Once again these different structures have at different times been incorporated into British social security provision and for long periods of time have apparently operated in tandem.

In addition to the disagreements over the aims of social security as a means of poverty prevention or poverty relief, or as means of redistributing resources or protecting income, some commentators have called into question the extent to which social security really is an antipoverty policy in modern industrial societies. Novak (1984, 1988) and Squires (1990) have argued that, rather than seeking to relieve or prevent poverty, the primary aim of social security policy has been to contain it, or even to reinforce it. This is because the payment of social security benefit is intended to support labour market discipline. Thus it is linked to stringent conditions requiring claimants to seek any form of paid work, and it carries a heavy stigma of dependency and inadequacy. As a result the administration of benefits is punitive and controlling, and is intended to reinforce the view that those relying on social security are the undeserving poor – as exemplified by the Poor Law notion of 'less-eligibility'.

Those who see in social security such a policy of containment and control, however, often overlook the genuine achievements that social security provisions have made in supporting the most vulnerable people in industrial societies and in redistributing resources within an unequal labour market. Whatever its limitations, social security does act as a form of redistribution and a means of preventing poverty. However at the same time those who recognise its achievements in this respect can also overlook its constraints and controls. Within a labour market economy social security policy does operate to reinforce labour market discipline and to control the poor. Social security is not just redistribution *or* control – it is *both*.

As an antipoverty policy therefore, social security in Britain is more complex and contradictory than one might expect. It is the product of conflicting aims and structures, and within these policies and priorities have shifted over time. Of course this is because social security policy has been created through political process, not scientific analysis. Changes in political power have resulted in changes in social security policy. Such changes have ebbed and flowed over time, and generally without the products of previous policies being abandoned or overhauled. Like all social phenomena social security policy is a product of history, not logic, and its aims and achievements must be assessed within that historical context.

The Development of State Support

Social security policy in modern British society can be traced back to the early seventeenth century and the introduction of the Poor Law in 1601, as we saw in Chapter 1. The Poor Law was a form of locally administered poverty relief providing support, plus discipline, to vagrants and beggars. It was initially a loosely structured system operating within a rural agrarian economy. With the growth of industrialisation it came under increasing pressure, and the 1834 reforms resulted in tighter national control over Poor Law provision and the introduction of clearer elements of labour market discipline.

The most significant element of this discipline was the principle of 'less eligibility' – the requirement that any support provided by the state must be set below the circumstances of the lowest wage labourer in order to ensure that dependence on state support remained undesirable. Linked to this was the assumption of family support – husbands, wives, parents and children were expected to provide mutual support during times of need to obviate the need to turn to the state. These restrictions on entitlement to state support were reinforced by the 'workhouse test', the grim and rigorous residential regime to which only those with no other potential source of support would subject themselves. Life in the workhouse was unpleasant – and it was intended to be. It also attracted fear and stigma. These elements of control were a central feature of early social security provision and, albeit in a less stringent form, they have remained at the centre of social security policy ever since.

Not surprisingly therefore the Poor Law was not a popular form of state support among the rapidly growing nineteenth-century working class. In practice it was also unable to provide support for all those who were unable to provide adequately for themselves, and in many areas workhouse provision was supplemented by direct provision of outdoor relief, despite the fact that this was intended to end after 1834. For more established workers, however, even this form of relief was undesirable, or largely unnecessary, and the latter half of the century saw the development of a range of private and voluntary schemes to provide income protection for such workers in times of labour market failure.

Most of these schemes were run by friendly societies or trade unions established within the working class. In return for contributions made during periods of employment they provided income support in times of sickness or in old age (see Thane, 1982, pp. 28–32). They often based the payment level on past contribution records, thus establishing the broader aim of income protection through benefit protection. Schemes such as these were limited in scope, however, and they were generally confined to particular industries or sections of workers. For the majority of workers, especially low-paid ones, there was no such protection.

By the end of the century additional support was being provided for some of the increasing number of poor workers and their families by a range of charitable ventures organised and controlled on a voluntary basis by concerned members of the middle class under the general auspices of an umbrella organisation called the Charity Organisation Society. Although partly motivated by concern for the deprivation experienced by Britain's new urban poor, charitable support was also linked to concern for the morality of the poor and their attitude to life and labour. Support was thus often accompanied by individual advice and moral pressure to conform to particular middle-class models of respectable family life.

By the end of the nineteenth century, therefore, state support through the Poor Law was operating alongside privately organised self-help and voluntary charitable aid to poor people. Provision of both was patchy however, and as the research of Booth and Rowntree graphically revealed it had not removed or prevented poverty. Moreover this revelation was accompanied by the growing political and economic strength of the organised working class, and by a fear of unrest from the less organised poor. There was thus increasing pressure on the government to do more to extend and co-ordinate state support.

By that time, too, Bismarck had introduced social reforms in Germany, where work-based insurance protection had been set-up on a national basis, coordinated and administered by the state, with the intention of relieving working-class pressure. The existance of this example and the privately organised insurance of the British friendly societies combined in the early twentieth century to create the precedents for the introduction of state-based insurance in Britain, although the first of such schemes – the old age pension, introduced in 1908 – was not in fact a contributory insurance benefit. In 1911, however, insurance-based benefits for sickness and unemployment based loosely on the Bismarck model were introduced into some industries, where benefits were paid during temporary absence from the labour market in return for contributions made whilst in work.

The intention was that this state insurance support would be actuarially sound and self-financing – there was thus, for instance, a lower rate of benefit for women, who were assumed to be a greater insurance risk. After the First World War the scheme was extended to include pensions and a wider range of workers and potential beneficiaries, but as unemployment rose dramatically during the depression of the 1920s and 1930s this became more difficult to sustain. There was pressure on the government to restrict entitlement and cut benefits, leading eventually to the defeat of the then Labour government. Restricted entitlement and increasing unemployment also meant that a growing number of poor people were forced to continue to rely on the inadequate and unpopular Poor Law.

Despite the critical recommendations of both the Majority and Minority Reports of the Royal Commission on the Poor Law of 1909 (see Thane, 1982, pp. 88–91), no significant changes had been made to the nineteenth-century scheme. It remained in local control and thus subject to local variation. Sometimes this led to relatively generous support, as in the controversial case of the Poor Law Guardians in the London Borough of Poplar (see Hill, 1990, p. 23), but in general provision was meagre. In part because of the controversy over local variation, the Poor Law was converted into the new means-tested Unemployment Assistance scheme in 1934, and later this was in turn converted into the National Assistance scheme.

Even after these changes, at the beginning of the Second World War social security provision in Britain was a confused mixture of partial insurance schemes and means-tested assistance, with the remnants of the Poor Law underlying the twentieth-century developments. There was need for a radical structural review, and eventually this was provided in the Report on Social Insurance and Allied Services by Sir William Beveridge. Beveridge's report was the first thorough review of state support and the role of social security in the alleviation or prevention of poverty, and although it was commissioned by the government, it was in practice largely his own work (Harris, 1977). It also became an international best-seller when it was released in 1942.

Beveridge's report was based on the general argument that state intervention was needed to tackle the major social problems of British society, and it contained what was in effect a blueprint for the reform of the social security system around the principle that he called 'social insurance'. In essence this involved a full state 'takeover' of the various insurance schemes developed earlier in the century, some aspects of which had remained under the administration of the friendly societies, and the extension of social insurance to provide a comprehensive cover for all circumstances of need arising from non-participation in the labour market (Silburn, 1995). It was a radical proposal, although its aim was to build on the successes of past policy development; and it was very much a product of its time and of Beveridge's own views about the role of social security protection (see Baldwin and Falkingham, 1994; Hills *et al.*, 1994).

The intention of the Beveridge plan was that nearly full employment, sustained by government policy, would provide support based on the labour market for most breadwinners. Their contributions into the scheme during employment could then be used to provide for the payment of benefits during times of sickness, retirement or temporary unemployment. As we saw in Chapter 9, however, Beveridge's plan was based on clear assumptions about family structure and gender roles. Married women, who had duties other than employment, were expected to receive support through their husbands' wages or benefits, and thus even when they were in employment they would be excluded from full participation in the insurance scheme (Lister, 1994).

Beveridge's aim was that through its link to the labour market and family structure the social insurance scheme would provide comprehensive protection for all. This link was central – social insurance was based on support for the labour market, not on some attempt to nationalise private self-protection (Atkinson, 1992). There was thus the potential problem of some poor people being excluded from both the labour market and the social insurance scheme, and for them Beveridge recommended the retention of a means-tested national assistance scheme, although he expected that this would have a declining, safety-net role.

After the end of the Second World War the Labour government introduced most of the changes recommended in the Beveridge plan and completely reformed benefit provision – although the scheme was retitled National Insurance (NI) and some adjustments were made to the benefit rates proposed by Beveridge. In order to avoid a situation in which currently retiring pensioners would be excluded from protection because they had not contributed to the scheme, all pensioners were automatically entitled to the new NI pension. This meant that current contributions had to be used to fund these benefits, rather than being invested to meet future benefit liabilities in the way a strict insurance scheme would operate. Thus from the outset the NI scheme was administered on a 'pay-as-you-go' basis, with the current benefit demand being met from current contribution payments. As we shall see, this created problems for the long-term viability of the social insurance plan.

Nevertheless the basic structures of the Beveridge plan have dominated postwar British social security provision. There have been reforms within the structure, and in effect a departure from Beveridge's vision of comprehensive insurance protection; but the broad labour-market insurance principle, supplemented by a means-tested safety net, are still the bases of entitlement to most social security benefits – and the main means of alleviating or preventing poverty. In practice, however, the comprehensiveness of the insurance scheme has never been realised, and the role of means-tested protection has risen to become the principle feature of state support in the 1990s (Alcock, 1996b) – an issue to which we shall return shortly.

Social Insurance

The Beveridge social insurance plan was in part based on the Bismarckian tradition of social reform to support existing social structures. Insurance protection has thus always been closely tied to support for labour market participation and has operated to provide support only in times of labour-market failure (Baldwin and Falkingham, 1994). Beveridge's report was also heavily influenced by Rowntree's research on poverty and in particular his notion of life-cycle poverty within families. If protection could be provided in such periods of high risk of poverty therefore, social security could operate not just to alleviate poverty, as had been the aim of the nineteenth-century Poor Law, but to prevent it.

Thus the aim of the social insurance scheme was to utilise contributions made through participation in the labour market to build an entitlement to benefit support in times of need. Social security would therefore provide for the horizontal distribution of resources through the state over the life cycle of its citizens, or rather its workers. This would operate on a collective basis in the NI scheme, but it would be based on individual contributions and individual entitlement. Indeed it was this individual investment in social security that Beveridge felt was its great popular appeal: 'The capacity and desire of British people to contribute for security are among the most certain and impressive social facts of today' (Beveridge, 1942, p. 119).

Despite the appeal of self-protection through contribution, however, the British NI scheme has never operated as a strict form of individual insurance protection. As stated above, in order to prevent existing pensioners from being excluded, since the start of the scheme contributions have been used to fund benefit payments on a pay-as-you-go basis. Thus although all individual contributions, together with a supplement from general taxation, are paid into a separate NI fund to meet benefit expenditure, and to make a small contribution towards the funding of the National Health Service, the resources in the fund are expended each year on current benefit payments, leaving future contributors to fund future benefit entitlement.

This may in practice, and in principle, be a reasonable way of financing benefit expenditure, in effect utilising NI contributions as a form of hypothecated tax for social security. However it is not what is generally understood as an insurance scheme and it does not mean that each individual's contributions will be available in the future in the form of guaranteed benefit entitlement, as many contributors may believe to be the case. Thus those who contribute to NI in the expectation that they are making an investment in their future protection have been seriously misled, although since the payment of contributions by employees and employers is compulsory the consequences of this deceit may not be so significant.

However, although NI contributions are not invested to meet future benefit payments, there is nevertheless a link within the scheme between individual contribution and benefit entitlement. In order to sustain the fiction that benefits are paid in return for contributions, and to limit the number of potential claimants on the NI fund, all NI benefits are subject to contribution tests that restrict entitlement to those who have paid the requisite number of contributions during the requisite period of employment. In practice these tests are complex and extremely difficult to understand and administer, the best summary being provided in the annual CPAG guide to non-means-tested benefits. They do include special rules for contributions to be credited during periods of unemployment and for people caring for dependent children or adults to be made exempt from some of the contribution conditions, but in general the contribution rules make entitlement to NI benefits conditional on payment into the fund during long periods of labour-market participation. They thus retain the logic of the labour-market support discussed by Atkinson (1992) and exclude from NI protection those who have not been able to maintain their contributions through paid employment (see Alcock, 1996c).

Consequently NI entitlement is exclusive to those who have not been able to contribute to it, significantly undermining the comprehensiveness of the scheme. In addition, as we have seen, this exclusion is not borne equally by all social groups because of inequalities in access to the labour market. Thus many black people, people with disabilities, the young unemployed and (because entitlement to NI protection during unemployment under the Jobseekers' Allowance is restricted to six months only) the long-term unemployed are all effectively excluded. As the unemployment level has generally grown in the latter decades of the twentieth century the size of these excluded groups has increased, and the comprehensive appeal of NI has further declined.

Beveridge's insurance plan was also based on a particular family structure in which married women were dependent on their husbands' support through wages or benefits. They were thus excluded from entitlement to benefits in their own right. This exclusion was removed by a later reform of the scheme, and single or married women in employment are now required to contribute, and are entitled to benefits in the same way as men. However for those married women who were not contributing fully prior to the reform the exclusion continues. Furthermore the formal introduction of equal treatment into the NI scheme has not prevented the unequal treatment of many other women, because their general exclusion from the labour market and concentration in low-paid jobs that fall below the threshold at which contributions are required, mean that many do not meet the conditions for entitlement to benefits (Lister, 1994).

Beveridge's recommendation, which was incorporated into the original NI scheme, was that flat-rate benefits would be paid in return for flat-rate contributions. All would be treated equally within the state scheme, and those who wanted additional protection could seek it separately through private insurance. He saw no contradiction between the principle of state protection for all and private protection for some, and in effect a partnership between the state and the private or occupational sector has developed over the past fifty years, in particular over the provision of additional pension protection, as discussed in Chapter 11.

In order to avoid benefits competing with low wages and thus discouraging labour market participation, Beveridge also recommended that the benefit rates be set at a low level, based initially on Rowntree's calculations of the weekly needs for subsistence living. This was followed when the NI scheme was introduced. It applied to all NI benefits, including pensions, and although benefit levels were later raised, this resulted in an overlap with entitlement to means-tested assistance benefits, which unlike NI included full payment for rent. This has meant that many of those receiving NI protection have also had to claim means-tested support, a point to which we shall return shortly.

In the 1960s and 1970s insurance protection was extended to include earnings-related benefit payments in return for earnings-related contributions, both for unemployment and (later) for pensions, following the model used in most other European countries. The earnings-related additions to unemployment and sickness benefit were phased out in the early 1980s, however, as part of a more general attempt to reduce the scope of the NI scheme. The state earnings-related pension scheme (SERPS) has been retained, despite the proposal in 1985 to abandon it; but future payments from it have been cut and it remains less generous than many private and occupational pension schemes.

The proposal to scrap SERPS in 1985 was largely based on a fear that the cost of the earnings-related benefits would place too high a burden on the contributors to the NI scheme in the early twenty-first century, as we saw in Chapter 11. This is of course one of the ever-present problems of the pay-as-you-go basis of the NI scheme, and in the 1980s the increased demands on the NI fund caused by the rising level of unemployment – together with the government's desire to remove the Treasury supplement to the fund from general taxation, which Beveridge had included as part of his original plan – meant that the contribution levels were increased at the same time as the benefit levels were cut. Following this the contribution conditions governing entitlement to benefit were tightened, further restricting the scope of insurance protection (Hill, 1990, ch. 5; Alcock, 1996c).

These changes to NI in the 1980s demonstrate most clearly that, whatever Beveridge's intentions or hopes may have been, the insurance scheme has never been independent of more general social security provision or benefit policy. The fund, now separately administered by the Contributions Agency, is a largely device for the financial management of NI benefits, and the contribution conditions are a means of ensuring that benefit entitlement is restricted to those who have some record of payment into the fund – albeit in a somewhat arbitrary fashion (see Dilnot *et al.*, 1984, pp. 28–34). In practice therefore NI is simply one part of a complex social security system, providing benefits without means tests for some claimants in some circumstances. For those who do benefit, avoidance of the means test is a significant advantage, but the low level of benefits and the large number of people excluded from protection mean that the former make up the minority of social security claimants.

Social Assistance

Beveridge recommended the retention of a social assistance scheme, actually called National Assistance (NA), alongside the new NI scheme because he recognised there may be some people with an inadequate income who would not be entitled to insurance benefit because they could not meet the contribution conditions. He saw assistance operating as a safety net below the basic state provision, and his expectation was that demand for it would be low and would decline as NI expanded.

The basis for entitlement to assistance was the means test. Only those who could prove they had no other source of adequate support would be able to receive state support under it. The means test was to be administered by the National Assistance Board (NAB) and was based on the assumption that married or cohabiting men and women and their children would support themselves, although the broader expectation that other family members would provide support in times of need, which had operated in the interwar scheme, was dropped (see Deacon and Bradshaw, 1983, ch. 2).

Unlike the Poor Law Guardians the NAB operated on a national basis, but in many other respects NA was a continuation of the Poor Law, which in effect it replaced. Benefit rates were fixed at a minimum subsistence level to avoid it being viewed as an attractive form of support, and in most cases receipt was conditional on submission to tests of labour market potential – adult claimants of working age were expected to be seeking employment. The principle of less eligibility thus continued into the assistance scheme, and with it went the negative imagery associated with dependence on state support for those unable to provide for themselves. Beveridge expected that stigma would accompany dependence on means testing; indeed this was indirectly a desirable feature for it would underline the attractions of the non-stigmatising NI scheme under which claimants had made provision for their support and thus had a *right* to claim benefit.

Assistance benefits were financed out of direct taxation rather than through individual contribution. Thus they transferred resources vertically from the (relatively) rich to the poor. It was because of this, however, that stringent eligibility criteria had to be included to ensure that only those who were really poor (and deserving) were able to benefit from them. The process of claiming means-tested benefits thus involved intrusive questioning into the circumstances and opportunities of potential claimants in a climate of suspicion that not all who presented themselves for support might necessarily be in need. This legacy has come to create serious problems for assistance claimants as the number of these has grown and grown over the last fifty years.

The stigma associated with dependency on means-tested benefits might have been a more manageable problem had such dependency remained, as Beveridge predicted, at a minor and declining level. This has not been the case however. Although the NA benefits were initially fixed at a minimum subsistence level, below that of NI benefits, they included separate provision for the cost of rent, which NI did not. This was because rent levels fluctuated widely and yet were an unavoidable cost for those with no adequate support; but it meant that even those who were entitled to NI benefits might also be able to claim NA to pay for their rent. There was thus, as we have seen, an inevitable overlap was built into the two schemes.

In addition to the overlap between NI and NA there was the problem of those who had not established an entitlement to NI benefits. For such people dependence on assistance was the only means of surviving in poverty, and contrary to Beveridge's expectations the number of claimants needing such means-tested support because of the inadequacy of the NI scheme grew rather than declined in the 1950s. In the famous study in which they 'rediscovered' poverty in the welfare state in the early 1960s, Abel Smith and Townsend (1965) found that over one million people had incomes on or below the NA scale.

In the 1960s many of those depending on NA were pensioners. Both Conservative and Labour governments during this period promised to improve pension provision to prevent the problem of high levels of means-test dependence in old age. For different reasons, however, neither succeeded in doing this, and in 1966 Labour decided instead to reform the still relatively unpopular NA scheme. It was retitled Supplementary Benefit (SB) and put under the administration of a new government body – the Supplementary Benefit Commission (SBC). In practice not much changed, although the SB scheme did include a fixed basic weekly rate that those with an income below this level would now have a right to claim, with extra payments available on a discretionary basis for extra needs.

The idea of the right to benefit was an attempt to overcome one of the major problems identified with means-tested benefits as a source of state support. Payment of them was not automatic, they had to be claimed; and the claiming of means-tested support involved an intrusive and uncomfortable process of questioning. Many were therefore deterred from claiming because of fear of the process, thus reducing the take-up of such benefits by those who needed them. The idea was that creating a right to the basic weekly rate would help to overcome this. After some initial improvement, however, there is little evidence that this was a successful move (see Deacon and Bradshaw, 1983, p. 107).

In the 1960s and 1970s dependence on the reformed SB scheme continued to increase, in particular as unemployment grew and those unemployed for long periods of time exhausted their entitlement to NI support. By the end of the 1970s the number dependent on SB had grown to four million. However there was also an extension in the scope of means-tested benefits to provide new forms of state support, including Family Income Supplement (FIS), rent and rate rebates, and a range of other specific benefits in areas such as health and education, for instance free school meals for the children of low-income parents. The reasoning behind the extension of means-tested assistance was the twin desire to tackle the problem that had come to be referred to as the 'unemployment trap', and to focus – or target – the limited funds presumed to be available for additional state support on those who could prove poverty or low income.

The unemployment trap was the presumed effect of the potentially significant SB entitlement of a large family with a high rent on the motivation of an unemployed breadwinner who might command only a low wage in employment. For them a low wage may have meant a drop in income (sometimes referred to as an insufficient 'replacement ratio' of wages to benefits), and thus such people were trapped into remaining unemployed, even though they wished to work. In the 1960s this was tackled through the use of the 'wage stop', whereby benefit entitlement was reduced to below the expected wage level, but it was an ineffective measure and in the 1970s it gave way to the use of means-tested FIS (paid to low-income workers with dependent children) and rent rebates to boost the incomes of families with low wages and high rents. This resulted in a significant increase in the scope of means tests in social security provision, and in 1976 the National Consumer Council reported that forty-five different means-tested benefits were operating in Britain (NCC, 1976).

The emphasis on targeting was the product of a shift in government policy on social security away from the universal principles of the NI scheme, under which all who paid into it were automatically entitled to claim benefit, towards a selective focus of state support on those in proven need (see MacGregor, 1981, ch. 5). This shift towards selectivity began on a gradual basis with the introduction of new means-tested benefits in the 1960s and 1970s. In the 1980s, however, it was taken much further by the social security policies of the Thatcher governments, whose members were quite outspoken in their support of selectivism in social security provision.

Policy changes in the 1980s reduced the scope of insurance protection, as we have already seen, but at the same time major changes were made to expand and rationalise means-tested benefits (see Alcock, 1996b). In 1980 SB was reformed to make additional payments a right rather than a matter of discretion, but with more and more SB claimants this only led to an escalation in the cost and administration of benefits. By the mid 1980s over eight million people were dependent on SB assistance and it was accounting for a significant proportion of social security expenditure, and so in 1985 the government introduced a review of much social security provision, including assistance payments.

The review, published initially as a Green Paper in 1985, did not suggest any fundamental reform of social security, but it did underline the central role that means testing was now playing in the delivery of benefit protection; and the reforms that followed in 1988 aimed to simplify the structure and administration of all the major means-tested benefits in order to encourage take-up and reduce administrative costs. As in the 1960s this involved some changing of names. SB was retitled Income Support (IS) and FIS became Family Credit (FC), but rent rebates, which had been renamed Housing Benefit (HB) a few years earlier, kept this new title. Critics at the time argued that the restructuring was motivated largely by a desire to cut costs, and that many claimants would lose out as a result of the changes (Berthoud, 1985, 1986; CPAG, 1985). This seems to have been borne out by subsequent research, which shows that in practice the changes involved only a degree of redistribution between claimants, whereby some lost out, rather than a more general increase in the targeting of resources onto the poor (Evans *et al.*, 1994).

The main effect of the 1988 changes, however, was to confirm the central role that means-tested support now had within the benefit system. Since then dependence on such benefits has continued to expand, with over a third of the population in receipt of some form of means-tested support and around ten million claiming IS in the mid 1990s (Field, 1995). This signifies a final departure from the principles of the Beveridge plan and the comprehensive role of social insurance in the provision of social security support, and a recognition that a mixture of insurance and assistance protection operates for many social security claimants. The benefit picture is even more complicated than this however, for there are other forms of state support that derive from neither the insurance nor the assistance traditions.

Universal Benefits

Universal benefits have sometimes been confused with insurance protection, and although the NI benefit scheme is informed by universal principles the benefits are not really universal. Despite the lack of a means test, receipt of NI benefits is dependent on meeting the contribution conditions. Genuine universal benefits should not require qualifying conditions. Beveridge was aware of this principle, and although he rejected it in favour of social insurance for his major benefit proposals, he did propose universal help towards the cost of child care through the introduction of family allowances.

The idea behind family allowances was that the state would provide a contribution towards the cost of rearing all children, in part as a recognition of their role as future citizens and workers and to encourage couples to have children, and in part to raise the overall income of families with children and thus reduce the hardship that might otherwise result in households that had low incomes or were dependent on benefits. Because no children had an income and all families experienced similar needs, allowances were paid universally to all. However the allowance scheme introduced after the Second World War provided only partial support – allowances were only paid for second and subsequent children and the rate payable was only a contribution towards the weekly needs of a child.

Despite its shortcomings the allowance scheme did introduce a universal benefit into the British social security system. Unfortunately the level of the benefit fluctuated and was allowed to fall below its original postwar levels. However it was not the only state support for children – relief against income tax was also available to tax-paying parents. As discussed in Chapter 13, one of the major focuses of CPAG campaigning in the 1960s and 1970s was the growing problem of child poverty in low-paid and claimant families. The CPAG proposed a reform of family allowances to tackle this, and after turbulent political debate changes were made with the introduction of Child Benefit (CB) in 1978 (Field, 1982).

CB is a universal benefit paid to the parents of all children, or rather to the nominated carer, usually the mother. It was based on an amalgamation of family allowances and tax relief, with the latter disappearing. However it remained only a contribution towards the cost of rearing a child, and the level of this contribution declined further in the 1980s when CB was not uprated in line with inflation as other benefits were. It has remained significantly below the cost of a child as calculated by researchers such as Piachaud (1979), but more significantly it is below the weekly rate provided for children in the means-tested assistance schemes. Thus for those in receipt of means-tested benefits CB is effectively discounted from their benefit entitlement and they receive only the higher level of means-tested support.

Child Benefit is the most well-known universal benefit in Britain, but it is not the only one. The benefits for the attendance and mobility costs of people with disabilities discussed in Chapter 12 are also paid on a universal basis, although they affect only a relatively small proportion of the population. What is more, as we have seen, there are problems with both the scope and the operation of these disability benefits and even for those who do receive them they play only a relatively minor role within the overall provision of state support, further adding to the complexity of overlapping benefit provisions.

Problems with Benefits

Despite its limitations and restrictions, and despite the other goals it often simultaneously pursues, social security remains the main anti-poverty measure in British social policy. In providing state support as either a substitute for or a supplement to income from the labour market, it aims to relieve or prevent poverty by ensuring that claimants and their families have what the government regards as an adequate income. As we have seen, there is much debate and dis-agreement about whether such an income is indeed adequate to prevent poverty. But leaving this to one side there are nevertheless serious problems with the current benefit system that lead to many people not receiving even the minimum amount that the system appears to provide – or even if they are, not benefiting significantly from these.

As suggested above there is the potential problem of non-take-up 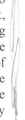 with any benefit system, especially one relying heavily on means-tested provision. Only those who identify themselves as poor enough to qualify for benefit, who recognise the potential of benefit entitlement, and who are prepared to undergo the rigorous process of submitting and defending their claim will be assessed for entitlement and receive benefits. Given the complexity of the benefit system and the range of means-tested and other benefits available, many may fail to recognise their potential entitlement; and given the application process and the stigma associated with dependence on means-tested benefits, many may choose not to claim even if they suspect they might benefit.

The problem of non-take-up exists with any form of benefit, and there is evidence that not all people with disabilities receive the universal disability benefits to which they are entitled (Martin and White, 1988). However in general take-up of universal and insurance benefits is high, with CB achieving nearly 100 per cent take-up. Most of the problems of take-up are associated with means-tested benefits, because of the complexity of entitlement and the stigma of depen-dency. The governments' own estimates of non-take-up of the major

means-tested benefits put average levels of take-up at 70–90 per cent
for IS, FC and HB in 1993/94, with as much as £3 billion in benefits
being left unclaimed by up to four million people (DSS, 1995c). This is
a serious flaw in the policy of targeting resources through means
testing, for it means that not all the people who most need income
support are receiving it; and it is a phenomenon that has been found to
be associated with social assistance benefits in other countries too (van
Orschot, 1995).

The other major failure of social security as an antipoverty measure
is also associated with the use of selectivity in determining benefit
entitlement. This is the problem of the 'poverty trap'; and it is a
problem that has grown in scope and scale as dependency on means-
testing within social security has expanded in the last two decades or
so. Unlike non-take-up, which perhaps could – and should – be
tackled by government, however, this problem is both inevitable and
ultimately unavoidable.

The poverty trap is a consequence of the use of means-tested
benefits to tackle poverty through the supplementing of low wages.
As we have seen, the introduction of a number of new means-tested
benefits in the 1970s and 1980s was aimed at supplementing wages in
order the tackle the unemployment trap – the lack of incentive for a
breadwinner to take paid employment because of the low replacement
ratio of wages to benefits. Benefits such as FC and HB relieve this
problem by making low-paid work more attractive. However the effect
of these benefits, together with the impact of tax liabilities on low-paid
workers, inevitably creates another, arguably more serious, problem in
the poverty trap.

The poverty trap was first 'discovered' in the early 1970s (Field and
Piachaud, 1971) at a time when means-tested benefits for those on low
wages were being rapidly extended, and it has been discussed in some
detail by Deacon and Bradshaw (1983, ch. 8). In simple terms the
problem arises because low-paid workers lose their entitlement to
means-tested benefit additions if their wages rise. Means-tested additions generally provide a proportion of the difference between low
wages and the income level fixed in the scheme: in the case of the now
defunct FIS 50 per cent of the difference was paid and in the case of
rent rebates up to 29 per cent. If wages rose these additions were
progressively lost, although in the case of FIS the effect was delayed
because it was paid for periods of twelve months at a time. In the early
1980s the combined effect of losing 50p of FIS and 29p rent rebate for
each extra pound earned, together with the need to pay income tax at

30p in the pound and NI contributions at 8p, as well as the potential loss of free school meals for children and other benefits, meant that people on low wages faced a 'marginal tax rate' (the amount of income forgone for each extra pound earned) of over 100 per cent. In other words, even if they were able to secure a rise in wages their overall income fell.

As Deacon and Bradshaw (ibid.) pointed out, the effect of this high marginal tax rate was to nullify the effect of any increase in family income over a wide range of low wages from around £70 to £120 a week. Thus those on these low wages were trapped in poverty. The receipt of benefits ensured that they had an income just above assistance benefit level, but the consequences of the criteria for entitlement kept them continually on this low income unless they could make a spectacular leap in employment earning. The reforms to means-tested benefits in 1988 did in part remove some of the worst aspects of this poverty trap for those on low wages, in particular by removing the problem of marginal tax rates of over 100 per cent. But rates of over 90 per cent have remained for some, and the consequence of removing the worst effects for some has spread the experience of relatively high rates of tax and benefit withdrawal over an even wider range of low wages, creating was has been referred to as a 'poverty plateau' (see Field, 1995).

It has also been recognised in the 1990s that this contradictory disincentive effect, caused by the withdrawal of means-tested support when wages rise, affects not only those on low wages. Most means-tests now take into account the capital holdings of claimants or the interest that accrues on savings above the allowable threshold, and so even those with relatively modest savings can lose entitlement to means-tested support or have their level of benefit reduced. Thus there is also a 'savings trap' associated with the expanded role of means-tested provision, affecting in particular those pensioners who have low state pensions, but have saved or invested money to help finance their retirement. As the recent changes to child maintenance provision brought about by the Child Support Agency have revealed, this problem can affect lone parents too, for money received from the agency in maintenance is deducted from any means-tested benefits paid to a parent – removing the advantage of and the incentive for securing such private support.

The problems of non-take-up and the poverty and savings traps seriously undermine the effectiveness of social security provision in alleviating poverty in a wage-labour economy. They are also a direct consequence of the expanding role of means testing in the benefits system over the last two decades. The apparent attractiveness of linking receipt of benefits to proof of poverty or low income is not effective in practice because of the failure of many people in need of benefits to recognise or pursue their entitlement to them, and because of the disincentive effects that flow from targeting state support only on the poor. These practical problems, and the confusion over the policy framework for social security from which they result, have led an increasing number of commentators to argue that social security provision in Britain is in need of radical reform if it is to continue to play an effective part in antipoverty strategy (see Parker, 1989; Field, 1995). We shall now look briefly at whether there are alternatives to the current social security structure that might better perform this task.

Alternative Models for Social Security

The debate over alternative structures for social security provision is not a new one. The Beveridge social insurance plan was itself presented as an alternative to the previous Poor Law and social assistance approaches to state support; and after the 'rediscovery' of poverty and the criticism of the postwar scheme in the 1960s, further discussion about potential structural reform of the benefits system began to reemerge in academic and political debate (see Atkinson, 1969). The extension of means testing in the early 1970s reopened the debate between the social assistance and social insurance approaches to benefit provision, and the Conservative government of 1970–4 seriously considered far-reaching reform to restructure benefit and taxation policy into a combined, means-tested, tax/benefit system (see Sandford, 1980), although in the end the plans were not realised.

In the 1980s the growing problems with means-tested benefits and the increasing failure of social insurance to provide comprehensive protection for all, both in Britain and in other Western European countries, prompted further discussion of the need for an alternative to both insurance and assistance approaches in the form of a basic income paid to all citizens as a means of preventing poverty and creating an incentive to take paid employment. Campaign and research networks were set up in Britain (the Basic Income Research Group, or BIRG) and Europe (the Basic Income European Network, or BIEN) to promote further exploration of this as an alternative to current social security systems.

By the end of the 1980s, therefore, the debate on social security reform had crystallised into three broad approaches to the role of the state in providing income support, which can be summarised as the tax credit approach, the basic income approach and the social insurance approach (see Alcock, 1987, ch. 11; Hill, 1990, ch. 9).

Tax Credits

The tax credit approach was considered by the Conservative government of the early 1970s and has since been promoted by the Institute
for Fiscal Studies (Dilnot *et al.*, 1984) and the Adam Smith Institute (ASI, 1984, 1989). It is based on an attempt to rationalise the relationship between current means-tested benefits and income taxation to create a single basis for state income support, thus replacing all current insurance and universal benefits with a new unified tax/benefit scheme. The basic aim is to target state support on the poor – those with no income or inadequate incomes – and to use the taxation system, which already contains records of income received, to do this.

The advantage of scrapping the current confusing and overlapping benefit system and replacing it with a unified means of income redistribution organised through the Inland Revenue is clearly an attractive one, at least in organisational terms. Benefit administration
would be simplified and perhaps therefore take-up could be improved. All income assessments would be made by one body and then tax would either be collected from households above a fixed income threshold, or benefits (or tax credits) paid to those below it. By this means poverty could be alleviated and income redistributed without state interference in wage levels or employment policy, and without the imposition of compulsory insurance. Income assessments and entitlement calculations could be made annually, or adjusted weekly if circumstances changed.

The superficial organisational attractions of the tax credit proposals are substantial, but as Collard (1980) and Sandford (1980) have discussed, they disguise serious practical and policy problems. Because they are based squarely on the principle of means testing, the tax credit proposals are likely to run the risk of reproducing in any reformed scheme the operational problems associated with existing means-tested provision. Even with a simplified administrative structure take-up could continue to be a problem, especially if stigma were to continue to be associated with receipt of credit. The rapidly changing circumstances of those at the bottom of the income scale and thus likely to be entitled to credit may also result in errors and under claiming. Even with simplified entitlement criteria, means testing requires complex and intrusive questioning to determine the right to benefit, together with the constant suspicion that some may be unjustly receiving state support.

The administrative and attitudinal problems of means testing are therefore likely to be reproduced in any tax credit scheme, as are the contradictory and perverse incentives of the poverty trap. If tax credit raises the income of those below the threshold up to a fixed income level, then the incentive for those below the level to improve their circumstances through their own efforts is entirely removed. Thus most tax credit proposals involve crediting only a proportion of income below the fixed level, thus leaving those in receipt of benefit still technically with an inadequate income. Nevertheless even such partial credit must be withdrawn if initial income rises, thus maintaining the poverty trap. As we have seen the poverty trap is an inevitable consequence of means-tested benefit support, and since tax credits would in effect institutionalise means testing they would also institutionalise the poverty trap. As a radical alternative to current social security provision, therefore, they may leave a lot to be desired.

Basic Income

The basic income proposals have emanated from attempts to get around the problem of the perverse incentives created by the poverty trap, and to appeal to the collective ethos of social insurance while at the same time avoiding the exclusive tendencies of the insurance contribution principle. In other words basic income would be an alternative to both means testing and insurance provision. The idea is that a standard benefit would be paid by the state to all individuals, irrespective of employment status, to provide for or contribute to a modest but adequate income, on top of which all wages from part-time or full-time work would be additional income. It would be a universal scheme like Child Benefit – but for adults. Basic income would mean avoidance of the poverty trap since all income from employment would be additional to state benefit, although obviously such income would have to be subject to relatively high levels of income tax in order to fund the basic benefit.

Supporters of the idea range from those on the left (Jordan, 1987; Purdy 1988), who propose that the payment level should be high enough to allow at least subsistence, to those towards the centre and right (Parker, 1989; Rhys Williams, 1989), who recommend only a partial basic income to replace current tax allowances for those in employment and to contribute towards benefit entitlement for those outside the labour market. This approach has attracted an increasingly wide range of supporters throughout Europe (see Van Parijs, 1992), including more recently Atkinson (1995), who in the past had been a strong supporter of the social insurance approaches.

Partial basic income could be introduced at a relatively low payment level without the need significantly to raise the current income tax rates; but it would not remove the need for additional means-tested benefits for those out of work, nor would it contribute towards housing costs. Full basic income would presumably replace all existing benefits, but it would require a tax rate of 60 per cent or more on any additional earned income, which could be a severe disincentive to employment. Full basic income would also replace, both in practice and in principle, wages as the main source of income for the majority of the population. Radical proponents such as Gorz (1982) argue that this is an inevitable step as we head towards a post-industrial world order, but it may be difficult to attract widespread support for such a radical reform in the current political and economic circumstances (see Alcock, 1989).

The problem with the basic income proposals, therefore, is that they are either so radical that they could only be introduced after a fundamental restructuring of the socioeconomic order, or they are so limited in scope that they could not replace the existing means-tested benefits and thus would not dispel all the difficulties associated with these. Certainly the proponents of the proposals in the BIRG and BIEN have grown in prominence in recent years, and they now publish a regular journal, *Citizen's Income*, and hold major international conferences; nevertheless they remain on the margins of the mainstream antipoverty policy debate.

Social Insurance

The undesirability or unachievability of tax credits and basic income have thus left many academics and politicians seeking a revitalisation of social insurance in order to overcome the contradictions and complexities of current benefit provision. Atkinson (1969) was an early proponent of a return to social insurance principles, and this path has also been largely supported by the main antipoverty campaign group, the CPAG (see Lister, 1975).

In the 1960s and 1970s, as the scope of means-tested benefits began to undermine the comprehensive aspirations of the NI scheme, the proponents of social insurance mainly based their proposals on a return to the ideas contained in the Beveridge plan for insurance – sometimes referred to as a 'Back-to-Beveridge' strategy. However most social policy academics are now aware of the serious limitations of the Beveridge insurance plan (see Baldwin and Falkingham, 1994), and even by the 1980s the proponents of social insurance had begun to explore the possibility of retaining a scheme of state support for those unable to provide for themselves through wages in the labour market without their having to be subject to contribution criteria as a condition of entitlement (Lister and Fimister, 1980).

The idea of social insurance in 1990s is thus presented not so much in order to make the case for a return to the Beveridge notion of benefits in return for contributions made, but rather to a revitalisation of the collectivist notion of social security, in which all who can contribute do contribute, so that all those in need can benefit (Alcock, 1996c). Such provision would not be insurance-based in the strict, self-protection sense of the term – but then as we have already seen the 'pay-as-you-go' British NI scheme has never in practice operated on such a basis anyway. Rather contributions could take the form of a hypothecated social insurance tax that is used to pay benefits to all who are not in full-time paid employment.

Social insurance proponents argue that such protection could gradually replace existing means-tested benefits for all those out of work, and could be linked to the introduction of a statutory minimum wage for those in work to ensure that low wages did not continue to be a cause of poverty. A statutory minimum wage, which would not need to be subsidised by benefit support, would also remove the problem of the poverty trap. Such a gradualist approach makes social insurance a politically more viable prospect than the radical reforms of tax credit and basic income. However it is just this gradualist appeal that may be a major cause of political weakness in practice. For, as most of the history of social security policy has so emphatically demonstrated, gradualist changes can be rapidly sidetracked or overturned as political or economic circumstances change and antipoverty policy becomes subject to the whims and vagaries of political fortune.

Whilst radical changes to social security policy may be unlikely in the foreseeable future, however, it is certainly the case that more minor reform is very much at the top of the social policy agenda in Britain in the late 1990s. Supported by the government, the Department of Social Security (DSS, 1993) has led a wide-ranging debate on the growing costs of benefit provision and the need for future reform; and the independent Commission on Social Justice (Borrie, 1994) published a review of various proposals for reform, some of which have been taken up by opposition parties. Nevertheless research evidence continues to suggest that the existing provisions have had only limited success in tackling poverty in affluent 1990s society (Barclay, 1995; Hills, 1995). This has led some to suggest that antipoverty policy might therefore better be concentrated on initiatives outside the social security system, and it is to some of these other initiatives that we now turn.

15

Targeted Antipoverty Strategies

Pockets of Poverty

Since the nineteenth century or earlier social security provision has been the major plank of antipoverty policy in Britain. State support through social security is a response to identification of the structural relationship between poverty, income and the labour market; and the payment of benefits to act as a substitute for or to supplement wages from the labour market is intended to prevent or relieve poverty. In modern welfare capitalist societies social security has become an extensive and expensive antipoverty strategy. In the mid 1990s social security expenditure in Britain was running at over £80 billion a year, by far the largest item of public expenditure. Without this expenditure it is certain that many people would experience significantly increased deprivation. However, as critics have frequently pointed out, it is debatable whether social security provision has succeeded in either preventing or relieving poverty.

Critics on the right, such as Murray (1984), have argued that social security has not prevented poverty because the provision of state support has encouraged dependency rather than promoting self-support through the labour market; whereas critics on the left, such as Townsend (1979, 1984), have argued that benefit provision has not prevented poverty because the benefit levels are too low, and that through means testing people have been trapped in poverty. Whilst there is little shared ground between such different approaches, both focus on the failings or limitations of social security provision and its impact on those who are still poor in an affluent society.

The failure of social security provision in an affluent society was very much the central theme of the 'rediscovery of poverty' in Britain in the 1960s. The research evidence and the political campaigning pointed to the continued experience of deprivation for a large number

236

of people despite the achievements of the welfare state, and suggested that further government action was needed to address this. In the 1960s, however, major expansion of social security protection was not perceived as a viable strategy – in particular because of the costs that such an expansion might incur. Alternative means of responding to the continuing problem of poverty in the midst of affluence were thus likely to be more attractive to the government.

The rediscovery of poverty in the 1960s was not just associated with a renewal of pressure for social security reform, however. As discussed in Chapter 2, it was also associated with a renewed emphasis on poverty as a pathological phenomenon in advanced industrial societies. Drawing on the 'culture of poverty' thesis developed by Lewis (1965, 1968), politicians such as Joseph (1972) argued that the continuation of poverty in an affluent welfare society might be a product of individual apathy and inadequate upbringing, a 'cycle of deprivation' rather than a policy failure. This 'blaming the victim' approach, as we have seen, has serious shortcomings, but in the 1960s it did begin to provide a framework for the development of a rather different approach towards state policy to combat poverty in a number of advanced industrial societies in the latter part of the twentieth century. As the quote from Ryan in Chapter 2 put it: 'define the difference [of the poor] as the cause of the problem. Finally, of course, assign a government bureaucrat to invent a humanitarian action programme to correct the difference' (Ryan, 1971, p. 8).

Implicit in this framework is a perception that poverty is caused not so much by the failings of social and economic policy planning, but rather by the inability of poor people to take advantage of the opportunities that such planning already offers. The action programme that is required, therefore, is not an extension of social security support and the further redistribution of resources to the poor, but rather the identifying of poor people and the use of state support to employ humanitarian professionals to work with them to encourage them to overcome the cultural and economic barriers that are trapping them in poverty. Resources focused on the poor should thus be used not to relieve their poverty but to help them escape from it.

This new approach to the focusing – or targeting – of resources was also a response to another feature of the research and campaigning thrown up by the 'rediscovery of poverty' debate. The research of Townsend (1979) and others on the experience of deprivation within affluent society revealed that income poverty was only a partial feature of the deprived environment in which many poor people found themselves, including poor housing, inadequate services, pollution and so on. These deprived environments were identified in particular with run-down inner city areas in many of Britain's decaying industrial conurbations. In inner cities, therefore, poverty and deprivation were concentrated in what commentators began to refer to as 'pockets of poverty'.

If limited state resources were to be focused on poor people to help them overcome their deprivation and take advantage of the opportunities of modern society, then the run-down inner city areas identified by the poverty researchers provided the obvious target for these resources. In pockets of urban poverty the cultural problems of transmitted deprivation were likely to be greatest, but at the same time the opportunities for escape would be close at hand. Professionals working in such concentrations of deprivation could thus influence a relatively large number of poor people within relatively limited overall costs, and so provide a model for self-help and upward mobility that could then be applied to other poor areas. Geographical targeting thus coincided with pathological perceptions of the problem of poverty to create a climate for a new approach to antipoverty policy in advanced industrial societies, which was taken up by governments in Britain and elsewhere from the 1960s onwards and remains a major feature of policy development in the 1990s.

The War on Poverty

Targeted antipoverty strategies in Britain were influenced significantly by the development of such approaches in the United States in the early 1960s. Indeed attempts were made to learn from and build on the American experiences – although, perhaps typically, the initiatives in the United States were rather grander than their later British counterparts, and they were presented as part of an apparently more substantial government commitment to the elimination of poverty.

In 1964, at more or less the same time as the United States was beginning to step up its involvement in the Vietnam War, President Johnson announced a 'national war on poverty', with the objective of 'total victory' in ensuring that every citizen shared 'all the opportunities of society' (James, 1970, p. 65). What the war on poverty represented in practice was federal government funding for locally targeted initiatives in which professionals would work in deprived areas to help poor people to take advantage of the opportunities of affluent American society. The money was channelled through a new government agency called, appropriately, the Office of Economic Opportunity (OEO). To use the jargon of the scheme the money was intended to provide 'doors, not floors' – an emphasis on education and job programmes to encourage mobility through self-help (*doors* out of the cellar of poverty) rather than the provision of additional resources to poor people themselves (a raising of the *floor* on which the poor stood) (see Higgins, 1978, pp. 108 ff).

The notion of self-help – 'helping the poor to help themselves' – was closely linked to pathological explanations of the causes of a trans-mitted culture of poverty and to the geographical targeting of re-sources on poor urban areas. In the United States this was furthermore overlain with perceptions of the racial dimension of the problem of urban poverty, which was at its worst in inner city areas with large black populations and high levels of urban unrest. Part of the not-so-hidden agenda of the OEO programme of antipoverty work, therefore, was avoidance or control of racial violence and urban protest, although this was a strategy with rather mixed achievements in the real world of black urban politics (see Wolfe, 1971).

Most of the resources of the OEO therefore went on a range of community action programmes in poor urban areas. They were designed to improve educational provision and job opportunities and to encourage local poor people to take advantage of these. Many of the programmes, such as Head Start and the Neighbourhood Youth Corps, focused particularly on children and youth as the logical point at which to seek to break the chain of transmitted deprivation.

There is little doubt that many youngsters in poor American inner city areas did benefit from some of the community action initiatives. However there is also little doubt that the initiatives did not succeed in providing total victory over urban poverty. As Marris and Rein (1974) pointed out, the community agencies had little power to challenge the local and central power structures within which urban poverty was located. Identifying the problems of urban poverty therefore often brought the agencies into conflict with entrenched social and economic interests. This conflict was inevitable – but it was one they could not hope to win.

Piven and Cloward's (1972) analysis was even more critical. In channelling antipoverty activity into limited initiatives to provide for the urban poor within existing welfare programmes, they pointed out, the war on poverty diverted attention away from any broader structural approaches to welfare problems and thus acted as a diversion from social and economic reform. In the 1970s the war on poverty in the United States was brought to an end without achieving the total victory that had been sought at its outset. In reality of course this victory was no less elusive than the victory in Vietnam had been; but in abandoning the war the lessons of the limitations of targeted anti-poverty strategies were only partially recognised. Yet in Britain the focus on community action to combat urban deprivation drew heavily on these American ideals of upward mobility out of the cellar of poverty.

Government Antipoverty Initiatives

In Britain in the 1960s debate on antipoverty strategy and fears of economic constraint provided a climate in which government initiatives to combat continuing poverty began to follow closely the targeting policies of the American war on poverty. The first example of such an approach emerged from the recommendations of the Plowden Report on the transition to secondary education, which proposed the targeting of additional resources to improve schooling in a number of identified priority areas (see Halsey, 1972).

As a result of these proposals the first government initiative on targeting was introduced in the form of the Educational Priority Area (EPA) programme in 1968. Drawing on the Head Start programme in the United States, the EPA scheme involved the provision of extra resources for primary schools in a small number of poor areas to ensure that educational disadvantage did not reinforce the cycle of poverty for children in these areas. The scheme was run on a small scale in a small number of areas and it lasted only for a few years; but it was subject to high-profile research analysis (Halsey, 1972) and it provided a model of targeted government support that was to be taken much further in a range of later initiatives with much wider horizons.

The most extensive and long lasting of these broader initiatives was the Urban Aid programme, which was also launched in 1968 and lasted until the mid 1990s. This too involved extra government resources being channelled into poor urban areas in order to help break the cycle of transmitted deprivation. However Urban Aid money was not restricted to resources for schools – grants could be obtained for any appropriate scheme aimed at neighbourhood-based action to work with local people to combat poverty. The idea was that local authorities and voluntary agencies would propose projects such as community centres, play schemes or remedial education, which would then receive Urban Aid funding and be run on a partnership basis by the authority and representatives of the local community. Some local authorities were understandably sceptical of the political motivation behind tying additional local funding to designated action programmes. It suggested to the authorities that they were not trusted to use rates and block grants to support such community initiatives; but the attraction of extra cash for projects in run-down areas was more than most could resist and Urban Aid grew rapidly to become a major source of support for a range of community-based activities in urban areas.

In the mid 1970s the idea of additional local resources for designated partnership schemes between central and local government and the voluntary sector was extended with the inner cities partnership programme. This was a more comprehensive attempt to harness neighbourhood-based activities in a selected number of city areas (see Berthoud *et al.*, 1981, pp. 273–4). However, both politically and symbolically, the most important of the government antipoverty initiatives of the 1960s and 1970s was the Community Development Project (CDP), which was based very closely on the American community action programme and ran for from 1968 to 1978. The CDPs were something of an experiment in the utilisation of government funding for community-based action, and although they were fairly limited in scope and number they received a great deal of attention from academics and politicians (see Lees and Smith, 1975; Loney, 1983).

The CDPs were in large part the brainchild of a senior civil servant in the Home Office, Derek Morrell. They were a response to a range of overlapping pressures – arguments for a more community-based focus in social work, pressure on the government to act on the problem of urban poverty, fears of racial violence and unrest stemming from immigration law changes and Enoch Powell's well-publicised attacks on Britain's black population, and acceptance that any new government measures must contain only minimal public spending commitments. Over their ten-year life the CDPs cost little more than £5 million.

They consisted of twelve projects in small areas of high unemployment, the largest being Canning Town in London with a population of 42 000, and they were administered directly by the Home Office. Each project comprised professionals recruited to engage in community development work in the area, and a research team – linked to a higher education establishment – to assess and analyse the success of the project. The research focus emphasised the experimental nature of the projects and they were given a budget to publish their findings. This helped to raise the profile of the CDPs, but it also contributed to their downfall.

As in the American community action programme the thinking that informed the CDPs was the concept of transmitted poverty. As one of the senior researchers put it:

> poverty and deprivation and consequent multi-problem families and individuals were conceptualised as the problems of a marginal minority who had slipped through the net of welfare, whether through personal or cultural inadequacy or through the services' own lack of co-ordination or administrative failures (Mayo, quoted in Loney, 1983, p. 49).

The idea was that highly specialised and focused community development could help overcome this marginalisation and restore the residents of the deprived areas concerned to active social and economic citizenship – but the idea backfired.

The newly recruited action and research teams in the CDPs were quickly made aware of the poverty and deprivation in the areas in which they were based. At the same time, however, they also quickly realised that much of this was the product not of individual inadequacy or service malfunctioning, but of wider social and economic policies leading to industrial decline, rising unemployment and deprived local environments (Corky and Craig, 1978). A handful of professionals with a few resources to support local activities could do little or nothing to counteract these wider forces. Indeed as one of the most famous of the CDP's numerous published reports – Coventry CDP's aptly titled *Gilding the Ghetto* (CDP, 1977) – pointed out, the mere existence of the project in the area could actually make things worse by confirming its reputation with potential investors as a neighbourhood in serious economic and social decline.

With their research back-up and high-profile publishing strategy the CDPs became a focus of debate on the theoretical and practical contradictions of utilising small-scale targeted resources to challenge large-scale urban poverty. The workers knew that the experiments were doomed to fail, and they said so. After ten years, during which time economic recession meant that in most of the areas the problem had become worse rather than better, an embarrassed government accepted the inevitable and terminated the project.

As with the American war on poverty, the CDPs were bound to be a temporary experiment – high-profile, targeted activity cannot be sustained for long. What is more, as with the American experiment they were bound to fail to eliminate poverty and deprivation – as we know, these are not the product of pathological inadequacy concentrated into a few run-down neighbourhoods. There are therefore inescapable contradictions to be faced when using targeted resources to combat poverty. However it would be shortsighted and unjust to conclude from this that the CDPs, and other targeted initiatives, achieved nothing in the struggle against poverty.

The CDP action teams included some highly motivated and innovative community development workers. During the ten years of the projects they developed some interesting and original community actions, some of which went a significant way towards tackling some of the problems of deprivation faced by local residents. For instance CDP workers collaborated in the establishment of pressure groups of local residents, such as tenants' associations that could challenge local housing departments to improve council housing and other amenities in the area. Perhaps most interestingly, CDP workers in Batley, Coventry and elsewhere worked to develop a welfare rights service with local residents, providing advice and advocacy to ensure that poor people were at least getting the basic state benefits to which they were entitled (Bradshaw, 1975). The welfare rights approach begun in some CDPs survived their demise and has developed since to become a major feature of targeted antipoverty activity.

Welfare Rights

Welfare rights work started as something of an experiment in some of the CDPs as a way of working with local people within the existing social and economic policy constraints to minimise their deprivation by ensuring that at least residents were getting the basic state benefits to which they entitled. Although with limited benefit provision this was not a transformatory achievement, it did lead to significant gains in the weekly income of some local people. Furthermore it provided an advice and advocacy service that neither the social security offices nor the local legal services had been willing or able to offer.

Thus when the CDPs were closed down in the mid to late 1970s some of the workers carried on this local advisory service from within revamped community-based agencies. Some of these agencies attracted funding from the local authority, which recognised the value of the service provided, and subsequently the number of these new advice and advocacy agencies began to grow, in some places building on the national Citizens' Advice Bureau (CAB) network, which had provided local information and advice on a voluntary basis since the Second World War. As well as local authority funding, local advice centres were also able to exploit the funding provided for local job-creation projects by the rapidly expanding Manpower Services Commission (MSC). This meant that the voluntary workers, who had always constituted the backbone of local advice and information work, could be supplemented by people on temporary employment contracts supported by the MSC, perhaps under the overall coordination of a supervisor paid by the local authority or the national CAB funding body, NACAB.

On this basis the number of local advice agencies providing welfare rights advice on social security, housing, homelessness and other areas of state welfare affecting poor people began to grow rapidly during the late 1970s and early 1980s. In Sheffield, for instance, the number of agencies grew from five to thirty-five between 1975 and 1985. Such generalist community-based agencies were also supplemented in many places by the development of specialist agencies concentrating on particular aspects of welfare rights work, such as tribunal appeals, housing cases or immigration law, sometimes on referral from local centres. These included housing aid centres (McDonnell, 1982) and especially law centres (Stephens, 1990).

Of course one of the reasons for the rapid growth of community-based welfare rights work was the speedily growing problem of low take-up of means-tested benefits in the 1970s and 1980s in the wake of the growth in the number of claimants and the expansion of means-tested benefits. Wherever agencies were set up they quickly attracted a large number of local enquiries about benefit rights, and they were often able to secure improved take-up, and thus additional resources, for local people. As a form of antipoverty activity, welfare rights work was thus flushed with early success, albeit as a result of the twin failures of economic policy and social security delivery.

The growing number of poor people and the growing dependency on means-tested benefits during this period also began to be recognised as a contributory factor to the problems experienced by many clients of social service departments (see Hill and Laing, 1979). Recognition that social services too may have a role to play in combating poverty by improving benefit take-up began in 1972 when the Manchester City Council appointed a welfare rights worker to its social services department. The idea was that such a worker could provide specialist advice and support in helping social workers to maximise their clients' incomes by improving their benefit take-up. The appointment in Manchester was quickly followed by other welfare rights workers being recruited to other social service departments, and by the development of welfare rights work as a part of the repertoire of social work tasks (see Cohen and Rushton, 1982; Fimister, 1986; CCETSW, 1989).

The number of welfare rights workers employed in local government grew rapidly in the early 1980s, and although most were placed in social service departments, some were given broader strategic responsibility for non-take-up and antipoverty work within the local area, and their work was extended beyond social service clientele. A study carried out by the PSI revealed a rapid growth in welfare rights work and a wide range of activities developed by workers (Berthoud *et al.*, 1986).

In addition to the increasing number of locally based welfare rights workers, at that time there was also a growth of national organisations providing support for local workers and a central focus for the development and dissemination of welfare rights initiatives. These included the NACAB, which rapidly expanded its role in providing local advice agencies with information and training, and the Citizens' Rights Office of the CPAG, which provided specialist support for welfare rights work and annually published comprehensive guides to benefit rights, which were used by all welfare rights workers. There were also specialist bodies providing support for work with particular groups of claimants, such as the Disability Alliance and the Campaign for the Homeless and Rootless (CHAR).

Because of the complexity of means-tested provision by the 1980s, welfare rights workers were able to secure significant increases in benefit for many claimants by encouraging them to make detailed claims for items of need specified in the various regulations. However providing such advice and encouragement to claimants on an individual basis was time-consuming and costly, and welfare rights workers began to experiment with ways of providing such information on a broader and more cost effective basis. The first attempt to do this was carried out by Strathclyde Regional Council, then the largest local authority in Britain, which mailed to all local residents a card advising them of benefit entitlements under the regulations and inviting them to make a claim by returning the card to the local social security office. The idea was that a large number of people would thus make claims that they would not otherwise have made, which the social security offices would then be required to process and, when appropriate, meet – thus massively increasing local take-up.

The idea of such blanket rights advice came to be called 'take-up campaigning'. In Strathclyde the organisers claimed that £1.3 million in additional benefits had been claimed locally as a result of the campaign, and following this lead other local authorities soon engaged in similar exercises. As local take-up campaigns expanded they also used increasingly sophisticated methods to encourage claims and target groups of potential claimants. The Greater London Council spent £2 million on a campaign that included television advertising and computer-based back-up advice; others used a variety of means of conveying information to groups known to be likely to be under-claiming particular benefits (see Alcock and Shepherd, 1987).

Take-up campaigns, like the welfare rights work from which they sprang, were relatively successful in increasing local benefit take-up, and thus combating local poverty. However they were of course only securing for people the relatively limited benefits the system was failing to deliver to them. This was an important gain for those who benefited from it, but it was also in one sense merely a transfer of benefit delivery work from central to local government. This transfer was also extremely patchy in its operation, since although many local authorities did develop benefit take-up initiatives during the 1980s, many did not, and in such areas a large number of people no doubt remained in more serious deprivation.

By increasing take-up, the campaigning also revealed quite starkly the failings of the state benefit system itself, which as we have seen is estimated to provide the major means-tested benefits to only 70–90 per cent of those entitled to them. Many of the more radical welfare rights workers saw in this a direct was to challenge the social security policy and practice of the government. Unfortunately this was a challenge that backfired – part of the reason for the reform of means-tested benefits in the late 1980s was a government fear of the escalating costs of the additional payments generated by take-up campaigning, and the changes made as part of the reform reduced the scope for such payments.

Nevertheless welfare rights work has continued to grow in both scale and scope in the 1990s. Indeed the rapid changes made to both benefit entitlement and benefit delivery have made the need for an independent source of advice and assistance ever more important for claimants, and welfare rights workers based in local authorities and in voluntary sector agencies have continued to secure significant additional benefits for their local citizens (Alcock, 1994). This has made welfare rights a central feature of targeted antipoverty action, and as such it has become a major element of many of the more coordinated responses to increased local poverty that have developed over the decade.

Local Antipoverty Strategies

Local authority support for welfare rights work was based in large part on the view of many, especially Labour-controlled, authorities that this would lead to significant increases in resources for local people. The GLC take-up campaign of the mid 1980s claimed to generate £10 million of additional income for Londoners (GLC, 1986). This represented, of course, potential additional revenue for local businesses, but it also significantly contributed towards reducing the deprivation experienced by local poor people. As with the government initiatives of the 1960s and 1970s therefore, it was in effect a form of antipoverty strategy, and local authorities engaged in supporting welfare rights work began to recognise that they might also be able to use other aspects of local services to combat local poverty.

In 1984 the CPAG devoted a special issue of its journal *Poverty* to the role local authorities might play in combating local poverty (CPAG, 1984). A range of local welfare rights and take-up initiatives were summarised, and in a more general discussion of a possible role for local authorities, Hume argued that there were a number of other areas of local services, such as housing, education and transport, where a focus on antipoverty initiatives might lead to new means of maximising income and improving services for the poor.

In the early 1980s the transfer of control of many of the larger urban authorities to more active, and more left-wing, Labour councillors created a climate in which such initiatives might also receive direct political support from local government. What some of these new councillors wanted to do was to use local Labour councils to provide an example to the Thatcher government that public services were popular and defensible, and that they played an important role in tackling the problem of local deprivation. Some, such as the GLC,

Sheffield and South Yorkshire, even presented this as an experiment in 'local socialism' (see Boddy and Fudge, 1984; Stoker, 1988).

Whatever their political motivation, many of the initiatives undertaken by local authorities during that period did have as a major aim the prevention or alleviation of local poverty. They also heralded a new role for local government in the development of local strategies for the economic and social regeneration of their local areas. By the end of the 1980s many local authorities had begun to appoint economic development officers and to enter into plans for the redevelopment of the local area in partnership with other agents, such as representatives of private industry and the voluntary sector. In the 1990s this was given further impetus by the shift within local government from a narrow service provider role to a strategic responsibility for 'enabling' the development and coordination of local service provision across a range of sectors (Clarke and Stewart, 1988; Cochrane, 1993).

Central government support for local development, which had been based largely on encouraging property speculation in the 1980s, also began to change in the 1990s. Additional funding was provided to local areas as part of the City Challenge and Single Regeneration Budget programmes, when these formed part of a coordinated plan for economic and social regeneration involving a partnership between local government, private industry and local voluntary sector agencies. Local social regeneration thus became increasingly closely linked to local economic development and a new strategic commitment by local government to secure a range of benefits for local people. In such a context antipoverty commitments increasingly came to be seen, and developed, within such a broader overall strategic framework.

Local antipoverty strategies, based in or led by local authorities, have expanded significantly as a major feature of targeted antipoverty action in the 1990s. At the end of the 1980s Balloch and Jones (1990) conducted a review of local authority antipoverty initiatives for the Association of Metropolitan Authorities and found that a range of different activities were being undertaken by a small number of authorities. By the mid 1990s this commitment to local antipoverty initiatives had expanded significantly, with over 140 authorities reporting an involvement in such work, almost half of which had formally adopted local antipoverty strategies as part of a corporate commitment to combating local poverty (see Pearson *et al.*, 1996).

Local antipoverty strategies in the 1990s include a wide range of local initiatives and activities, such as welfare rights and take-up work, policies to reduce or rebate fees and charges for services for the poor, support for debt support and the development of credit unions lending money at low interest, moves to decentralise and democratise services into poor areas, community development initiatives with local disadvantaged groups, and economic development work to increase local job opportunities (Alcock *et al.*, 1995). These strategic commitments are also supported by a national agency, the Local Government Anti-Poverty Unit, which is funded by the Local Government Association; and examples of good practice are reported in the unit's magazine, *Antipoverty Matters.*

A major reason for the increased in local authority attempts to combat poverty in their areas, of course, has been the growing scale of the problem of poverty and exclusion within local communities, as discussed in Chapter 1. The process of social polarisation accompanying this has meant that the experience of poverty has become much more concentrated in particular local areas (Green, 1994; Philo, 1995). This has resulted in many local authorities engaging in research to measure and map the extent of poverty in their areas. This in turn has led to a major increase in research activity into the distribution of poverty, although this has generally produced a depressing picture of growing deprivation and polarisation, against which local politicians and activists must struggle (Alcock *et al.*, 1995, ch. 4).

Backed by such local research findings and often involving other local agencies, local authority antipoverty strategies are therefore now an established feature of targeted antipoverty activity within social policy. They are also, however, subject to many of the fundamental problems and contradictions which were revealed by the early attempts at targeting, such as the CDPs – in particular the problem of where to draw the line between the targets.

Missing Targets

The main aim of targeted antipoverty strategies has been to expose and to challenge the limitations and failings of existing state provision in preventing or relieving poverty, by channelling limited resources into work in local areas to improve the delivery and receipt of existing services. Important though these initiatives have been in revealing the problems of providing protection for the poor and securing much-needed extra support for those experiencing extreme deprivation, there are nevertheless serious problems and contradictions inherent in targeted initiatives to challenge poverty.

For a start, in overall terms the resources that have gone into targeted initiatives have been relatively small. It was the low cost of a small number of targeted projects that first attracted the governments of the 1960s and 1970s to such initiatives, at a time when pressure to curb the overall rise in state welfare expenditure was growing; and in the 1990s local authority commitment to antipoverty activity has not generally involved the allocation of large budgets to support such work. Targeted strategies are cheap because they are small-scale. This is a structural feature; but it is also a structural problem. If the strategies were to be extended in scope they would no longer be targeted; they would also no longer be cheap, and questions might be asked about whether such large amounts of money might not be better spent in other ways, such as on improved social security benefits.

What is more, most of the limited resources of the targeted initiatives have gone not to local poor people, but on the salaries of the professionals involved, such as welfare rights workers. No doubt welfare rights workers would justify the money spent on them by pointing to the extra benefits they have been able to secure for local clients. These extra benefits have come from the social security system, not from the antipoverty initiative funding, so if such funding can 'lever in' extra funds from other sources, then perhaps the expenditure on professionals is justified; but if it can not, then some might sceptically ask why the money could not be given straight to those who need it most.

The assumption behind the use of targeted resources to employ professionals to 'help the poor to help themselves' is also to some extent linked to a pathological model of the causes of urban poverty in affluent society, stemming from the culture of poverty and cycle of deprivation theses discussed in Chapter 2. The CDP workers were generally well aware of the shortcomings and contradictions of such approaches, and the consequences of these for their work in local communities – and no doubt most other antipoverty workers are too. Nevertheless focusing targeted initiatives on poor people and poor communities inevitably means focusing on the symptoms rather than the causes of continuing poverty. The workers may argue, as they did in the CDPs, that what is really needed are changes to the broader economic and social policies; but then this is not what targeted initiatives are intended to achieve – as the CDP workers discovered.

Finally, and perhaps most importantly, the most fundamental problem with targeted antipoverty initiatives is the fact that they are targeted on particular – usually urban – areas. Of course large numbers of poor people do live in run-down inner city areas, but many – indeed most – do not. For those outside the target area, or the particular local authority, the resources are of no benefit to them. This is especially the case for the rural poor, who tend to live in small isolated communities, often with less active local authorities that are less likely to pursue antipoverty strategies (Cloke *et al.*, 1994). These people are probably also poorly provided with local services such as education and transport. Their deprivation and exclusion is likely to be acute, but they are unlikely to be the beneficiaries of targeted antipoverty action.

Thus in hitting one target, targeted antipoverty strategies inevitably miss many others. Of course this is not a reason for not undertaking them, but it is a reason for recognising the intrinsic limitations of the targeting approach. For instance the widespread development of advice agencies and welfare rights work has created expectations, among benefit administrators in particular, that such independent advice and advocacy work is available to all claimants, and as a result the Benefits Agency has to some extent withdrawn from its commitment to provide take-up advice, for instance most claim forms now contain a suggestion that claimants might wish to seek independent assistance from an advice agency. For those who do not benefit from such local antipoverty services this represents a double deprivation.

Against the significant gains achieved by some targeted antipoverty initiatives, therefore, must be balanced the structural limitations of strategies to target activities and resources at defined geographical areas or social groups, especially when, as is frequently the case, these initiatives only operate for specific periods of time. Such targeting can only meet the needs of some of the people for some of the time. Where targeting is undertaken therefore, there should be clear recognition of the limitations of the potential achievements, and activities should be monitored and evaluated to ensure that real progress is made. Within such limits progress in combating local poverty through local action can be significant and important, but many of the causes of – and therefore the solutions to – the problems of local poverty and exclusion lie well outside the control of local activists or local politicians. They are part of the broader social and economic context of the British state and the wider international order, and it is to this broader context that we now turn.

16

Poverty, Inequality and Welfare

The Problem of Poverty

Throughout this book we have argued consistently that poverty is a problem and that academic and political concern with poverty has been predicated upon the assumption that something should be done in response to this problem. Poverty is therefore identified and measured in order to provide a basis for antipoverty policy; and as we have discussed, the disagreements over both definition and measurement are inextricably intertwined with disagreements over the policies that should or should not flow from these.

Our understanding of poverty therefore involves recognition of the political context of the problem and the links within this between definition and policy. As we have seen, however, understanding poverty also involves understanding the broader context of the inequality and exclusion within which it is situated. Poverty is the unacceptable face of broader inequalities; and although they may not be aimed at producing equality, policies to combat poverty must also seek to change the wider patterns of inequality, even if only minimally. What is more, material poverty is only one aspect of the broader social structures and processes within which some individuals and social groups experience marginalisation, disadvantage and social exclusion; so policies that aim to combat poverty must also aim to challenge the structures and processes that accompany it.

Therefore poverty and antipoverty policy must be addressed within the wider context of social and economic trends and policies in society and beyond. In practice, however, throughout most of the twentieth century the poverty and antipoverty debate in Britain has been dominated by two general approaches to defining and solving the problem of poverty, and these approaches have been reflected in the main antipoverty policies developed by British policy makers.

Those who argue in favour of a largely *absolute* measure of poverty claim that the problem is restricted to extremes of inequality that leave some without the resources to survive, and following this approach antipoverty policy is limited to the redistribution of just enough resources to provide for some measure of basic subsistence for those in need. Such policies also usually seek to restrict the redistribution of resources to those in proven poverty through the use of means tests, and to ensure that those who do receive support are encouraged by a variety of means to continue to seek self-support rather than rely on state assistance.

Those who argue in favour of a more *relative* measure of poverty, or deprivation, suggest that the problem of poverty is an exaggerated aspect of an unequal distribution of resources in which some are so far below the rest that they are excluded from many important aspects of modern living. From this perspective antipoverty policy is extended to include the redistribution of a range of resources to assist those who cannot participate fully to become more integrated into society. Such policies usually seek to extend redistribution to reduce more general inequalities in society and provide guaranteed support for a range of people who may be in circumstances that are likely to place them at the bottom in the distribution of resources.

There are differences within these two broad approaches of course, and some protagonists at the extremes who may not fit readily into either. There is also conflict between the two in both theory and practice. Nevertheless the focus of both is similar in that it directs antipoverty action at policies designed to provide support for those in, or at risk of, poverty. By and large the measures that are promoted to achieve this are also similar and involve a central, dominant role for the state in directing and resourcing support for the poor. Even when private sector protection or voluntary activity has been encouraged within antipoverty policy, it is still generally controlled and regulated through the powers of the state.

Thus debate on the problem of poverty and its solution has largely been a debate on the identifying and measuring of inequality and deprivation in order to provide a basis for state policy to intervene, directly or indirectly, so as to redistribute the resources to alleviate these. The evidence from research such as that by the Rowntree Foundation in the 1990s (Barclay, 1995; Hills, 1995) also suggests that in general terms this has not resulted in complete success in removing the problem of poverty from present-day Britain. In part this may be because the policies introduced are not working as intended or that they do not go quite far enough; but it may also, and more importantly, be because such antipoverty policy initiatives do not take account of the broader context within which the problem of poverty is situated.

Antipoverty policies by and large focus on poor people and seek to provide support or the redistribution of resources to those who are poor. However, as Ferge and Millar have cogently stressed, 'Who becomes or stays poor is a *structural social consequence*' (1987, p. 298, emphasis in original). The causes of poverty are not rooted in individual action, or inaction, although this may be a contributory factor at times. They are to be found in the dynamics of change of the social and economic forces within societies that structure the production and distribution of resources. Poverty is the unacceptable consequence of these social forces, and antipoverty policies that focus on this consequence are concentrating on the *symptoms* of the problem of poverty, not the *causes*.

Certainly policies concentrating on the redistribution of resources to the poor can and do mitigate the problems resulting from the inequalities of the initial distribution of resources in society; and of course at this level antipoverty policies have indeed done much to reduce some of the harshest consequences of an inequitable social order. However, as long as their focus is on poverty and redistribution, such policies can only play a mitigating role. If mitigation is to be replaced by prevention, then the focus of policy must move beyond the redistribution of resources to address their production and initial distribution.

Marxists such as Novak (1988, 1995) argue that the forces of production and distribution are the product of the capitalist economic system that dominates a society such as Britain, and that only when that economic system is overthrown and replaced with an egalitarian system of production and distribution will poverty disappear. This is a rather Utopian perspective however. It generally tells us little about how such revolutionary change might be achieved, and still less about whether such changes would indeed remove poverty. Furthermore, although capitalist investment and profit does exercise a predominant influence over the British economy and its consequent labour market, capital is not the only structuring feature of what is in practice a complex social and economic order, and its removal is neither a precondition for combating poverty nor a guarantee of it – as the different levels of poverty in both capitalist and non-capitalist societies demonstrate.

Where the Marxists are partially correct, however, is in their focus on the need for broader structural change to prevent poverty. Structural inequities must be tackled if poverty is to be prevented. This requires a broader strategic approach to policy development than measures that focus only on redistribution to the poor. Any attempt to challenge the structural dynamics of poverty requires attention to the broader context of inequality within which poverty is produced, and an attempt to develop a 'strategy of equality' to combat these structural forces at a number of levels. The case for such a strategy of equality has been argued by a number of academics and politicians concerned with the problem of poverty throughout this century, and it has formed the basis of some of the most important aspects of social and economic policy development pursued by governments in Britain and elsewhere.

The Strategy of Equality

The Fabian campaigners, such as Sydney and Beatrice Webb, who sought to promote the politics of poverty in the early twentieth century were aware that the prevention of poverty and the achievement of socialist reform required a concerted strategy by government to secure greater equality within British society. Evidence of the problem of poverty was used by Fabians to persuade governments to act to prevent it; but the actions the Fabians championed were intended to produce wide-ranging reform through the extension of state provision of welfare to improve the overall standards for all in society. Their aim was not just the elimination of poverty, but the greater efficiency of the entire social order through the enhancement of state intervention and control – the development, in other words, of a *welfare state*.

The pursuit of state welfare as part of a broader strategy to remove poverty through structural reform was also promoted by academics and politicians outside the fairly narrow utilitarian perspective of Fabian politics. These included in particular influential writers such as Tawney (1931) and Marshall (1950).

Tawney was a Christian socialist who saw the struggle against poverty in moral as well as practical terms. He believed that greater equality could be achieved by state action to extend welfare in order to minimise the privileges enjoyed exclusively by the rich and raise the standards of the bulk of the population. He did not think that absolute equality was either achievable or necessarily desirable and he believed that all had a duty to contribute to the welfare of society as well as to benefit from it; but his belief in common values and common standards for all people led him to argue for state welfare as a means of reducing differentials and eliminating deprivation. Although they were not intended to produce an egalitarian social order therefore, Tawney referred to the development of welfare policies through the state as a 'strategy of equality'.

The main focus of Marshall's work was the development of citizenship within society. He argued that as industrial society developed, then the rights of citizens within it became more extensive, thus creating greater social cohesion. He argued that *civil* rights of freedom of speech and of property had developed in the eighteenth century, and that *political* rights in the democratisation of public power had developed in the nineteenth century. In the twentieth century, he argued, citizenship should be extended to include *social* rights to welfare, security and economic participation, and that this would be achieved by the development of a welfare state granting welfare rights to all citizens, and by reducing social divisions. Marshall saw this as leading to 'an equalisation between the more and the less fortunate at all levels – between the healthy and the sick, the employed and the unemployed, the old and the active, the bachelor and the large family' (Marshall, 1950, p. 56). Thus like Tawney he saw in the achievement of social citizenship a strategy to reduce inequality by guaranteeing minimum standards through state welfare.

Both Tawney and Marshall were writing at a time when the role of state welfare was being reconsidered at the government level during and after the Second World War. Beveridge's (1942) report on social security reform, commissioned by the wartime coalition government, shared their support for the extension of state welfare to remove all social ills. Beveridge referred to these as the 'five giants' – disease, idleness, ignorance, squalor and want – and he expected the state to ensure that after the war all would be the objects of welfare reforms, including the social security proposals that he himself was recommending.

In large part the postwar Labour government did introduce Beveridge's social security reforms. It also tackled the other 'giants' with the development of the National Health Service, free state education, a public housing programme and a commitment to full employment. Together these policies have generally been referred to as the 'welfare state'. They did much to fulfil Marshall's hopes of social citizenship, although in practice many citizens did not benefit fully from all the welfare reforms; and they did much to translate Tawney's strategy of equality into a wide-ranging reform of the whole social and economic order. Despite the change to Conservative governments in the 1950s the basic structure of the welfare state was maintained throughout the decades following the war, and politicians from both major parties pledged support for its aims and achievements (see Glennerster, 1995).

However the welfare state and its strategy of equality were not without their critics. As we have seen, by the 1960s Fabian academics were once again arguing that poverty was a serious problem in British society and that state welfare reform was needed to eliminate it (Abel Smith and Townsend, 1965; Townsend, 1979). This suggested that the strategy of equality had failed because state welfare reforms had not sufficiently raised the standards of all. Other critics of the strategy went further, arguing that the state welfare reforms had actually operated to benefit the better off.

This criticism of the perverse achievements of state welfare in promoting inequality has been argued most persuasively by Le Grand (1982). Le Grand claims that the strategy of equality was never properly developed to ensure equality of outcome, as opposed to equality of opportunity, and that when the evidence is examined it reveals that much of the growth of public expenditure on state welfare services, such as health and education, has not gone towards raising standards for all but to benefit the more active and articulate middle classes, who are most able to benefit from these services. He concludes that public expenditure on welfare has therefore not reduced the differences flowing from inequalities in monetary income, but has tended to multiply them, and that consequently the strategy of equality has failed.

The tendency of welfare expenditure to promote inequality was identified as early as 1958 by one of the most famous of the postwar Fabians, Titmuss. He argued that there were in effect divisions within state welfare between expenditure on state services for all, which benefited the poor, and expenditure in the form of tax relief to support individual services for the few, which benefited those wealthy enough to purchase such services in the first place (Titmuss, 1958). This 'fiscal welfare' has grown in significance throughout the postwar period, providing a major counterbalancing influence on the equalising impact of direct welfare spending. Taylor Gooby (1991, p. 26) estimated that the extent of the major tax reliefs on an annual basis at the end of the 1980s was £10.9 billion on mortgage interest relief to owner-occupiers, £12.9 billion on occupational and personal pensions, £300 million on support for private schools and £100 million on support for private medical insurance.

All these forms of tax relief disproportionately benefit the better-off, and they constitute government support for welfare services that seem to be in direct contradiction to the supposed aims of the strategy of equality in utilising state welfare expenditure to reduce differentials by raising common standards for all. Thus Le Grand's conclusion that the strategy of equality has failed seems to be vindicated; and the evidence of continued and growing problems of poverty and depriva- tion suggests that expectations of Tawney, Marshall, Beveridge and the early Fabians that state welfare would prevent want were mis- placed. However much of the increased poverty experienced in Britain in the 1970s and 1980s was associated not so much with the failings of postwar welfare services, but with the onset of economic recession and the adaptation of welfare provision in changed political and economic circumstances. By the 1980s it was not at all clear that a strategy of equality was underpinning state welfare policy, indeed some critics were arguing that a 'strategy of inequality' had come to dominate social and economic policy in Britain.

The Strategy of Inequality

Criticism of the postwar welfare state's failure to combat the problem of poverty came not only from Fabian and other left-wing critics. There have also been critics on the right who, following on from the early arguments of Hayek (1944) that state welfare would inevitably conflict with economic freedom, have maintained that welfare reforms could not succeed in removing poverty and raising the living standard of all in society. These criticisms have been articulated most widely in Britain by members the right-wing think tank, the Institute of Eco- nomic Affairs (see Green, 1990); but they have also been voiced by some prominent Conservative Party politicians, such as Keith Joseph (Joseph and Sumption, 1979) and Rhodes Boyson (1971).

In general terms the right-wing critics argue that state welfare has an inevitable tendency to push the overall cost of public expenditure beyond the limits a market economy can afford. This is because a wide range of state welfare activity providing services for large sections of the population naturally becomes expensive when seeking to meet more and more needs; and in the absence of any overall assessment of the broader impact of this, it receives popular support for such expansion. The problem is that such activity cannot continually expand without endangering overall economic growth – as was revealed by the economic recession in Britain and other advanced industrial countries in the 1970s, as a result of which public welfare expenditure had to be curtailed.

Some critics, such as Murray (1984) in the United States, have gone further than this, however, and have argued that redistributive welfare spending also destroys the incentive that individuals would otherwise have to provide for themselves and their families, and that it provides 'perverse incentives' for them to remain dependent on further state support. This notion of the creation through state welfare of a 'dependency culture' was central to Rhodes Boyson's earlier criticisms of the welfare state, which 'saps the collective moral fibre of our people as a nation' (Boyson, 1971, p. 385), and to Secretary of State John Moore's speech attacking the poverty lobby and the notion of relative poverty in 1989. As we saw in Chapter 2, it also informs some of the pathological approaches to the problem of poverty that have underlain recent debates on the problem of a growing underclass in affluent welfare capitalist societies.

The conclusions the right-wing academics and politicians draw from these failings within state welfare are not just that public welfare expenditure will need to be curtailed in times of recession in order to support economic growth, but also that redistributive policies that result in increased welfare dependency should be withdrawn, or redrawn, in order to reduce or at least minimise the extent of the dependency culture. This leads to an increased unwillingness to support state welfare expenditure and to calls for the transfer of welfare services to the private or voluntary sectors leaving only a residuum of those who could not afford self-protection to depend on reduced, and targeted state support. The consequence of these conclusions in policy terms is an attempt to reverse the strategy of equality and the growth of state welfare expenditure in order to support market-led economic growth and to provide incentives for self-protection, which will itself encourage further growth.

In Britain in the 1980s the Thatcher governments did attempt such a strategy, at least to some extent. Their aim was to reduce state expenditure by reducing state dependency and encouraging private protection through the market. Of course the cuts in state expenditure that resulted from this and the reduction in tax rates, aimed especially at creating incentives for the rich, resulted in the increased inequality and polarisation discussed in Chapter 1. Nevertheless the government believed that this would lead to greater overall economic growth, and that the benefits of this – greater overall wealth – would 'trickle down' to the poor at the bottom.

However not much did trickle down to the poor in the 1980s and early 1990s. As the government's own figures on the changes in the real value of incomes since 1979 revealed, whilst average incomes had risen by 38 per cent and those of the wealthiest 10 per cent had increased by 62 per cent, the incomes of the bottom decile of the population had *declined* by 17 per cent (DSS, 1995a).

Furthermore it is impossible to know whether the economic growth that was achieved over this period could have been matched, or bettered, had redistributive welfare policies continued to be actively followed – although other Western European countries achieved growth rates equal to or better than Britain's during the same period without equivalent retrenchment of welfare policy. Nevertheless it is arguable that right-wing critics were successful in Britain in the 1980s in persuading the Thatcher governments to attempt such a policy reversal and to institute a 'strategy of inequality', the aim of which was to use economic growth supported by free market policies, rather than redistributive welfare spending, to raise overall standards – neatly encapsulated by Joseph and Sumption's (1979, p. 22) assertion that, 'You cannot make the poor richer by making the rich poorer'.

In one sense of course Joseph and Sumption are clearly wrong. In the short run at least, redistribution would raise the living standards of the poor, whereas the trickle down policies of the 1980s appear to have reduced them, and to have contributed to the broader problems of exclusion and polarisation. The argument behind the right-wing support for a growth-led rise in overall standards, however, rests on the assumption that in the longer run *only* free markets and non-interventionist states can produce sustained economic growth.

The record of the British economy over the latter half of the twentieth century however, and that of most other major industrial societies, lends little credence to such beliefs. Growth has been sustained in economies with high welfare spending, such as Sweden, and recession has been experienced in those with minimal state welfare, such as the United States. Indeed the improved growth that Britain experienced in the 1980s was followed in the early 1990s with a severe recession, which the Conservative government attributed to international economic trends rather than public expenditure patterns in Britain.

Furthermore the attempt to reverse the expansionary tendencies of state welfare could hardly be counted as successful. State expenditure on the major welfare services such as social security, health and education has continued to grow, and despite the minor growth of private protection in some areas, no alternative to state welfare as a means of meeting these major welfare needs has emerged. What is more surveys on social attitudes towards welfare reveal continued support for the expansion of state welfare expenditure (Taylor Gooby, 1991).

So we might conclude that the strategy of inequality pursued in Britain in the 1980s has failed. It did not produce sustained growth. It did not raise the living standards of all. It removed neither the need nor the support for increased state welfare. By the early the 1990s it is arguable that, with the replacement of Thatcher by Major as prime minister, it was no longer supported so strongly within the government; and outside government the deliberations of bodies such as the Commission on Social Justice (Borrie, 1994) were once again raising the demand for welfare policies to be used to challenge social inequality.

As with the failings of the strategy of equality in the 1970s therefore, it seems that welfare policies of the 1980s were unable to escape from the broader context, and consequences, of the changing balance of social and economic forces. This is because, just as with the creation and recreation of poverty, welfare policy too is shaped by these economic forces. At the same time, however, once introduced, welfare policy also operates to shape economic forces – the two are inevitably and inextricably interrelated. It is in this interrelationship between welfare and economic policy that strategic planning for equality or inequality must take place; and if in the past strategies appear to have failed, it may be because they have failed to appreciate the importance of this broader canvas of social relations.

Welfare State and Welfare Capitalism

Once we recognise that poverty is the product of the operation of social and economic forces, in which individual choices or individual responsibility may be important but in general can never be decisive, then we must look for the solutions to poverty in antipoverty policies that take account of and seek to influence these major social and economic forces. Both the strategy of equality and the strategy of inequality were attempts to engineer such changes, but both failed because they did not extend far enough in tackling the relationship between social and economic forces in a complex industrial society, and because in practice therefore they were never really fully explored.

Curiously enough both the strategy of equality and the strategy of inequality saw the introduction of state welfare as the focus of antipoverty policy, either as the means of engineering greater equality or as the cause of lower overall standards. State welfare was seen as the use of social policy to adjust the consequences of economic forces within a capitalist economy. What this overlooked, however, is the fact that the welfare state is *not* merely the product of benevolent, or misguided, social policy. As Gough (1979) has argued, the introduction of state welfare is the product of a process of economic adjustment within capitalist society in which state intervention in the reproduction and maintenance of a range of major services, such as health and education, has become a necessary means of ensuring the continuation of existing economic forces, just as much as a means of redistributing resources to the poor.

Thus the introduction of state welfare results in a transformation of economic forces, indeed in a transformation of the social and economic structure itself, into what Esping-Andersen (1990) has called 'welfare capitalism'. The major extension of state intervention into the reproduction of social forces – and in many countries into production too through the nationalisation of major industries such as energy, steel and transport – transforms capitalist economies into some form of mixed market economy in which state policies are a major determinant of economic as well as social trends. As the work of Esping-Andersen (ibid.) demonstrates, despite some variations in the forms of state welfare its extension has been a consistent trend in all the major advanced industrial economies in the latter half of the twentieth century; and antipoverty policy must be seen, and developed, within the broader structural role that state welfare now plays in shaping social and economic forces.

This casts a new light on the criticisms of Le Grand (1982) and others of the failure of the strategy of equality. As Hindess (1987) for instance has pointed out, Le Grand's criticisms are really misplaced since their assumption that state welfare was introduced merely as the vehicle for a strategy of equality cannot be justified. Tawney and the Fabians may have wished state welfare to play such an equalising role in the combating of poverty, but this has only ever been one part of what state welfare has been designed and developed to accomplish.

Indeed, as Hindess suggested, the fact that so little was done to monitor the impact of state welfare in achieving equalisation is evidence not so much of failure, but of a lack of attention to this as a relevant goal for services such as education, health and even social security. Thus the strategy of equality has not really failed, because it has not really been attempted.

The failure of the strategy of inequality too is based on a misconception of the role and extent of state welfare. The welfare state is not, as right-wing critics such as Rhodes Boyson (1971) have argued, merely a means of taking resources from the rich and successful and transferring them to the poor and dependent. It is a part of the broader structure of production and reproduction in advanced industrial societies, on which the rich and successful are equally dependent for providing the social and economic environment in which their industries and investments can flourish. Economic forces depend on state welfare, and political forces reflect this reality. As Therborn and Roebroek (1986) have argued, state welfare services have become *irreversible* features of advanced industrial societies not just because of their economic role but also because the services they provide secure political support across a wide range of the social structure, and too many people know that they would lose too much if these were to be withdrawn completely.

It is not surprising therefore that the attitude survey evidence discussed by Taylor Gooby (1991) revealed continued high levels of support in Britain for state welfare services despite over a decade of a supposed strategy of inequality. Nor is it surprising therefore that most critics argue that despite significant cuts and privatisations, Thatcherism was unable to remove, or even reverse, the growth of state welfare in Britain in the late twentieth century (see Johnson, 1990). Indeed, as with the strategy of equality, it could be argued that in the extreme form promoted by critics such as Green (1990) or Murray (1984) a strategy of inequality aimed at removing the major features of state welfare in favour of entirely market-based or voluntary provision has also not thus far been attempted in Britain.

British welfare capitalism has therefore been driven exclusively neither by the pursuit of equality nor the promotion of inequality. It is the product of much more complex and contradictory social and economic forces, and its consequences have been the recreation of poverty and social exclusion as well as their amelioration. As discussed above, however, the predominant focus of antipoverty policy within British welfare has been on the symptoms of inequality and deprivation rather than their causes or their context. This has resulted in what critics such as Townsend (1984) have referred to as the adoption of a 'casualty approach' to welfare services.

The casualty approach is particularly true of a social security policy that has sought to identify and compensate the victims of harsh inequalities within the wage labour market and the broader distribution of wealth via the redistribution of cash through benefits, rather than to alter or influence the initial distribution of wealth or the operation of the labour market that has largely produced it. The central role of means testing, or selectivity, reveals most starkly the casualty philosophy with its requirement of proof of need before resources can be made available, and with its stigmatising undertones of social and economic failure

An antipoverty policy that seeks to transcend such a casualty approach to welfare, therefore, would have to develop, policies on wealth and income as well as policies on need and benefits. An income and wealth policy would require intervention into the labour market to influence both the availability of employment as a source of income and the level of wages that employment might provide. It would also require policies of taxation and investment to direct wealth into productive industries or social services, rather than it being squandered on private affluence. An income and wealth policy would therefore require intervention in economic forces as well as social structures; it would require the welfare state planning directly for production and distribution, and not only for redistribution. Only in this way might welfare policy be able to achieve economic as well as social change, and to advance a strategy of equality as a means of challenging the problem of poverty.

Such a shift in welfare policy may appear to imply a significant transition from the casualty-based policy developments of twentieth-century welfare – even perhaps a revolutionary change. In practice, however, moves towards a more interventionist social and economic strategy for welfare are neither revolutionary nor untried.

British governments have variously tried to influence investment policies and practices throughout most of the postwar period, albeit often without any clear overall strategic objectives. British governments have also tried to influence wealth and income distribution, for instance through legislating minimum wage levels in certain industries and in seeking to control prices and wage rises. In other welfare capitalist countries similar policies have been developed, and often taken further. For instance many Western European countries impose statutory minimum wages and control overall wage levels, and many use government investment in industries and services to shape and direct economic growth and development. Indeed such strategies are commonplace within the nations of the EU and are now promoted by the European Commission as part of a wider European programme for social and economic development, including for instance the Social Charter.

In the future it is likely that the further integration of Britain into the EU will require the greater development of such social and economic strategies in this country too, despite the government's hostility to this in the early 1990s. Britain is now a member of the single European market and it benefits from EU investment strategies both nationally and on a regional basis. Despite securing the right to opt out of the Social Charter, Britain is likely to come under increasing pressure to guarantee a range of social rights in common with other member states; and in order to meet the requirements for economic and currency union Britain will also be pressed to pursue broader economic policy goals and policy measures that complement those of the other member states on the continent. The further integration and development of social and economic policies within British welfare capitalism are not revolutionary therefore – rather they are inevitable.

Of course greater social and economic policy integration within Europe will not immediately remove the problem of poverty in Britain, just as it has not in the other EU member states. However it is to such a future integration that those who wish to see the removal of poverty and the reduction of social exclusion must look – and not to the poor themselves. We must recognise that those approaches that seek to identify an underclass of poor individuals – who are the willing or unwilling victims of dependency – in order to focus antipoverty policies onto them *only* are ignoring the broader structural context in which some people become or remain poor. Therefore we must widen our focus to encompass the social and economic forces that shape the social structure that affects us *all*. Only by challenging these social forces will we be able to change the position of the poor within them. As Tawney succinctly put it in his famous statement of 1913, quoted in the Preface, the problem of poverty is a 'problem of riches' too.

References

ABEL SMITH, B. and TOWNSEND, P. (1965) *The Poor and the Poorest* (G. Bell and Sons).

ADAM SMITH INSTITUTE (ASI) (1984) *Omega Report: Social Security Policy* (ASI).

ADAM SMITH INSTITUTE (ASI) (1989) *Needs Reform: The Overhaul of Social Security* (ASI).

AHMAD, W. and ATKIN, K. (eds) (1996) *'Race' and Community Care* (Open University Press).

ALCOCK, P. (1987) *Poverty and State Support* (Longman).

ALCOCK, P. (1989) 'Unconditional Benefits: Misplaced Optimism in Income Maintenance', *Capital and Class*, no. 37 (Spring).

ALCOCK, P. (1994) 'Welfare Rights and Wrongs: The Limits of Local Anti-Poverty Strategies', *Local Economy*, vol. 9, no. 2.

ALCOCK, P. (1996a) *Social Policy in Britain: Themes and Issues* (Macmillan).

ALCOCK, P. (1996b) 'Development of Social Security Policy', in J. Ditch (ed.), *Poverty and Social Security: Issues and Research* (Harvester/Wheatsheaf).

ALCOCK, P. (1996c) 'The advantages and disadvantages of the contribution base in targeting benefits: A social analysis of the insurance scheme in the United Kingdom', *International Social Security Review*, vol. 49, no. 1 (Geneva).

ALCOCK, P. *et al.* (1995) *Combating Local Poverty: The Management of Anti-Poverty Strategies by Local Government* (Local Government Management Board).

ALCOCK, P. and SHEPHERD, J. (1987) 'Take–up Campaigns: Fighting Poverty Through the Post', *Critical Social Policy*, issue 19 (Summer).

AMIN, K. and OPPENHEIM, C. (1992) *Poverty in Black and White: Deprivation and Ethnic Minorities* (CPAG/Runnymede Trust).

ATKINSON, A. B. (1969) *Poverty in Britain and the Reform of Social Security* (Cambridge University Press).

ATKINSON, A. B. (1983) *The Economics of Inequality*, 2nd edn (Oxford University Press).

ATKINSON, A. B. (1989) *Poverty and Social Security* (Harvester Wheatsheaf).

ATKINSON, A. B. (1990a) *A National Minimum? A History of Ambiguity in the Determination of Benefit Scales in Britain* (LSE/STICERD, WSP/47).

ATKINSON, A. B. (1990b) *Comparing Poverty Rates Internationally: Lessons from Recent Studies in OECD Countries* (LSE/STICERD, WSP/53).

ATKINSON, A. B. (1991a) *Poverty, Statistics, and Progress in Europe* (LSE/STICERD, WSP/60).

ATKINSON, A. B. (1991b) *The Development of State Pensions in the United Kingdom* (LSE/STICERD, WSP/58).

ATKINSON, A. B. (1992) *Social Insurance* (LSE/STICERD, WSP/65).

ATKINSON, A. B. (1995) *Public Economics in Action: The Basic Income/Flat Tax Proposal* (Clarendon Press).

ATKINSON, A. B. and SUTHERLAND, H. (1984) 'TAXMOD: User Manual' (LSE).

ATKINSON, A. B. and SUTHERLAND, H. (1991) *Two Nations in Early Retirement?: The Case of Britain* (LSE/STICERD, WSP/56).

AULETTA, K. (1982) *The Underclass* (New York: Random House).

BALDWIN, S. and COOKE, K. (1984) *How Much is Enough?* (Family Policy Studies Centre).

BALDWIN, S. and FALKINGHAM, J. (eds) (1994) *Social Security and Social Change: New Challenges to the Beveridge Model* (Harvester/Wheatsheaf).

BALDWIN, S. and PARKER, G. (1991) 'Support for informal carers – the role of social security', in G. Dalley (ed.), *Disability and Social Policy* (PSI).

BALLOCH, S. and JONES, B. (1990) *Poverty and Anti-Poverty Strategy: the Local Government Response* (Association of Metropolitan Authorities).

BARCLAY, Sir P. (1995) *JR Foundation Inquiry into Income and Wealth*, vol. 1, (JR Foundation).

BARRETT, M. and MACINTOSH, M. (1982) *The Anti-Social Family* (Verso).

BARRON, R. G. and NORRIS, G. M. (1976) 'Sexual Divisions and the Dual Labour Market', in D. L. Barker and S. Allen (eds), *Dependence and Exploitation in Work and Marriage* (Longman).

BARRY, N. (1987) *The New Right* (Croom Helm).

BECKER, S. (ed.) (1991) *Windows of Opportunity: Public Policy and the Poor* (CPAG).

BECKERMAN, W. (1980) *National Income Analysis*, 3rd edn (Weidenfeld & Nicolson).

BECKERMAN, W. and CLARK, S. (1982) *Poverty and Social Security in Britain Since 1961* (Oxford University Press).

BEECHEY, V. (1978) 'Women and production: a critical analysis of some sociological theories of women's work', in A. Kuhn and A. Wolpe (eds), *Feminism and Materialism: Women and Modes of Production* (Routledge & Kegan Paul).

BEECHEY, V. (1987) *Unequal Work* (Verso).

BERESFORD, P. and CROFT, S. (1995) 'It's our problem too! Challenging the exclusion of poor people from poverty discourse', *Critical Social Policy*, issue 44/45 (Autumn).

BERGHMAN, J. (1995) 'Social Exclusion in Europe: Policy Context and Analytical Framework', in G. Room (ed.), *Beyond the Threshold: The Measurement and Analysis of Social Exclusion* (Policy Press).

BERTHOUD, R. (1985) *The Examination of Social Security* (PSI).

BERTHOUD, R. (1986) *Selective Social Security: an Analysis of the Government's Plan* (PSI).

BERTHOUD, R. (1991) 'Meeting the costs of disability', in G. Dalley (ed.), *Disability and Social Policy* (PSI).

BERTHOUD, R., BENSON, S. and WILLIAMS, S. (1986) *Standing up for Claimants: Welfare Rights Work in Local Authorities* (PSI).

BERTHOUD, R., BROWN, J. and COOPER, S. (1981) *Poverty and the Development of Anti-Poverty Policy in the UK* (Heinemann EB).

BERTHOUD, R. and KEMPSON, E. (1992) *Credit and Debt: The PSI Report* (PSI).

BERTHOUD, R., LAKEY, J. and MCKAY, S. (1993) *The Economic Problems of Disabled People* (PSI).

BEVERIDGE, SIR W. (1942) *Report on Social Insurance and Allied Services*, Cmd 6404 (HMSO).

BINNEY, V., HARKELL, G. and NIXON, J. (1981) *Leaving Violent Men: a Study of Refuges and Housing for Battered Women* (Women's Aid Federation).

BLACKBURN, C. (1991) *Poverty and Health: Working with Families* (Open University Press).

BODDY, M. and FUDGE, C. (eds) (1984) *Local Socialism? Labour Councils and New Left Alternatives* (Macmillan).

BOOTH, C. (1889) *The Life and Labour of the People* (Williams and Northgate).

BOOTH, C. (1892) *Pauperism: a Picture of the Endowment of Old Age: an Argument* (Macmillan).

BOOTH, C. (1894) *The Aged Poor: Condition* (Macmillan).

BORRIE, Sir G. (1994) *Social Justice: Strategies for National Renewal – The Report of the Commission on Social Justice* (Vintage).

BOSANQUET, N. and TOWNSEND, P. (1980) *Labour and Equality* (Heinemann EB).

BOWLEY, A. L. and BURNETT-HURST, A. R. (1915) *Livelihood and Poverty* (G. Bell and Sons).

BOYSON, R. (1971) *Down with the Poor* (Churchill).

BRADSHAW, J. (1975) 'Welfare rights: an experimental approach', in R. Lees and G. Smith (eds), *Action Research in Community Development* (Routledge & Kegan Paul).

BRADSHAW, J. (ed.) (1993a) *Budget Standards for the United Kingdom* (Avebury).

BRADSHAW, J. (ed.) (1993b) *Household Budgets and Living Standards* (JR Foundation).

BRADSHAW, J. and HOLMES, H. (1989) *Living on the Edge: a Study of the Living Standards of Families on Benefit in Tyne and Wear* (Tyneside CPAG).

BRADSHAW, J. and MILLAR, J. (1991) *Lone-Parent Families in the UK* (HMSO).

BRADSHAW, J., MITCHELL, D. and MORGAN, J. (1987) 'Evaluating Adequacy: the Potential of Budget Standards', *Journal of Social Policy*, vol. 16, no. 2.

BRADSHAW, J. and MORGAN, J. (1987) *Budgeting on Benefit: the Consumption of Families on Social Security* (Family Policy Studies Centre).

BROWN, C. (1984) *Black and White Britain: the Third PSI Survey* (Heinemann EB).

BROWN, M. and MADGE, N. (1982) *Despite the Welfare State* (Heinemann EB).

BROWN, P. and SCASE, R. (eds) (1991) *Poor Work: Disadvantage and the Division of Labour* (Open University Press).

BRUEGEL, E. (1989) 'Sex and Race in the Labour Market', *Feminist Review*, no. 32.

BYTHEWAY, B. and JOHNSON J. (1990) 'On defining ageism', *Critical Social Policy*, issue 29 (Autumn).

CALLENDER, C. (1992) 'Redundancy, Unemployment and Poverty', in C. Glendinning and J. Millar (eds), *Women and Poverty in Britain: the 1990s* (Harvester/Wheatsheaf).

CCETSW (1989) *Welfare Rights in Social Work Education: Report by a Curriculum Development Group*, Central Council for Education and Training in Social Work, paper 28.1.

CHILD POVERTY ACTION GROUP (CPAG) (Annual) *National Welfare Benefits Handbook* (CPAG).

CHILD POVERTY ACTION GROUP (CPAG) (Annual) *Rights Guide to Non-Means-tested Benefits* (CPAG).

CHILD POVERTY ACTION GROUP (CPAG) (1984) *Poverty*, no. 57 (CPAG).

CHILD POVERTY ACTION GROUP (CPAG) (1985) *Burying Beveridge: a Detailed Response to the Green Paper – Reform of Social Security* (CPAG).

CLAPHAM, D., KEMP, P. and SMITH, S. J. (1990) *Housing and Social Policy* (Macmillan).

CLARKE, K., CRAIG, G. and GLENDINNING, C. (1996) *Small Change: The Impact of the Child Support Act on Lone Mothers and Children* (Family Policy Studies Centre).

CLARKE, M. and STEWART, J. (1988) *The Enabling Council* (Local Government Training Board).

CLOKE, P., MILBOURNE, P. and THOMAS, C. (1994) *Lifestyles in Rural England* (Rural Development Commission/Department of Environment).

COATES, D. and SILBURN, R. (1970) *Poverty: the Forgotten Englishmen* (Penguin).

COCHRANE, A. (1993) *Whatever Happened to Local Government?* (Open University P.).

COHEN, R., COXALL, J., CRAIG, G. and SADIQ-SANGSTER, A. (1992) *Hardship Britain: Being Poor in the 1990s* (CPAG).

COHEN, R. and RUSHTON, A. (1982) *Welfare Rights* (Heinemann EB).

COHEN, R. and TARPEY, M. (1986) 'Are We up on Take-up?', *Poverty*, no. 63.

COLE, I. and FURBEY, R. (1994) *The Eclipse of Council Housing* (Routledge).

COLLARD, D. (1980) 'Social dividend and negative income tax', in C. Sandford, C. Pond and R. Walker (eds), *Taxation and Social Policy* (Heinemann EB).

COMMUNITY DEVELOPMENT PROJECT (CDP) (1977) *Gilding the Ghetto: the State and the Poverty Experiments* (CDP).

COOKE, K. (1987) 'The Withdrawal from Paid Work of the Wives of Unemployed Men: a Review of Research', *Journal of Social Policy*, vol. 16, no. 3.

COOPER, S. (1985) *Observations in Supplementary Offices: the Reform of Supplementary Benefit Working Paper C* (PSI).

CORKEY, D. and CRAIG, G. (1978) 'CDP: Community Work or Class Politics?', in P. Curno (ed.), *Political Issues in Community Work* (Routledge Kegan Paul).

COWAN, R. (1988) 'Blaming the Buildings', *Roof*, March/April.

CROSLAND, C. A. R. (1956) *The Future of Socialism* (Jonathon Cape).

DAHRENDORF, R. (1987) 'The erosion of citizenship and its consequences for us all', *New Statesman*, 12 June.

DALLEY, G. (ed.) (1991) *Disability and Social Policy* (PSI).

DAVIES, R., ELIAS, P. and PENN, R. (1994) 'The Relationship between a Husband's Unemployment and his Wife's Particpation in the Labour Force', in D. Gallie, C. Marsh and C. Vogler, *Social Change and the Experience of Unemployment* (Oxford University Press).

DEACON, A. and BRADSHAW, J. (1983) *Reserved for the Poor: the Means-test in British Social Policy* (Basil Blackwell and Martin Robertson).

DEAN, H. (1991) 'In search of the underclass', in P. Brown and R. Scase (eds), *Poor Work: Disadvantage and the Division of Labour* (Open University Press).

DENNETT, J. *et al.* (1982) *Europe against Poverty: The European Poverty Programme 1975–1980* (Bedford Square Press).

DEPARTMENT FOR EDUCATION AND EMPLOYMENT (DEE) (1996) *Labour Market Trends, March 1996* (HMSO).

DEPARTMENT OF SOCIAL SECURITY (DSS) (1988) *Low Income Statistics: Report of a Technical Review* (HMSO).

DEPARTMENT OF SOCIAL SECURITY (DSS) (1993) *The Growth of Social Security* (HMSO).

DEPARTMENT OF SOCIAL SECURITY (DSS) (1995a) *Households below Average Income: a Statistical Analysis 1979–1992/3* (HMSO).

DEPARTMENT OF SOCIAL SECURITY (DSS) (1995b) *Family Resources Survey, Great Britain 1993/4* (HMSO).

DEPARTMENT OF SOCIAL SECURITY (DSS) (1995c) *Income Related Benefits Estimates of Take-up in 1993/4* (HMSO).

DESAI, M. (1986) 'Drawing the line: on defining the poverty threshold', in P. Golding (ed.), *Excluding the Poor* (CPAG).

DE TOMBEUR, C. and LADEWIG, N. (1994) *LIS Information Guide* (Luxembourg: LIS).

DEX, S. (1985) *The Sexual Division of Work* (Wheatsheaf).

DEY, I. (1996) *The Poverty of Feminisation* (University of Edinburgh, Department of Social Policy).

DILNOT, A., KAY, J. and MORRIS, C. (1984) *The Reform of Social Security* (Oxford University Press).

DISABILITY ALLIANCE (1990) *Disability Rights Handbook* (Disability Alliance).

DISABILITY ALLIANCE (1992) *A Way out of Poverty and Disability: Moving Towards a Comprehensive Disability Income Scheme* (Disability Alliance).

DOBSON, B. *et al.* (1994) *Diet, Choice and Poverty: Social Cultural and Nutritional Aspects of Food Consumption among Low Income Families* (Family Policy Studies Centre).

DONNISON, D. (1982) *The Politics of Poverty* (Martin Robertson).

DONNISON, D. (1988) 'Defining and Measuring Poverty: a Reply to Stein Ringen', *Journal of Social Policy*, vol. 17, no. 3.

EDGELL, S. and DUKE, V. (1983) 'Gender and Social Policy: the impact of the public expenditure cuts and reactions to them', *Journal of Social Policy*, vol. 12, no. 3.

ESAM, P and BERTHOUD, R. (1991) *Independent Benefits for Men and Women* (PSI).

ESPING ANDERSEN, G. (1990) *The Three Worlds of Welfare Capitalism* (Polity).

EUROPEAN COMMISSION (EC) (1977) *The Perception of Poverty in Europe* (EC).

EUROPEAN COMMISSION (EC) (1989) *Medium-term community action programme to foster the economic and social integration of the least privileged groups*, EC Commission Bulletin, Supplement 4/89.

EUROPEAN COMMISSION (EC) (1990) *The Perception of Poverty in Europe in 1989* (EC).

EUROPEAN COMMISSION (EC) (1991) *Final Report on the Second European Poverty Programme 1985–89* (EC).

EUROPEAN COMMISSION (EC) (1994) *The Perception of Poverty and Social Exclusion in Europe 1994* (EC).

EUROSTAT (1993) *European Community Household Panel: Strategy and Policy* (EC).

EVANS, M., PIACHAUD, D and SUTHERLAND, H. (1994) *Designed for the Poor – Poorer by Design: The Effects of the 1986 Social Security Act on Family Incomes* (LSE/STICERD WSP/105).

EVASON, E. (1980) *Ends That Won't Meet* (CPAG).

FALKINGHAM, J. (1989) 'Dependency and Ageing in Britain: a Re-Examination of the Evidence', *Journal of Social Policy*, vol. 18, no. 2.

FALKINGHAM, J. and VICTOR, C. (1991) *The Myth of the Woopie?: Incomes, the Elderly, and Targeting Welfare* (LSE/STICERD, WSP/55).

FERGE, Z. and MILLAR, S.M. (eds) (1987) *Dynamics of Deprivation* (Gower).

FIEGEHEN, G.C., LANSLEY, P.S. and SMITH, A.D. (1977) *Poverty and Progress in Britain 1953–7* (Cambridge University Press).

FIELD, F. (1982) *Poverty and Politics: the Inside Story of the CPAG's Campaigns in the 1970s* (Heinemann EB).

FIELD, F. (1989) *Losing Out: the Emergence of Britain's Underclass* (Blackwell).

FIELD, F. (1995) *Making Welfare Work: Reconstructing Welfare for the Millennium* (Institute of Community Studies).

FIELD, F. and PIACHAUD, D. (1971), 'The Poverty Trap', *New Statesman*, 3 December.

FIMISTER, G. (1986) *Welfare Rights Work in Social Services* (Macmillan).

FINCH, J. and GROVES, D. (eds) (1983) *A Labour of Love: Women, Work and Caring* (Routledge & Kegan Paul).

FISHER COMMITTEE (1973) *Report of the Committee on Abuse of Social Security Benefits*, Cmnd 5228 (HMSO).

FLOYD, M. (1991) 'Overcoming barriers to employment', in G. Dalley (ed.), *Disability and Social Policy* (PSI).

FORD, J. (1991) *Consuming Credit: Debt and Poverty in the UK* (CPAG).

FRAYMAN, H. (1992) *Breadline Britain 1990s: the Findings of the Television Series* (London Weekend Television).

FRIEDMAN, M. (1962) *Capitalism and Freedom* (Unversity of Chicago Press).

GALLIE, D. (1988) 'Employment, Unemployment and Social Stratification', in *Employment in Britain* (Basil Blackwell).

GAMBLE, A. (1989) *The Free Economy and the Strong State: the Politics of Thatcherism* (Macmillan).

GARNHAM, A. and KNIGHTS, E. (1994) *Putting the Treasury First: The Truth about Child Support* (CPAG).

GEORGE, V. (1988) *Wealth, Poverty and Starvation: an International Perspective* (Harvester Wheatsheaf).

GEORGE, V. and HOWARDS, I. (1991) *Poverty Amidst Affluence: Britain and the United States* (Edward Elgar).

GEORGE, V. and LAWSON, R. (1980) *Poverty and Inequality in Common Market Countries* (Routledge & Kegan Paul).

GEORGE, V. and WILDING, P. (1994) *Welfare and Ideology* (Harvester/ Wheatsheaf).

GINSBURG, N. (1992) 'Racism and Housing: Concepts and Reality', in P. Braham, A. Rattansi and R. Skellington (eds), *Racism and Antiracism: Inequalities, Opportunities and Policies* (Sage).

GITTINS, D. (1993) *The Family in Question: Changing Households and Familiar Ideologies*, 2nd edn (Macmillan).

GLENDINNING, C. (1990) 'Dependency and Interdependency: the Incomes of Informal Carers and the Impact of Social Security', *Journal of Social Policy*, vol. 19, no. 4.

GLENDINNING, C. and BALDWIN, S. (1988) 'The Costs of Disability', in R. Walker and G. Parker (eds), *Money Matters: Income, Wealth and Financial Welfare* (Sage).

GLENDINNING, C. and MILLAR, J. (eds) (1987) *Women and Poverty in Britain* (Wheatsheaf).

GLENDINNING, C. and MILLAR, J. (eds) (1992) *Women and Poverty in Britain: the 1990s* (Harvester/Wheatsheaf).

GLENNERSTER, H. (1995) *British Social Policy Since 1945* (Blackwell).

GOLDING, P. (ed.) (1986) *Excluding the Poor* (CPAG).

GOLDING, P. and MIDDLETON, S. (1982) *Images of Welfare: Press and Public Attitudes to Welfare* (Basil Blackwell and Martin Robertson).

GOODMAN, A and WEBB, S. (1994) *For Richer for Poorer: The Changing Distribution of Income in the United Kingdom 1961–1991* (IFS).

GORDON, P. and NEWNHAM, A. (1985) *Passport to Benefits: Racism in Social Security* (CPAG/Runnymede Trust).

GORZ, A. (1982) *Farewell to the Working Class* (Pluto P).

GORZ, A. (1991) 'The New Agenda', *New Left Review*, no. 184 (January).

GOSLING, A., MACHIN, S. and MEGHIR, C. (1994) *The Changing Distribution of Wages in the UK 1966–1992* (IFS).

GOUGH, I. (1979) *The Political Economy of the Welfare State* (Macmillan).

GRAHAM, H. (1986) *Caring for the Family*, Research Report no. 1 (Health Education Council).

GRAHAM, H. (1987) 'Women's Poverty and Caring', in C. Glendinning and J. Millar (eds), *Women and Poverty in Britain* (Wheatsheaf).

GRAHAM, H. (1992) 'Budgeting for Health: Mothers in Low Income Households', in C. Glendinning and J. Millar (eds), *Women and Poverty in Britain: the 1990s* (Harvester/Wheatsheaf).

GRAHL, J. and TEAGUE, P. (1990) *1992 – The Big Market: the Future of the European Community* (Lawrence and Wishart).

GRANT, L. (1995) *Disability and Debt: The Experience of Disabled People in Debt* (Sheffield Citizens Advice Bureau).

GREATER LONDON COUNCIL (GLC) (1986) *The Work of the GLC Welfare Benefits Project* (GLC).

GREEN, A. (1994) *The Geography of Poverty and Wealth* (Institute for Employment Research, University of Warwick).

GREEN, D. G. (1987) *The New Right: The Counter Revolution in Political, Economic and Social Thought* (Wheatsheaf).

GREEN, D. G. (1990) *Equalizing People: Why Social Justice Threatens Liberty* (IEA).

GREEN, D. G. (1996) *Community without Politics: A Market Approach to Welfare Reform* (IEA).

GREEN, H. (1988) *Informal Carers*, General Household Survey 1985 (HMSO).

GREEN PAPER (1985) *Reform of Social Security*, vols 1, 2 and 3, Cmnd 9517, 9518, 9519 (HMSO).

GREENWICH BOROUGH COUNCIL (1994) *Breadline Greenwich* (BMRB International Ltd).

GREGG, P. and WADSWORTH, J. (1994) *More Work in Fewer Households?* (National Insitute of Economic and Social Research).

GRIFFITHS, S. (1994) *Poverty on your Doorstep* (Newham Borough Council).

GROVES, D. (1988) 'Poverty, disability and social services', in S. Becker and S. MacPherson (eds), *Public issues and Private Pain: Poverty, Social Work and Social Policy* (Insight).

GROVES, D. (1992) 'Occupational Pension Provision and Women's Poverty in Old Age', in C. Glendinning and J. Millar (eds), *Women and Poverty in Britain: the 1990s* (Harvester/Wheatsheaf).

HADJIPATERAS, A. (1992) 'Reforming Social Security Provision for People with Disabilities: Ways to Move Beyond Mere Tinkering', *Benefits*, issue 3.

HADJIPATERAS, A. and HOWARD, M. (1993) *Too Little – Too Late: A national survey of claimants and advisers' experiences following the introduction of Disabilty Living Allowance and Disabilty Working Allowance* (Disability Alliance/RADAR).

HALSEY, A. H. (ed.) (1972) *Educational Priority: EPA Problems and Policies* (HMSO).

HANTRAIS, L. (1995) *Social Policy in the European Union* (Macmillan).

HARKER, L. (1996) *A Secure Future? Social Security and the Family in a Changing World* (CPAG).

HARRIS, C. C. (1991) 'Recession, Redundancy and Age', in P. Brown and R. Scase (eds), *Poor Work: Disadvantage and the Division of Labour* (Open University Press).

HARRIS, J. (1977) *William Beveridge: a Biography* (Oxford University Press).

HARRISON, P. (1983) *Inside the Inner City* (Penguin).

HAYEK, F. A. (1944) *The Road to Serfdom* (Routledge & Kegan Paul).

HENWOOD, M., RIMMER L. and WICKS M. (1987) *Inside the Family: Changing Roles of Men and Women* (Family Policy Studies Centre).

HIGGINS, J. (1978) *The Poverty Business: Britain and America* (Basil Blackwell and Martin Robertson).

HILL, M. (1990) *Social Security Policy in Britain* (Edward Elgar).

HILL, M. and LAING, P. (1979) *Social Work and Money* (George Allen and Unwin).

HILLS, J. (1989) *Distributional Effects of Housing Subsidies in the United Kingdom* (LSE/STICERD, WSP/44).

HILLS, J. (1990) 'Conditional Response', *Roof*, September/October.

HILLS, J. (1995) *JR Foundation Inquiry into Income and Wealth*, vol. 2 (JR Foundation).

HILLS, J., DITCH, J. and GLENNERSTER, H. (eds) (1994) *Beveridge and Social Security: An International Retrospective* (Clarendon Press).

HINDESS, B. (1987) *Freedom, Equality and the Market: Arguments on Social Policy* (Tavistock).

HOLMAN, R. (1978) *Poverty: Explanations of Social Deprivation* (Martin Robertson).

HOMER, M., LEONARD, A. E. and TAYLOR, M. P. (1984) *Private Violence: Public Shame* (Cleveland Refuge and Aid for Women and Children).

JAMES, E. (1970) *America Against Poverty* (Routledge & Kegan Paul).

JARVIS, S. and JENKINS, S. (1995) *Do the Poor Stay Poor?* (University of Essex).

JENKINS, S. (1994) *Winners and Losers: A Portrait of the UK Income Distribution during the 1980s* (University College of Wales, Swansea).

JENNINGS, J. (1994) *Understanding the Nature of Poverty in Urban America* (Connecticut: Praeger).

JOHNSON, N. (1990) *Reconstructing the Welfare State: a Decade of Change 1980–1990* (Harvester/Wheatsheaf).

JOHNSON, P. and WEBB, S. (1990) *Counting People with Low Incomes: the impact of recent changes in official statistics* (Institute for Fiscal Studies).

JONES, T. (1993) *Britain's Ethnic Minorities* (PSI).

JORDAN, B. (1987) *Rethinking Welfare* (Basil Blackwell).

JOSEPH, K. (1972) 'The Cycle of Deprivation', speech to Pre-School Playgroups Association, 29 June.

JOSEPH, K. and SUMPTION, J. (1979) *Equality* (John Murray).

JOSHI, H. (1988) *The cash opportunity costs of childbearing* (Centre for Economic Policy Research), Discussion Paper 208.

JOSHI, H. (1992) 'The Cost of Caring', in C. Glendinning and J. Millar (eds), *Women and Poverty in Britain: the 1990s* (Harvester/Wheatsheaf).

KELL, M. and WRIGHT, J. (1990) 'Benefits and the Labour Supply of Women Married to Unemployed Men', *Economic Journal*, Conference Papers Supplement.

KEMPSON, E. (1996) *Life on a Low Income* (JR Foundation).

KEMPSON, E., BRYSON, A. and ROWLINGSON, K. (1994) *Hard Times? How Poor Families Make Ends Meet* (PSI).

KIERNAN, K. (1991) 'Men and Women and Work at home', in R. Jowell *et al.* (eds), *British Social Attitudes, the 8th Report, 1991/92* (SCPR, Dartmouth).

LAND, H. and ROSE, H. (1985) 'Compulsory altruism for all, or an altruistic society for some?', in P. Bean, J. Ferris and D. Whynes (eds), *In Defence of Welfare* (Tavistock).

LAW, I. *et al.* (1994) 'The Effect of Ethnicity on Claiming Benefits: Evidence from Chinese and Bangladeshi Communities', *Benefits*, issue 9.

LEES, R. and SMITH, G. (eds) (1975) *Action Research in Community Development* (Routledge & Kegan Paul).

LE GRAND, J. (1982) *The Strategy of Equality* (Allen and Unwin).

LEIBFRIED, S. (1993) 'Towards a European Welfare State?', in C. Jones (ed.), *New Perspectives on the Welfare State in Europe* (Routledge).

LEVITAS, R. (ed.) (1986) *The Ideology of the New Right* (Polity).

LEWIS, J. (ed.) (1993) *Women and Social Policies in Europe: Work, Family and the State* (Edward Elgar).

LEWIS, J. and PIACHAUD, D. (1992) 'Women and Poverty in the Twentieth Century', in C. Glendinning and J. Millar (eds), *Women and Poverty in Britain: the 1990s* (Harvester/Wheatsheaf).

LEWIS, O. (1965) *The Children of Sanchez* (Penguin).

LEWIS, O. (1968) *La Vida* (Panther).

LISTER, R. (1975) *Social Security: the Case for Reform* (CPAG).

LISTER, R. (1990) 'Women, Economic Dependency and Citizenship', *Journal of Social Policy*, vol. 19, no. 4.

LISTER, R. (1992) *Women's Economic Dependency and Social Security* (Equal Opportunities Commission).

LISTER, R. (1994) '"She has other duties" – Women, Citizenship and Social Security', in S. Baldwin and J. Falkingham (eds), *Social Security and Social Change: New Challenges to the Beveridge Model* (Harvester/Wheatsheaf).

LISTER, R. and BERESFORD, P. (1991) *Working Together Against Poverty: Involving Poor People in Action Against Poverty* (Open Services Project/University of Bradford).

LISTER, R. and FIMISTER, G. (1980) *The Case Against Contribution Tests* (CPAG).

LISTER, R. *et al.* (1996) *Poverty First Hand* (forthcoming).

LIVERPOOL CITY COUNCIL (1991) *The Liverpool Quality of Life Survey* (Liverpool County Council).

LOCAL ECONOMY (1994) *Special Issue – Poverty, the Local Economy and Local Anti-Poverty Initiatives*, vol. 9, no. 2.

LONEY, M. (1983) *Community Against Government: the British Community Development Project 1968–78* (Heinemann).

LONSDALE, S. (1992) 'Patterns of Paid Work', in C. Glendinning and J. Millar (eds), *Women and Poverty in Britain: the 1990s* (Harvester/Wheatsheaf).

LONSDALE, S. and WALKER, A. (1984) *A Right to Work: Disability and Employment* (LPU).

MacGREGOR, S. (1981) *The Politics of Poverty* (Longman).

MACHIN, S. and WALDFOGEL, J. (1994) *The Decline of the Male Breadwinner* (LSE/STICERD WSP/103).

MACK, J. and LANSLEY, S. (1985) *Poor Britain* (George Allen and Unwin).

MACNICOL, J. (1980) *The Movement for Family Allowances 1918–1945: A Study in Social Policy Development* (Heinemann).

MACNICOL, J. (1987) 'In Pursuit of the Underclass', *Journal of Social Policy*, vol. 16, no. 3.

MANN, K. (1992) *The Making of an English 'Underclass'? The Social Divisions of Welfare and Labour* (Open University Press).

MANN, K. and ANSTEE, J. (1989) *Growing Fringes: Hypotheses in the Development of Occupational Welfare* (Armley).

MARRIS, P. and REIN, M. (1974) *Dilemmas of Social Reform* (Penguin).

MARSHALL, T. H. (1950) *Citizenship and Social Class* (Cambridge University Press).

MARTIN, J., MELZER, H. and ELLIOTT, D. (1988) *OPCS Report 1, the Prevalence of Disability among Adults* (HMSO).

MARTIN, J. and WHITE, A. (1988) *OPCS Report 2, the Financial Circumstances of Disabled Adults living in Private Households* (HMSO).

MARTIN, J., WHITE, A. and MELTZER, H. (1989) *OPCS Report 4, Disabled Adults: Services, Transport and Employment* (HMSO).

MARX, K. (1952) *Wage Labour and Capital* (Progress).

MATTHEWS, A. and TRUSCOTT, P. (1990) *Disability, Household Income and Expenditure: a Follow-up Survey of Disabled Adults in the Family Expenditure Survey*, DSS Research Report no. 2 (HMSO).

McCARTHY, M. (1986) *Campaigning for the Poor: CPAG and the Politics of Welfare* (Croom Helm).

McCLELLAND, J. (ed.) (1982) *A Little Pride and Dignity: the Importance of Child Benefit* (CPAG).

McDONNELL K. (1982) 'Working in Housing Aid', *Critical Social Policy*, vol. 2, no. 1.

McGLONE, F. (1992) *Disability and Dependency in Old Age: A Demographic and Social Audit* (Family Policy Studies Centre).

McLAUGHLIN, E. (1992) 'Mixed Blessings? The Invalid Care Allowance and Carer's Income Needs', *Benefits*, issue 3.

MIDDLETON, S., ASHWORTH, K. and WALKER, R. (1994) *Family Fortunes: Pressures on Parents and Children in the 1990s* (CPAG).

MILLAR, J. (1988) 'The Costs of Marital Breakdown', in R. Walker and G. Parker (eds), *Money Matters: Income, Wealth and Financial Welfare* (Sage).

MILLAR, J. (1989a) *Poverty and the Lone Parent Family: the challenge to Social Policy* (Avebury).

MILLAR, J. (1989b) 'Social Security, Equality and Women in the UK', *Policy and Politics*, vol. 17, no. 4.

MILLAR, J. (1992) 'Lone Mothers and Poverty', in C. Glendinning and J. Millar (eds), *Women and Poverty in Britain: the 1990s* (Harvester/Wheatsheaf).

MILLAR, J. and GLENDINNING, G. (1989) 'Gender and Poverty', *Journal of Social Policy*, vol. 18, no. 3.

MITCHELL, D. (1991) *Income Transfers in Ten Welfare States* (Avebury).

MOORE, J. (1989) 'The End of the Line for Poverty', speech to Greater London Area CPC, 11 May.

MOORE, R. and WALLACE, T. (1975) *Slamming the Door* (Martin Robertson).

MORRIS, A. E. and NOTT, S. M. (1991) *Working Women and the Law: Equality and Discrimination in Theory and Practice* (Routledge).

MORRIS, L. (1989) *The Workings of the Household* (Polity).

MORRIS, L. (1991) 'Women's Poor Work', in P. Brown and R. Scase (eds), *Poor Work: Disadvantage and the Division of Labour* (Open University Press).

MORRIS, L. (1994) *Dangerous Classes: The Underclass and Social Citizenship* (Routledge).

MORRIS, L. (1995) *Social Divisions: Economic Decline and Social Structural Change* (University College London Press).

MORRIS, L. and IRWIN, S. (1992) 'Employment Histories and the Concept of the Underclass', *Sociology*, vol. 26, pp. 401–20.

MORRIS, L. and RUANE, S. (1989) *Household Financial Management and the Labour Market* (Gower).

MOYNIHAN, D. P. (1965) *The Negro Family: the Case for National Action* (Office of Policy Planning and Research, US Department of Labor).

MURRAY, C. (1984) *Losing Ground: American Social Policy 1950–1980* (New York: Basic Books).

MURRAY, C. (1990) *The Emerging British Underclass* (IEA).

MURRAY, C. (1994) *Underclass: The Crisis Deepens* (IEA).

NATIONAL ASSOCIATION OF CITIZENS ADVICE BUREAUX (NACAB) (1991) *Barriers to Benefit: Black Claimants and Social Security* (NACAB).

NATIONAL CONSUMER COUNCIL (NCC) (1976) *Means-tested Benefits: a Discussion Paper* (NCC).

NOVAK, T. (1984) *Poverty and Social Security* (Pluto).

NOVAK, T. (1988) *Poverty and the State: an Historical Sociology* (Open University Press).

NOVAK, T. (1995) 'Rethinking Poverty', *Critical Social Policy*, issue 44/45 (Autumn).

O'HIGGINS, M., BRADSHAW, J. and WALKER, R. (1988) 'Income Distribution over the Life Cycle', in R. Walker and G. Parker (eds), *Money Matters: Income, Wealth and Financial Welfare* (Sage).

OLDFIELD, N. and YU, A. (1993) *The Cost of a Child: Living Standards for the 1990s* (CPAG).

OLIVER, M. (1990) *The Politics of Disablement: a Sociological Approach* (Macmillan).

OLIVER, M. (1991a) 'Speaking Out: disabled people and state welfare', in G. Dalley (ed.), *Disability and Social Policy* (PSI).

OLIVER, M. (1991b) 'Disability and participation in the labour market', in P. Brown and R. Scase (eds), *Poor Work: Disadvantage and the Division of Labour* (Open University Press).

OPPENHEIM, C. (1994) *The Welfare State: Putting the Record Straight* (CPAG).

OPPENHEIM, C. and HARKER, L. (1996) *Poverty: the Facts, Revised and Updated*, 3rd edn (CPAG).

ORSHANSKY, M. (1965) 'Counting the Poor: Another Look at the Poverty Profile', *Social Security Bulletin*, vol. 28.

ORSHANSKY, M. (1969) 'How Poverty is Measured', *Monthly Labour Review*, vol. 92.

PAHL, J. (1989) *Money and Marriage* (Macmillan).

PARKER, G. (1988) 'Indebtedness', in R. Walker and G. Parker (eds), *Money Matters: Income, Wealth and Financial Welfare* (Sage).

PARKER, G. (1990) *With due care and attention: a review of research on informal care* (Family Policy Studies Centre).

PARKER, H. (1989) *Instead of the Dole: an Enquiry into the Integration of the Tax and Benefit Systems* (Routledge).

PEARSON, S., ALCOCK, P. and CRAIG, G. (1996) 'Welfare Rights and Local Authority Anti-Poverty Strategies', *Benefits*, issue 16.

PEN, J. (1971) 'A Parade of Dwarfs (and a few Giants)', in T. S. Preston (ed.), *Income Distribution* (Penguin).

PHILLIPS, K. (1990) *The Politics of Rich and Poor: Wealth and the American Electorate in the Reagan Aftermath* (New York: Random House).

PHILLIPSON, C. (1993) 'Older Workers and Retirement: A Review of Current Trends', *Benefits*, issue 8.

PHILO, C. (ed.) (1995) *Off the Map: The Social Geography of Poverty in the UK*, (CPAG).

PIACHAUD, D. (1979) *The Cost of a Child* (CPAG).

PIACHAUD, D. (1981a) 'Peter Townsend and the Holy Grail', *New Society*, 10 September.

PIACHAUD, D. (1981b) *Children and Poverty* (CPAG).

PIACHAUD, D. (1982a) 'Patterns of Income and Expenditure within Families', *Journal of Social Policy*, vol. 11, no. 4.

PIACHAUD, D. (1982b) *Family Incomes since the War* (Study Commission on the Family).

PIACHAUD, D. (1984) *Round about 50 hours a week: the time costs of children* (CPAG).

PIACHAUD, D. (1987) 'Problems in the Definition and Measurement of Poverty', *Journal of Social Policy*, vol. 16, no. 2.

PIACHAUD, D. (1988) 'Poverty in Britain 1899 to 1983', *Journal of Social Policy*, vol. 17, no. 3.

PILLINGER, J. (1992) *Feminising the Market: Women's Pay and Employment in the EC* (Macmillan).

PIVEN, F. and CLOWARD, R. (1972) *Regulating the Poor: the Functions of Public Welfare* (Tavistock).

PLOWDEN REPORT (1967) *Children and their Primary Schools, Report of Central Advisory Council for Education*, vols I and II (HMSO).

PRESCOTT-CLARKE, P. (1990) *Employment and Handicap* (Social and Community Planning Research).

PURDY, D. (1988) *Social Power and the Labour Market* (Macmillan).

QURESHI, H. and WALKER, A. (1989) *The Caring Relationship: Elderly People and their Families* (Macmillan).

RADAR (1993) *Disability and Discrimination in Employment* (RADAR).

REX, J. (1973) *Race, Colonialism and the City* (Routledge & Kegan Paul).

REX, J. (1979) 'Black Militancy and Class Conflict', in R. Miles and A. Phizaklea (eds), *Racism and Political Action in Britain* (Routledge & Kegan Paul).

RHYS WILLIAMS, B. (1989) *Stepping Stones to Independence: National Insurance after 1990* (Aberdeen University Press).

RINGEN, S. (1988) 'Direct and Indirect Measures of Poverty', *Journal of Social Policy*, vol. 17, no. 3.

ROBBINS, D. (1994) *Social Europe. Towards a Europe of Solidarity: Combating Social Exclusion* (EC).

ROBBINS, D. *et al.* (1994) *Observatory on National Policies to Combat Social Exclusion, Third Annual Report* (EC).

ROLL, J. (1986) *Babies and Money: Birth Trends and Costs* (Family Policy Studies Centre).

ROLL, J. (1989) 'Social and Economic Change and Women's Poverty', in H. Graham and J. Popay (eds), *Women and Poverty: Exploring the Research and Policy Agenda* (Thomas Coram Research Unit/University of Warwick).

ROOM, G. (ed.) (1995) *Beyond the Threshold: The Measurement and Analysis of Social Exclusion* (Policy Press).

ROOM, G. *et al.* (1990) *'New Poverty', in the European Community* (Macmillan).

ROOM, G. *et al.* (eds) (1991) *National Policies to Combat Social Exclusion: First Annual Report of the European Community Observatory* (CRESEP, University of Bath).

ROOM, G. *et al.* (1993) *Anti-Poverty Action Research in Europe* (School of Advanced Urban Studies, University of Bristol).

ROOM, G., LAWSON, R. and LACZKO, F. (1989) '"New Poverty", in the European Community', *Policy and Politics*, vol. 17, no. 2.

ROWLINGSON, K. and BERTHOUD, R. (1994) *Evaluating the Disability Working Allowance: First Findings* (PSI).

ROWNTREE, B. S. (1901) *Poverty: a Study of Town Life* (Macmillan).

ROWNTREE, B. S. (1941) *Poverty and Progress: a Second Social Survey of York* (Longman).

ROWNTREE, B. S. and LAVERS, G. (1951) *Poverty and the Welfare State* (Longman).

ROYAL COMMISSION (1980) *An A to Z of Income and Wealth, Royal Commission on the Distribution of Income and Wealth* (HMSO).

RUNCIMAN, W. G. (1966) *Relative Deprivation and Social Justice: a study of attitudes to social inequality in twentieth-century* England (Penguin).

RUNCIMAN, W. G. (1990) 'How many classes are there in British society?', *Sociology*, vol. 24, pp. 378–96.

RUTTER, M. and MADGE, N. (1976) *Cycles of Disadvantage* (Heinemann).

RYAN, W. (1971) *Blaming the Victim* (Orbach and Chambers).

SANDFORD, C. (1980) 'The Tax Credit Scheme', in C. Sandford, C. Pond and R. Walker (eds), *Taxation and Social Policy* (Heinemann EB).

SEABROOK, J. (1984) *Landscapes of Poverty* (Blackwell).

SEN, A. (1983) 'Poor, Relatively Speaking', *Oxford Economic Papers*, vol. 35, no. 1.

SHERRADEN, M. (1991) *Assets and the Poor: a New American Welfare Policy* (New York: Sharpe).

SILBURN, R. (1995) 'Social Insurance: Key Themes form the First Phase', in R. Silburn (ed.), *Social Insurance: The Way Forward* (University of Nottingham).

SIMPSON, R. and WALKER, R. (1993) *Europe for Richer for Poorer?* (CPAG).

SKELLINGTON, R. and MORRIS, P. (1992) *'Race' in Britain Today* (Sage).

SMEEDING, T., O'HIGGINS, M. and RAINWATER, L. (eds) (1990) *Poverty, Inequality and Income Distribution in Comparative Perspective: the Luxembourg Income Study (LIS)* (Harvester/Wheatsheaf).

SMITH, A. (1776) *An inquiry into the nature and causes of the wealth of nations*, 1892 edn (Routledge).

SMITH, D. (ed.) (1992) *Understanding the Underclass* (PSI).

SMITH, G. (1995) *Geography, Ethnicity and Poverty: Newham in the 1991 Census* (Newham Borough Council).

SMITH, R. (1985) 'Who's Fiddling? Fraud and Abuse', in S. Ward (ed.), *DHSS in Crisis: Social Security – Under Pressure and Under Review* (CPAG).

SMITH, S. (1992) *Disabled in the Labour Market, Economic Report, 7.1* (Employment Policy Institute).

SMITH, T. and NOBLE, M. (1995) *Education Divides: Poverty and Schooling in the 1990s* (CPAG).

SPICKER, P. (1990) 'Charles Booth: the examination of poverty', *Social Policy and Administration*, vol. 24, no. 1.

SPICKER, P. (1993) *Poverty and Social Security* (Routledge).

SQUIRES, P. (1990) *Anti-Social Policy: Welfare, Ideology and the Disciplinary State* (Harvester/Wheatsheaf).

STEDMAN JONES, G. (1971) *Outcast London* (Oxford University Press).

STEPHENS, M. (1990) *Community Law Centres: a Critical Appraisal* (Avebury).

STITT, S. and GRANT, D. (1993) *Poverty: Rowntree Revisited* (Avebury).

STOKER, G. (1988) *The Politics of Local Government* (Macmillan).

SWANN REPORT (1985) *Education for All: the Report of the Committee of Enquiry into the Education of Children from Ethnic Minority Groups*, Cmnd 9453 (HMSO).

TAWNEY, R. H. (1913) 'Inaugural Lecture "Poverty as an Industrial Problem"', reproduced in *Memoranda on the Problems of Poverty*, vol. 2 (William Morris Press).

TAWNEY, R. H. (1931) *Equality* (Allen and Unwin).

TAYLOR GOOBY, P. (1991) *Social Change, Social Welfare and Social Science* (Harvester/Wheatsheaf).

TEAGUE, P. (1989) *The European Community: the Social Dimension. Labour Market Policies for 1992* (Kogan Page).

TEEKENS, R. and VAN PRAAG, B. (eds) (1990) *Analysing Poverty in the European Community: Policy issues, Research Options and Data Sources* (Eurostat).

THANE, P. (1982) *The Foundations of the Welfare State* (Longman).

THERBORN, G. and ROEBROEK, J. (1986) 'The Irreversible Welfare State: Its Recent Maturation, Its Encounter with the Economic Crisis, and Its Future Prospects', *International Journal of Health Services*, vol. 16, no. 3.

THOMPSON, P., LAVERY, M. and CURTICE, C. (1990) *Short Changed by Disability* (DIG).

TITMUSS, R. M. (1955) 'Age and Society: Some Fundamental Assumptions', in *Old Age in the Modern World*, Report of the Third Congress of International Association of Gerontology, Edinburgh (Livingstone).

TITMUSS, R. M. (1958) 'The Social Division of Welfare', in R. M. Titmuss, *Essays on the Welfare State* (Allen and Unwin).

TOMLINSON, A. (1986) 'Playing away from home: leisure, disadvantage and issues of income and access', in P. Golding (ed.), *Excluding the Poor* (CPAG).

TOPLISS, E. (1979) *Provision for the Disabled*, 2nd edn (Blackwell Scientific with Martin Robertson).

TOPOROWSKI, J. (1986) 'Beyond banking: financial institutions and the poor', in P. Golding (ed.), *Excluding the Poor* (CPAG).

TOWNSEND, P. (1954) 'The Meaning of Poverty', *British Journal of Sociology*, June.

TOWNSEND, P. (1979) *Poverty in the United Kingdom: a Survey of Household Resources and Standards of Living* (Penguin).

TOWNSEND, P. (1984) *Why are the Many Poor*, Fabian Tract 500 (Fabian Society).

TOWNSEND, P. (1987) 'Deprivation', *Journal of Social Policy*, vol. 16, no. 2.

TOWNSEND, P. (1993) *The International Analysis of Poverty* (Harvester/Wheatsheaf).

TOWNSEND, P. (1995) *The Rise of International Social Policy* (Policy Press).

TOWNSEND, P. and BOSANQUET, N. (1972) *Labour and Inequality* (Fabian Society).

TOWNSEND, P., CORRIGAN, P. and KOWARZIK, U. (1987) *Poverty and Labour in London: Interim Report of a Centenary Survey* (Low Pay Unit).

TOWNSEND, P. and DAVIDSON, N. and WHITEHEAD, M. (eds) (1988) *Inequalities in Health: the Black Report and the Health Divide* (Penguin).

TOWNSEND, P. and WALKER, A. (1995) *New Directions for Pensions: How to Revitalise National Insurance* (European Forum).

VAN OORSCHOT, W. (1995) *Realizing Rights: A multi-level approach to non-take-up of means-tested benefits* (Avebury).

VAN PARIJS, P. (ed.) (1992) *Arguing for Basic Income: Ethical Foundations for a Radical Reform* (Verso).

VAN PRAAG, B., HAGENAARS, A. and VAN WEEREN, H. (1982) 'Poverty in Europe', *Review of Income and Wealth*, vol. 28.

VEIT-WILSON, J. (1986) 'Paradigms of Poverty: a Rehabilitation of B. S. Rowntree', *Journal of Social Policy*, vol. 15, no. 1.

VEIT-WILSON, J. (1987) 'Consensual Approaches to Poverty Lines and Social Security', *Journal of Social Policy*, vol. 16, no. 2.

VINCENT, D. (1991) *Poor Citizens: the State and the Poor in Twentieth Century Britain* (Longman).

WALKER, A. (1980) 'The Social Creation of Poverty and Dependency in Old Age', *Journal of Social Policy*, vol. 9, no. 1.

WALKER, A. (1986) 'Pensions and the Production of Poverty in Old Age', in A. Walker and C. Phillipson (eds), *Ageing and Social Policy: a Critical Assessment* (Gower).

WALKER, A. (1993) 'Poverty and Inequality in Old Age', in J. Bond, P. Coleman and S. Peace (eds), *Ageing in Society: an Introduction to Social Gerontology*, 2nd edn (Sage).

WALKER, A. and PHILLIPSON, C. (eds) (1986) *Ageing and Social Policy: a Critical Assessment* (Gower).

WALKER, A. and WALKER, L. (1991) 'Disability and financial need – the failure of the social security system', in G. Dalley (ed.), *Disability and Social Policy* (PSI).

WALKER, C. (1993) *Managing Poverty: The Limits of Social Assistance* (Routledge).

WALKER, R. (1987) 'Consensual Approaches to the Definition of Poverty: Towards an Alternative Methodology', *Journal of Social Policy*, vol. 16, no. 2.

WALKER, R. (1988) 'The Costs of Household Formation', in R. Walker and G. Parker (eds), *Money Matters: Income, Wealth and Financial Welfare* (Sage).

WALKER, R. (1994) *Poverty Dynamics: Issues and Examples* (Avebury).

WALKER, R., LAWSON, R. and TOWNSEND, P. (eds) (1984) *Responses to Poverty: Lessons from Europe* (Heinemann EB).

WALKER, R. and PARKER, G. (eds) (1988) *Money Matters: Income, Wealth and Financial Welfare* (Sage).

WARD, S. (1986) 'Power, politics and poverty', in P. Golding (ed.), *Excluding the Poor* (CPAG).

WHEELER, R. (1986) 'Housing Policy and Elderly People', in A. Walker and C. Phillipson (eds), *Ageing and Social Policy: a Critical Assessment* (Gower).

WHITELEY, P. and WINYARD, S. (1983) 'Influencing Social Policy: the Effectiveness of the Poverty Lobby in Britain', *Journal of Social Policy*, vol. 12, no. 1.

WHITE PAPER (1990) *The Way Ahead: Benefits for Disabled People, Department of Social Security*, Cmnd 917 (HMSO).

WILLIAMS, F. (1989) *Social Policy: A Critical Introduction* (Polity).

WILLIAMS, S. (1986) 'Exclusion: the hidden face of poverty', in P. Golding (ed.), *Excluding the Poor* (CPAG).

WILSON, R. (1994) 'Sectoral and Occupational Change: Prospects for Women's Employment', in R. Lindley (ed.), *Labour Market Structures and Prospects for Women* (Equal Opportunities Commission).

WILSON, W. J. (1987) *The Truly Disadvantaged: the Inner city, the Underclass and Public Policy* (University of Chicago Press).

WOLFE, T. (1971) *Radical Chic and Mau-mauing the Flak Catchers* (New York: Bantam Books).

YOUNG, J. (1986) *The Islington Crime Survey* (Gower).

Index